AMAZING
TALES FROM THE
CLEVELAND INDIANS
DUGOUT

AMAZING
TALES FROM THE
CLEVELAND INDIANS
DUGOUT

A COLLECTION OF THE GREATEST
TRIBE STORIES EVER TOLD

RUSSELL SCHNEIDER

SPORTS
PUBLISHING

Sports Publishing books may be purchased in bulk at special discounts for sales promotion, corporate gifts, fund-raising, or educational purposes. Special editions can also be created to specifications. For details, contact the Special Sales Department, Sports Publishing, 307 West 36th Street, 11th Floor, New York, NY 10018 or sportspubbooks@skyhorsepublishing.com.

Sports Publishing® is a registered trademark of Skyhorse Publishing, Inc.®, a Delaware corporation.

Visit our website at www.sportspubbooks.com.

10 9 8 7 6 5 4 3 2 1

Library of Congress Cataloging-in-Publication Data is available on file.

ISBN: 978-1-61321-196-0

Printed in the United States of America

Table of Contents

Introduction xi

Joe Adcock 1
Andy Allanson. 1
Robbie Alomar 2
Sandy Alomar, Jr. 2
Max Alvis 3
Tony Amato 5
Brian Anderson 5
Alan Ashby 7
Ken Aspromonte. 7
Bobby Avila. 8
Joe Azcue. 9
Carlos Baerga 13
Danys Baez 13
Scott Bailes 12
Len Barker. 16
Gene Bearden 17
Buddy Bell 19
Gary Bell. 21
Albert Belle 23
Ron Belliard 23
Casey Blake. 23
Bert Blyleven. 25
Alva T. "Ted" Bonda 26
Aaron Boone. 27
Ray Boone. 28
Dick Bosman 29
Lou Boudreau 30
Alva Bradley 33

Milton Bradley 34
Bobby Bragan 35
Ben Broussard 35
Jackie Brown 35
Larry Brown 36
Dave Burba 38
Ellis Burks 39
Cy Buynak 40
Ernie Camacho 42
Tom Candiotti 43
Rico Carty 43
Joe Charboneau 44
Allie Clark 45
Rocky Colavito 46
Vince Colbert 48
Pat Corrales 50
Del Crandall 50
Coco Crisp 51
Alvin Dark 52
Jeff Datz 53
Jason Davis 54
Bob DiBiasio 54
Larry Doby 55
Larry Dolan 57
Frank Duffy 57
Dave Duncan 59
Steve Dunning 59
Dennis Eckersley 60
Doc Edwards 62
Harry Eisenstat 64
Ed Farmer 66
Bob Feller 69
Ray Fosse 74
Julio Franco 77
Tito Francona 78

Vern Fuller 80
Richie Garcia. 80
Wayne Garland 81
Jody Gerut 82
Pedro Gonzalez 83
Joe Gordon 83
Johnny Goryl 84
Jim "Mudcat" Grant 85
Hank Greenberg 86
Alfredo Griffin. 87
Steve Gromek 87
Travis Hafner 89
Sammy "Bad News" Hale 91
Mel Harder 92
Mike Hargrove 93
Ken "The Hawk" Harrelson. 93
John Hart 94
Ron Hassey 96
Von Hayes. 96
Jim Hegan. 97
Woodie Held. 97
George Hendrick. 98
Orel Hershiser. 99
Chuck Hinton. 100
Harold "Gomer" Hodge 101
Willis Hudlin 102
Luis Isaac. 103
Brook Jacoby. 103
David Jacobs 104
Charley Jamieson 104
Tommy John. 105
Alex Johnson. 105
Mike Kekich 106
Bob Kennedy 106
Jim Kern 108

Ralph Kiner. 108
Wayne Kirby 109
Duane Kuiper 109
Frank LaBono 110
Napoleon Lajoie 113
Frank Lane 114
Matt Lawton 115
Hal Lebovitz 117
Bob Lemon 117
Eddie Leon 119
Johnny Lipon 120
Joe Lis 120
Al Lopez 121
John Lowenstein 126
Ditto Lucarelli. 126
Candy Maldonado 129
Rick Manning. 130
Jeff Manto. 132
Charlie Manuel 133
Tom McCraw 135
Sam McDowell 136
Tom McGough 140
Cal McLish 141
Don McMahon. 143
Jose Mesa 143
Al Milnar 143
Saturnino Orestes "Minnie" Minoso 145
Fernando Montes 146
Terry Mulholland 147
Eddie Murray 149
Ray Murray. 149
Hal Naragon 150
Ray Narleski 153
Graig Nettles. 154
Hal Newhouser 155

Phil Niekro 157
Jesse Orosco 158
Satchel Paige 158
Gabe Paul 160
Mike Paul 160
Tony Peña 162
Gaylord Perry 163
Jim Perry 166
Hank Peters 167
Dave Philley 169
Jim Piersall 169
Lou Piniella 170
Boog Powell 171
Vic Power 171
Dick Radatz 172
Manny Ramirez 173
Pedro Ramos 174
Rudy Regalado 175
Kevin Rhomberg 177
Eddie Robinson 178
Frank Robinson 179
John Rocker 180
Ricardo Rodriguez 181
Rich Rollins 181
John Romano 182
Al Rosen 184
Hank Ruszkowski 189
C.C. Sabathia 190
Chico Salmon 190
Richie Scheinblum 192
Jim Schlemmer 193
Herb Score 194
Phil Seghi 196
Richie Sexson 196
Mark Shapiro 197

Sonny Siebert 198
Duke Sims. 200
Grady Sizemore. 204
Joel Skinner. 204
C. C. Slapnicka 205
Shane Spencer 205
Charlie Spikes 206
Scott Stewart. 207
George Strickland 207
Pat Tabler 209
Ed Taubensee 211
Birdie Tebbetts 211
Jim Thome 213
Andre Thornton 213
Luis Tiant 215
Bill Veeck 217
Mickey Vernon 218
Omar Vizquel 218
Rick Waits. 219
Bill Wambsganss 221
Jim Warfield 222
Eric Wedge 223
Fred Weisman 224
Jed Weisman 225
Jake Westbrook 226
Dr. William Wilder 227
Stan Williams 229
Rick Wise 230
Early Wynn. 232

Introduction

Some would call it a labor of love, which in many ways—and *days*—it was during the nearly quarter of a century that I covered the Cleveland Indians for the (Cleveland) *Plain Dealer*.

On the other hand, also in many ways—and, again, many *days*, during the period after the Tribe's losing efforts—it wasn't really a labor of love.

But the stories that follow often were a large part of the reason for my alleged love affair with the Indians and baseball in general.

Why so? Because most of them took place in the clubhouse or other semi-private sites, though not always off the field or even out of sight, and/or unheard by the fans in the stands or in front of their television sets.

Whatever, if nothing else they prove (or *should*) that ball players are human, too, with their foibles and fables, eccentricities and exaggerations, all of which seldom, if ever, are seen or heard by fans in the stands or those watching in their living room.

In the case of the Indians, a franchise that began as a charter member of the American League in 1901 and often lost more games than they won (especially during the seasons I covered them), the stories and anecdotes told by a few were better than the way they played the games, and are repeated in this book.

But the best of the gems were those told by Bob Feller, Gaylord Perry, Al Lopez, Frank Robinson, Dennis Eckersley, and Larry Doby, all of whom (not coincidentally) are in the Hall of Fame; as well as some by several who should be (or *could* have made it to the hallowed hall of baseball immortals), including Mel Harder, Herb Score, Rocky Colavito, and Sam McDowell. Others are included because . . . well, just because they were very quotable (and not the least of which, they're very good guys).

Of course, there are many more Cleveland Indians with stories to tell, and perhaps someday we'll catch up with them and their amazing stories, too.

But for now, read and enjoy these guys, as I did for more than a quarter of a century.

And still do.

Russell Schneider, 2013

AMAZING
TALES FROM THE
CLEVELAND INDIANS
DUGOUT

Joe Adcock
(First baseman, 1963; manager, 1967)

On Opening Day, 1967, Joe Adcock's first—and only—season as a Major League manager, the Indians played the Athletics, who were then based in Kansas City. The A's were owned by flamboyant Charles O. Finley, who introduced to baseball what he called "wedding gown white" uniforms trimmed in green and gold.

Finley's players also wore white shoes, which was another drastic style change. Until then professional baseball teams wore black spikes.

So when "Jumbo Jim" Nash took the mound and made his first pitch, Adcock bolted out of the Indians dugout, complaining to umpire Larry Napp that the pitcher's white shoes were "distracting" the Tribe batters. Maybe they did, as Kansas City won, 4–3, with the Indians getting only five hits off Nash.

Adcock formally protested the loss, citing the distraction of Nash's white shoes, but it was disallowed by then-American League president Joe Cronin.

Among Adcock's problems was his inability to deal with the media. Early on, when asked by a sportswriter if he thought a certain umpire blew a call against the Indians, he replied, "Does a bear [defecate] in the woods?" which, thereafter, became his standard response to questions he chose to avoid answering.

Andy Allanson
(Catcher, 1986–1989)

After he was selected by the Indians as their second choice in the 1983 amateur draft and was named the catcher on the Major League All-Rookie team in 1986, Andy Allanson's career quickly careened downhill. At the end, it consisted of 512 games over parts of eight seasons with five teams, including Detroit, Milwaukee, San Francisco, and California, in addition to Cleveland.

The fault might have been that success came too soon for Allanson. After he batted .263 with five homers and 50 RBIs in 133 games in 1988, Allanson became embroiled in a protracted hassle with the Indians on the contract they offered for 1989. He filed for salary arbitration and, to the dismay of Tribe General Manager Hank Peters, won a healthy increase.

However, it also cost Allanson his job, which Peters made clear in the wake of the arbitrator's decision favoring the catcher.

When asked what Allanson's future with the Indians would be, Peters replied, "His future is in the past," and when the 1989 season ended, Allanson was released.

Robbie Alomar
(Second baseman, 1999–2001)

"Even though my brother Sandy is playing for the Chicago White Sox, we stay in touch regularly. We talk on the phone a couple of times a week, although I'm usually the one who does the calling. Sandy always tells me that I should be calling him, because I make more money."

Upon joining the Indians in 1999, Robbie said, "I'm not only a player of the game, I'm a student of the game. I watch and learn," to which Jack McKeon, Alomar's former manager (San Diego Padres) commented, "You never had to tell Robbie Alomar a thing. He always knew what to do."

Sandy Alomar, Jr.
(Catcher, 1990–2000)

Upon his acquisition (with Carlos Baerga and Chris James for Joe Carter) from San Diego in 1990, Sandy Alomar played a prominent role in the Indians' resurgence in winning five consecutive American League Central Division championships.

After the Indians reached the postseason playoffs in 1995 for the first time in 41 years, clinching the AL Central title on September 8, 1995, Alomar said, "I cried, thinking of all we'd gone through to get to where we are."

Sandy Alomar's primary problem with the Indians was neither hitting nor catching, but staying healthy, which ended his stint in Cleveland. After his eighth trip to the disabled list with another knee injury in 1999, he shrugged and said, "If 50 guys are standing around in a group and somebody throws a bomb, you can bet it'll hit me—only me. That's been the story of my career."

Alomar admitted he cried—although he shed what he called "happy" tears—upon being greeted with a standing ovation by the fans in his return to Jacobs Field as a member of the Chicago White Sox on April 2, 2001.

"It was a very touching, very sentimental time for me, after so many years with the Indians, and going through so many tough times [1990–1994] and then so many very good times [1995–2000]," he said. "I'll always remember being a part of the family of this city."

Max Alvis
(Third baseman, 1962–1969)

"Once, early in my career when my sons Max and Steve were very young, they were playing ball in the backyard and trying to identify with big leaguers. I heard Max say, 'I'm going to be Rocky Colavito,' and then David said, 'OK, I'll be Fred Whitfield.'

"I hollered out the window, 'Hey, you guys, why don't you want to be Max Alvis?' and one of them replied, 'Aw, dad, you strike out too much.'"

"Everybody knows that Chicago is called the 'Windy City,' but nobody knows it better than I do—from personal experience.

"We were playing the White Sox in Chicago [in 1966] and the wind caused me the greatest embarrassment of my baseball career. It was late in the game, we were in the field and a foul ball was popped up in my direction [third base]. I backpedaled to get under it, but the wind started taking the ball out toward left field. The thought crossed my mind that the ball was drifting quite a bit, but I figured I was OK, because I was in foul territory.

"So I kept backpedaling and, just as I reached up to catch the ball, I tripped over third base and fell backwards. The back of my head hit the ground, and the ball landed a couple of feet away. It was still foul, but the batter got a life and subsequently got a hit. I was very embarrassed . . . and the fact that we lost the game made it worse.

"In a way—make that a couple of ways—it was kind of funny, as I found out later. While I was backpedaling to get under the ball, Herb Score, who was broadcasting the game on the radio, saw what was developing and was hollering into the microphone, 'Watch out for the bag! Watch out for the bag!' I know that because people in Cleveland who were listening to the game told me.

"Something else that's funny—now, but not then—is that Brownie [Larry Brown] was playing shortstop and [Manager] Birdie Tebbetts jumped all over him for not backing me up and catching the ball himself. But to my face, Birdie just shook his head and said, 'Max, I've been in baseball 30 years and I've never seen anything like that. Never.' I never did either.

"But that still wasn't the end of it. After the game we flew to California to play the Angels. When I went out on the field for batting practice, [Angels shortstop] Jim Fregosi saw me and flopped down on the ground and started rolling around, laughing. He told me, 'Max, that was the funniest thing I ever saw the first time, and it was even funnier on instant replay.'

"See, the game was on national television and, not only did they show it when it happened, they kept on replaying it."

★ ★ ★ ★ ★

After being traded by the Tribe and then retiring from the Milwaukee Brewers in 1970, Max Alvis went to work for a bank in Jasper, Texas, and eventually became its president.

"I guess you can say I got to be president of the bank kind of like the way I learned to play third base. You get enough bad hops, and pretty soon you can handle them. I made enough mistakes at the bank and learned from them, just as I did in baseball."

Tony Amato
(Indians clubhouse manager, 2002–)

Tony Amato's memories of Albert Belle remain vivid—particularly an incident that occurred in 1995.

"A. B. [Belle] complained that it was too cold in the clubhouse and asked me, 'Tony, did you do this? . . . Did you turn the thermostat down during the game?' I told him I didn't, and he went around the clubhouse asking guys if they did it, but nobody admitted they'd turned it down.

"So he went to his locker, grabbed a bat, and said, 'I'll make sure no one turns it down again,' and smashed the thermostat to pieces. That was it. We all looked at each other, but nobody said anything until A. B. left the room. Then it was like, 'Holy cow!' We couldn't believe what he did."

(In his next paycheck, Belle was docked the cost of replacing the thermostat and repairing the damage done to the wall.)

Brian Anderson
(Pitcher, 1996–1997, 2003)

During a Spring Training bus trip to Vero Beach, Florida, to play Los Angeles in 2003, Brian Anderson suddenly realized he'd forgotten his equipment bag. It meant he had no baseball cleats and no glove, which he needed because he was scheduled to pitch against the Dodgers that day.

"When we got to Vero," he said, "I borrowed a car and went shopping at a Wal-Mart and Champs Sporting Goods store. I bought a glove at Wal-Mart for $24.95 and a pair of spikes at Champs for $65. The glove was beautiful two-tone ready-to-play leather—but it was a softball glove, nothing I would use if I didn't have to."

As it turned out, Anderson ruefully recalled, "Naturally, I got three comebackers that day, although I've got to say, the glove worked fine."

Afterward he gave it away.

"When I was growing up in Geneva, [Ohio], the Indians were the team my family and I always rooted for, always hoped they'd do well. I listened to all their games on the radio, and I'll never forget the time—I was three or four years old—when my sister and I had our pictures taken with Brett Butler. It was at one of those photo days at the old Stadium, and he had each of us on his knees. That was really neat. My mom still has that photo.

"Those were what [the media] call the 'bad old days,' but to me they were good. I mean the players were good. All of them.

"I was very disappointed when the Indians let me get away in the [1997] expansion draft [to Arizona], but it turned out to be a tremendous break for me. The Diamondbacks gave me the ball and gave me the opportunity to pitch, which I probably would not have gotten in Cleveland. In those days if you had a rough outing, they'd send you back to Buffalo and bring up somebody else."

Anderson returned to the Tribe as a free agent in 2003, but with a record of 9–10 on August 25, he was traded to Kansas City for two minor leaguers and subsequently re-signed with the Royals in 2004.

However, Anderson struggled early in the season and, with a 7.71 earned run average, was demoted by the Royals to the bullpen, after which he was his own severest critic. "Nobody is this bad . . . I mean nobody in pro ball," he said. "You could take some kid in rookie ball, give him 10 or 11 starts and he would not do what I've done. Nobody can possibly be this bad—but I am.

"It's no fun being me . . . not this season."

Alan Ashby
(Catcher, 1973–1976)

"I often think about our teams of the early 1970s, all the good young players we had and how great it might have been if we could have stayed together longer than we did," Alan Ashby said.

Among them were former teammates Ray Fosse, Rick Manning, Duane Kuiper, Buddy Bell, George Hendrick, Dennis Eckersley, Chris Chambliss, Dick Tidrow, Charlie Spikes, John Lowenstein, and Rick Waits, along with veterans Gaylord Perry and Frank Robinson, who took over as Tribe manager in 1975.

During Ashby's four seasons in Cleveland, the Indians finished above .500 only once, 81–78 in 1976, but as he pointed out, "A lot of the guys we had back then went on to have good careers with other teams.

"We also had some guys who are now talking good games."

The former players turned broadcasters are Kuiper for the San Francisco Giants, Fosse for the Oakland Athletics, Manning for the Indians, Lowenstein, a former radio and television "voice" of the Baltimore Orioles, and Ashby for the Houston Astros.

Ashby has been calling Astros games on the air since 1998 after retiring from a 17-year playing career with the Indians, Toronto, and Houston.

Ken Aspromonte
(Second baseman, 1960–1962; manager, 1972–1974)

"I grew up in Brooklyn in a very tough neighborhood where it was always a dog-eat-dog atmosphere, which probably was the reason I was so hot-tempered as a player," Ken Aspromonte said. "In retrospect, I realize my temper kept me on the bench a lot. I took everything so personally.

"I think I was a pretty good player. . . . I had good statistics, especially in the minor leagues, but once I got to the big leagues, I let my temper get the best of me. I started fighting myself. I took everything too personally, which hurt me as a player, especially after I got to the big leagues."

After a mediocre seven-year playing career with six Major League teams and three seasons in the Japanese Central League, Aspromonte managed in the minor leagues for four years. He was hired by Gabe Paul to pilot the Indians in 1972, a job he held for three seasons, compiling an overall won-lost record of 220-260.

Looking back at the time he was fired and replaced by Frank Robinson, who became Major League Baseball's first black manager, Aspromonte said, "Attendance was down and the team was bad. A fall guy was needed, and I was it.

"But I have no regrets about not being in baseball anymore. It probably will mean I'll live a little longer than if I were still in the game."

Bobby Avila
(Second baseman, 1949–1958)

Late in the Indians' pennant-winning season of 1954, when they set an American League record (since broken) by winning 111 games, Bobby Avila was batting in the high .380s and told reporters, "If I hit .375 or better, I will run for president of Mexico."

As it turned out, Avila did neither, although he won the batting championship with a .341 average, was a member of the AL All-Star team, and finished third in the balloting for the Most Valuable Player award.

"I was only kidding about running for president. . . . I was not a politician," he said during a recent visit to Cleveland.

But still, after he retired from baseball, Avila served a term as mayor of Vera Cruz, his hometown.

"I was born in Vera Cruz, I grew up in Vera Cruz, I was married in Vera Cruz, I was the mayor of Vera Cruz, and when I die, I will be buried in Vera Cruz," he said.

A few months after attending a reunion of the 1954 Indians in Cleveland, Avila died in Vera Cruz on October 26, 2004, of complications from diabetes. He was 84.

Joe Azcue
(Catcher, 1963–1969)

"When the Indians got me, I was playing at [Class AAA] Portland [in the Kansas City Athletics] farm system. I had started with Cincinnati, they traded me to Kansas City [in 1962]. When Spring Training ended in 1963, they said they were sending me to Portland to get me in better shape because they were going to do some changing around. I joined the Portland team in Hawaii, which was very nice, and then I returned to Portland with the team.

"My wife and daughter Angela, who had just been bom, met me there, and we got an apartment. A couple days later I was told, 'Joe, we traded you to the Indians, and you have to go to Cleveland right away.' I thought they were kidding. I said, 'Bull—. I just got here, so did my wife and baby. We just bought a car, and now I have to go to Cleveland?' Then I said it again. 'Bull—. I just got here, and I am not going to Cleveland.'

"But then [Indians General Manager] Gabe Paul called me. He and [Manager] Birdie Tebbetts knew me from when they were in Cincinnati and Gabe signed me, and I knew I had to go. So I flew all night—about seven hours in a propeller plane—with my wife and baby to Cleveland. I had to leave my car at the airport in Portland and ask a guy to sell it for me. We didn't know a soul in Cleveland, and we got there just in time for me to go to the ballpark for a double-header.

"The only person I knew on the team was Pedro Ramos. He let my wife and baby stay with his family because, right after the double header, the Indians were leaving on a road trip. It was crazy. There's my wife with a brand new baby and she doesn't know anybody in town. Isn't that amazing?

"When I got to the ballpark, I told [Coach] Mel Harder that I flew all night and did not get any sleep. He said, 'Why don't you just go out to the bullpen and take a nap. We won't use you unless we need you.'

"So I'm out in the bullpen sleeping, and in the fourth inning of the first game [catcher John] Romano got hit with a foul tip and broke his hand. They woke me up and said I had to go in the game to catch. I think it was either Gary Bell or Mudcat Grant who was pitching. I was still half asleep; I didn't know any of the pitchers, not even their names.

"But I had a great day. I hit a home run and got a couple more hits, and we won both games. With Romano hurt I was the only [healthy] catcher for almost a month. But I had a great season, and that's when somebody started calling me the 'Immortal Cuban.' The rest is history. I was making $8,500 that season, which was a lot of money then, and I was very happy with it."

"Here's what it was like to catch Sam McDowell, how he always wanted to call his own pitches. He'd brush up or down with his glove against his uniform shirt to add or subtract from the number I would give him. Sometimes he would cross himself up—not just me, but himself. I don't know why. Maybe because he didn't know how to add or subtract.

"A lot of times I didn't know what Sam was going to throw, and I would tell the umpire and the hitter that I didn't. They would say, 'What! Are you crazy or something?' I'd say, 'No, I'm serious,' and the hitter would say, 'Aw, come on,' and I would say again, 'No, really I don't know.' Maybe that helped Sam. I don't know.

"Sometimes, when I didn't know what was coming, I'd just duck and the ball would go back to the backstop. When that would happen, Sam would call me out to the mound and I'd yell to him, 'No, no, you come here,' and the umpire would get mad and say, 'You guys better get together.'

"That was Sam. But he was a helluva pitcher. The best left-hander I ever caught."

"Let me tell you about [Manager] Birdie Tebbetts. Anytime somebody on the team would say that famous big word, you know, the four letter one that starts with an 'F,' Birdie would fine him $50. And if we used the famous big word with 'mother' in front of it, it would cost us twice as much, $100. So what we did, we changed it around and instead of saying the words, we'd call somebody, 'Hey, you two big words,' and Birdie couldn't fine us.

"One time in Chicago a guy was ragging on me. I got mad and yelled to him, 'Hey, shut up you mother . . . you know.' But before I could finish it, Birdie stopped me and said, 'Joe, it'll cost you a hundred to finish it. But I was so mad at the guy, I said to Birdie, 'That's OK. Put me down for two hundred,' and I called the guy those two big words twice.

"After the game Birdie called me into his office and said, 'Joe, my son, be a professional. Don't say things like that,' and after that I didn't."

It was during the "bad old days" of Cleveland baseball that Joe Azcue—a.k.a. the "Immortal Cuban"—played for the Indians and still finds it hard to understand why the team was so bad back then.

"Look at the starting pitchers we had," said Azcue, naming Sam McDowell, Luis Tiant, Sonny Siebert, and Steve Hargan. "We should have won a couple of pennants because nobody in the league had better starters, except we didn't have the middle relievers we needed.

"I'll never forget the time Tiant came up [from Class AAA Portland on July 19, 1964,] and blew away the Yankees [3–0, with a four-hitter, striking out 11]. It was amazing, although I wasn't surprised because I had faced him in Cuba before we both came to the United States, and I knew how good he was."

"Another game I'll never forget was one that McDowell pitched for us in 1963. [Manager] Birdie Tebbetts called Sam and me into his office before the game and told Sam, 'If you throw anything except a fastball or a change-up, it will cost each of you $100,' which was a lot of money then. We followed Birdie's orders, and Sam shut out the Yankees even though they figured out what was happening—that Sam wasn't going to throw anything but fastballs and change-ups.

"Yogi Berra came up to the plate late in the game and said, 'Geez, Joe, we know what's coming, and we still can't hit it. The kid is too tough.'"

"When I got traded to Boston in 1969 the guy who was the manager, Dick Williams, told me, 'Look at the way we pitch over here,' like it was something real good. I said to him, 'Damn, you must play with a different kind of ball, or something, huh?' I guess he didn't like the way I said it, because a week passed and I did not play very much. They were using me as mop-up. Not like what they told me when they traded for me.

"[Then] we went to Minnesota and in the last game of the series Williams called me in from the bullpen to pinch hit. I walked all the way to the plate and [umpire] Tom Haller said, 'What are you doing? Hurry up, the beer is getting warm.' I said, 'This is my last game with this team, why should I hurry?' He didn't believe me, but it was.

"I swung three times and went back to the dugout. Williams screamed at me, 'You so and so, that will cost you $100.' I said to him, 'You know what you can do—you can kiss my Cuban ass,' and I put all my stuff in a grocery sack and walked out. He yelled, 'You cannot walk out on us, you cannot quit,' and I said, 'Watch me. Watch the door hit my ass,' and I did. I walked out.

"I called my wife to come and pick me up and we drove back to Overland Park, [Kansas]. That was sometime in May. Then my phone started to ring. The reporters in Boston called me. Lots of people called me. Other teams, too. They wanted to know if something was wrong with me. I said no, not with me, with Williams. I said I wouldn't play for that guy. All they wrote in Boston was that I was hard to handle, stuff like that. Finally they made a deal for me with California for Tom Satriano.

"When I got to Boston with the Angels, all the fans booed me, worst I ever was booed. But I just smiled and doffed my hat and then they liked me again. They started clapping their hands. But Williams never said anything to me, and I didn't say anything to him. He was still pissed off at me, and I was still pissed off at him. "But then, 30-some years later I was at one of those old-timers games and so was Williams. When he saw me he asked, 'Hey, are you still a grouch?' and I said to him, 'My God, get a life,' and then I called him a name, but he didn't hear that part, which was a good thing."

Carlos Baerga
(Second and third baseman, 1990–1996, 1999)

"I was shocked when the Indians traded me [on July 29, 1996], but it probably was the best thing that ever happened to me because I became a Christian after leaving Cleveland," Carlos Baerga said. (His free-wheeling lifestyle was the reason he was dealt to the New York Mets.)

And, just as the trade initially upset Baerga, Tribe fans also were outspokenly angered by the deal. The day after it was made an airplane circled Jacobs Field pulling a banner that read, "Trade [John] Hart, Not Baerga."

One of the reasons they hated to see Baerga leave was best elicited in a comment by longtime play-by-play announcer and former pitcher Herb Score, who once said about Baerga: "He's fearless. If a freight train were bearing down on him [at second base], I wouldn't be surprised if he'd stay in there and complete the double play."

Danys Baez
(Pitcher, 2001–2003)

Before he was allowed to leave as a free agent to sign with the Tampa Bay Devil Rays, Danys Baez looked back on his career in Cleveland and said, "The toughest hitter I've faced is [Seattle's] Edgar Martinez. He always seemed to be so comfortable at the plate against me. It was like he looked out at me and said, 'Danys Baez . . . who is he? I'm going to hit this guy, and I don't care how hard he throws the ball or what he throws.'

"And then he did hit me, usually."

Scott Bailes
(Pitcher, 1986–1989)

"One of the biggest thrills of my baseball career was in 1987 when I was on the same pitching staff as two Hall of Famers, Steve Carlton and Phil Niekro," Scott Bailes said. "I tried not to show it ... you know, I tried to be real cool around them, but it was hard. Especially after I saved a game for Niekro.

"It was against the Detroit Tigers [on June 1, 1987]. We beat them 9-6, and it gave Phil and his brother Joe the record for the most Major League victories [530] by two brothers. Until that game they had lost four or five games in a row, and their families had been flying all over both leagues to be with one of them when he would have won the game that broke the record.

"When I replaced Phil in the eighth inning, he warned me, 'Don't blow this [expletive] game. ... Joe and I have been trying too long to win one.' Afterward Phil autographed one of his gloves, and he also gave me the pair of spikes he wore. I have them in my trophy room at home."

Bailes went on to pitch for California from 1990 to 1992 and retired.

Well, *sort of.*

As he admitted, "I went home to Springfield, Missouri, and didn't touch a baseball, not even to play catch, until the summer of 1996 when I started playing in an over-30 league, pitching and playing some first base. It was just a beer league; we never practiced, just played one night a week, and at the end of the season we spent our own money to go to a tournament in Arizona. We played three games, lost two of them and were eliminated, then played golf for three more days, and went home.

"At the time Dan O'Brien, Jr. was the assistant general manager of the Texas Rangers and saw me pitch in the tournament. He called me and said, 'Hey, you're throwing harder now than you ever did,' and asked if I'd be interested in playing pro ball again. At first I said no, that I had gone to the tournament only to be with my buddies and play some golf with them. He told me, 'Well, if you decide you have an interest [in making a comeback], call me.' "When I told my wife and kids about it they encouraged me to give it a try. My kids were at the age then where it was kind of cool for them to know someone in the big leagues, especially if it was their father, so I called O'Brien and asked if he was serious. He said he was, and I told him, 'If I try it, I'd need at least a month to work out and get in shape because I don't want to embarrass myself.'

"He agreed, and I went to winter ball [1996-1997] and pitched great. I had an ERA of two-something against a lot of Major League hitters and went to Spring Training with the Rangers as a non-roster invitee. I had a great Spring Training; I think I gave up only one run in 14 or 15 innings and agreed to go to [Class AAA] Oklahoma City because it was close to home. The wife and kids could come down to see me and then go home when I went on the road. I kind of planned to finish the season in Triple A and enjoy myself and then fade into the sunset as a washed-up 35-year-old left-hander.

"But in the middle of the [1997] season, injuries to a couple of [Texas] pitchers changed my plans. The Rangers' plans, too. They called me up, and I had the best three-month run that I ever had in the big leagues. I was relieving, pitching the seventh and eighth innings and setting up for [closer] John Wetteland, and did great. I had a two-something ERA and made the team again in 1998.

"But then, about three-quarters through the season I got a sore shoulder and the Rangers' doctor started giving me cortisone shots. We were winning and heading into the playoffs, where I'd never been, and I was determined to stay on the roster and go to Yankee Stadium to pitch against New York. So I kept pitching—and getting cortisone—but when we got swept by the Yankees in the first round of the playoffs, that proved to be it for me.

"I had arm surgery to repair a couple of small tears in the rotator cuff that had become major tears, and my biceps tendon also had become detached, and they fixed that, too. I went to Spring Training in 1999, and although my arm didn't hurt anymore, it was dead. I couldn't throw 70 miles an hour, and it was all over for me.

"But I guess it was a pretty amazing comeback while it lasted. Some PR guy somewhere told me that it was the longest non-injury layoff or retirement from baseball ever in the Major Leagues, except for during World War I and World War II when guys came back from the service to resume their careers."

Len Barker
(Pitcher, 1979–1983)

"A week or so before I pitched my perfect game [May 15, 1981], we were playing the Blue Jays in Toronto and Bert Blyleven was pitching. He had a no-hitter going for eight innings, and when the [last half of the] ninth began, Dave Garcia, our manager, took Joe Charboneau out of left field and put Larry Littleton in for defense. So what happens? The first ball hit to left field—a catchable ball—Littleton lost it in the lights, or whatever, and it fell for a double, which turned out to be the only hit off Blyleven.

"The following week we were playing Toronto again, this time in Cleveland, and I had the perfect game going for eight innings. Between innings, while we were batting, I felt like I had the plague. Once, I sat down next to [Manager] Dave Garcia and he got up and walked away without saying a word. Then, before I went out for the ninth, Garcia came over to me and said, 'You want me to take Joe [Charboneau] out of left field and put Larry [Littleton] in for defense?' He was serious, and I immediately thought about what happened a week earlier in Toronto.

"I said to Dave, 'If you take out Joe, take me out, too.' I remembered how Littleton screwed up Blyleven's no-hitter. So Garcia didn't take Joe out of the game, though he wouldn't have gotten a chance to screw it up anyway. I got the first two batters, and then Ernie Whitt, a pinch hitter, was the last one. He hit a routine fly to center, and I knew it was over because Rick Manning was out there—not Littleton."

Gene Bearden
(Pitcher, 1947–1950)

As a rookie left-hander, Gene Bearden pitched—and won—perhaps the single-most important game in the Indians' first 100 years. He beat the Red Sox, 8–3, in Boston's Fenway Park, with a five-hitter in an unprecedented, one-game playoff for the pennant in 1948 for his 20th victory of the season.

Then Bearden went on to win the third game of the World Series, beating the Boston Braves, 2–0, and three days later, working in relief of Bob Lemon, saved the Indians' 4–3 victory in the deciding sixth game.

Bearden threw all the standard pitches—fastball, curve, slider, change-up—though there were two others that might have contributed more heavily to his success, at least in 1948. That was the only one of his seven Major League seasons in which he won more than eight games.

"I had a pretty good spitball," he later confessed, "though my knuckleball was my best pitch. It was the knuckleball that got me where I went. It had a downward rotation that made the ball drop when it got to the plate."

Comparing the way the game was played during his career (1947–53), Bearden said, "Times are so different now. If you're a pitcher, you can't pitch inside, or the batters will come out after you. They also did in my day, though they never got far, because Mr. Hegan [Tribe catcher Jim Hegan] would stop them before they got halfway.

"One who tried was Dave Philley [an outfielder who played for the White Sox in 1948, and became a member of the Indians in 1954]. Mr. Philley didn't like it that I was pitching him tight and started out [to the mound], but he didn't make it. Mr. Hegan made sure of that."

Bearden had pitched Philley "tight"—or as he subsequently admitted, even tighter—to "protect" Larry Doby who, as the American

League's first black player in 1947, was the target of much verbal abuse by opposing players.

"I had thrown the ball tighter than tight to Mr. Philley, actually behind him, and I guarantee it wasn't a knuckleball either. That's the way we protected Larry against the guys who gave him a bad time. They usually got the message. If they didn't the first time, we kept sending it to them.

"There were a few who were pretty bad in St. Louis, Bob Dillinger and Al Zarilla in particular. But we handled them in our own way. We threw behind them. Sometimes even between their legs."

It was a well-known fact that Boudreau and Indians vice president Hank Greenberg were not on the best of terms in 1948, and team owner Bill Veeck, of course, usually sided with Greenberg. Prior to the playoff game in Boston against the Red Sox, Bearden overheard Boudreau arguing with Greenberg and Veeck as he walked through the dugout to go to the bullpen to warm up.

"They [Veeck and Greenberg] were raising hell with Lou because he was going to play [outfielder] Allie Clark at first base. I don't think they were mad because I was pitching; it's just that they wanted Eddie Robinson to play first base.

"Finally I heard Lou say, '[Clark] is going to play first base . . . you can fire me if you want, but it will have to be after the game,' and that's the way it was left.

"Something else I'll never forget was what Clark said to me before I made my first pitch: 'Don't you dare throw over here and try to pick somebody off. Remember—I never played first base before.'

"I was crazy about Bill [Veeck], but I didn't have that same opinion of Greenberg. I never argued with him. . . . I just tell people what I think. What I told Greenberg [during contract negotiations in 1950]

was that everybody couldn't be a Hall of Famer like he was, and that he ought to learn how to treat people. That was it. Just a clash of personalities between him and me."

Buddy Bell
(Third baseman/outfielder, 1972–1978; coach, 1994–1995, 2003–2005)

"It was the start of my Major League career, and it should have been one of the best times of my life, but it wasn't. Not at first. It was scary. We didn't know what to do," recalled Buddy Bell about 1972 when he and two fellow rookies, pitcher Dick Tidrow and second baseman Jack Brohamer, made the team and were heading to Cleveland to open the season.

"The three of us had played at [Class AAA] Wichita in 1971, and you can imagine how excited we were to be in the big leagues. But before we were to go to Cleveland, we played exhibition games en route, after leaving Tucson [Spring Training], and the last two were in New Orleans against the Chicago Cubs.

"It was right after the first game—I don't remember if we won or lost—that Steve Mingori and Ray Fosse, who were our player representatives, held a meeting and told us that the players association was going on strike. The three of us had no clue as to what it meant for us, but as we found out, we were stuck in New Orleans with about $30 among the three of us and no credit cards.

"What happened was that Hammer's [Brohammer's] dad drove Jack's car over from Spring Training and then flew back to his home in California, and we started for Cleveland. But to make matters worse, we almost got in a wreck. I was driving, Tidrow was in the passenger seat, and Hammer was in the back, sleeping. It happened near Newport, Kentucky. The car was a [Plymouth] Duster, and the brakes were the kind that, you know, if you pushed on the pedal real hard, the brakes locked up and the car would skid, which is what happened. We wound up doing a 360 in the median [of the freeway].

Fortunately, we didn't hit anything. All of our suitcases fell on top of Hammer in the backseat, but otherwise, we were OK.

"Somehow we made it to my parents' home in Cincinnati before we ran out of money. My mom and dad took us in, and we stayed with them a couple of days, but, being rookies, we still didn't know what to do. Finally, we drove to Cleveland. The strike was still on, so we stayed with friends and waited to see what was going to happen.

"A couple of days later an agreement was reached, and the season started. Graig Nettles was the Indians' third baseman then, and a couple of outfielders got hurt in Spring Training so [Manager] Ken Aspromonte put me in right field, even though I had never played the outfield before that spring. I was scared that I'd screw up, but I never let anybody know. Actually, I told [Aspromonte and the coaches] that I had played some in the outfield because I really wanted to make the team and figured that was my only chance.

"As it turned out, I was OK. The first few games I was a little hesitant, but after that I was fine. My only complaint about playing the outfield is that it gets kind of boring. It's not as intense as it is when you're playing the infield. I even moved over to center field when the Indians traded Del Unser."

Bell returned to his natural position at third base when Nettles was traded to the New York Yankees on November 27, 1972.

"As every longtime old Tribe fan will remember, the Indians were rebuilding damned near every year," he lamented. "But the truth be told, I wouldn't trade any of those years for anything. They were great seasons— except for that first week when the players association went on strike."

One of the Tribe's former coaches, Dave Garcia, recalled instructions he received from then-General Manager Phil Seghi when Bell was a young third baseman.

"Phil told me," Garcia said, "'I want you to work with Buddy Bell. He catches every ground ball with one hand.' So I hit Buddy about 5,000 grounders the next two days, and then I went to Seghi and said, 'You're right. He does catch everything with one hand—just leave him alone.'"

Which was well said. Bell went on to win six Gold Glove awards as a (sometimes one-handed) third baseman.

"When I took this job with the Rockies [as manager in 2000], I wanted to hire Dave Garcia, because he'd been around so long and had seen everything there is to see in baseball. I loved him when he was a coach for us in Cleveland.

"I had trouble reaching him by telephone, and when I finally did, I told him, 'Dave, this is Buddy Bell. I'm going to manage the Rockies, and I want you to come with me.' Dave said, 'What! Buddy, do you realize I'm 79 years old!' I told him, 'I don't want you to play second base, I want you as a coach.'"

Garcia accepted the job.

Gary Bell
(Pitcher, 1958–1967)

"One of my favorite games was against the Boston Red Sox in Cleveland in 1958 or 1959, and every time I see Bill Monboquette he reminds me about it. He pitched against me that day. We were ahead, 1–0, going into the ninth inning, and up to then I'd struck out Ted Williams three times in a row. Pete Runnels was the leadoff hitter in the ninth, and while he was up at the plate getting ready to hit, Williams was stalking around in the dugout and looking out at me kind of weird. It scared the hell out of me.

"Runnels got a hit to bring up Williams, and as he dug in at the plate, he was still glaring at me. I was thinking that I'd just blow his big ass away again.

"But this time he hit a ball that made it to the upper deck of the old Stadium, which was a helluva long way, and the Red Sox won, 2–1. Somebody said I should have chased him around the bases. I didn't. . . . I respected him too much.

"Besides, I was afraid he'd come after me and hit me—not the ball—again."

"Before I was traded [in 1967] to Boston, I played for Joe Adcock [then the rookie manager of the Indians]. We were in Spring Training that season, and after playing a game in Palm Springs we were going to Holtville [California] for another exhibition game the next day. The team bus was scheduled to leave at 10 o'clock in the morning.

"So, right after breakfast a couple of us came out of the hotel and were walking toward the bus—it was just going on 10 o'clock and we were only like 10 or 15 feet away from it—and Joe had the bus driver slam the door and take off.

"There we were, almost ready to get aboard, and he left us standing there. We had to rent a car to get to Holtville, which I guess was about 100 miles away. I never asked him why he did it; I just figured he was a big jerk.

"Another time, when Adcock was still playing for us [1963], we were in a game against the Red Sox, and Joe went up to hit against Dick Radatz, who was then in his prime. They called him 'The Monster,' because he was so big and threw so hard.

"Adcock stepped in to the batter's box, and Radatz threw him three 500 mph pieces of cheese [fastballs]. Adcock never took the bat off his shoulder [and was called out on strikes]. When he came back to the dugout he said, 'A fly landed on my bat and I couldn't pull the trigger.' He was serious! Just about everybody in the dugout fell on the ground laughing."

Albert Belle
(Outfielder, 1989–1996)

A reporter for the *Arizona Republic* in Phoenix was given an assignment to visit the Scottsdale home of former Indian Albert Belle to ask him his opinion on Sammy Sosa's 2003 use of a corked bat.

Belle, who was caught using a corked bat in 1994, told the reporter, "Isn't it interesting that you and your editor care enough to find my house and ask me about this, but no one cares that I've been taking classes at Arizona State University and that I'm about to get my undergraduate accounting degree."

Ron Belliard
(Second baseman, 2004–2006)

Through the first month and a half of his first season with the Indians, Ron Belliard seemingly could do nothing wrong at the plate, flirting with a .400 batting average and remaining in the high .300s until midseason.

"Sometimes every ball you hit turns into good luck," he said. "I just go up there and swing the bat. I've been hitting the ball in the right place [on the field]."

And sometimes even on the wrong place of the bat.

"I've never broken so many bats that went for base hits in such a short period before, at least 15 or 20, but that's OK. I'll trade a bat for a hit anytime."

A career .266 hitter in his five previous seasons in the National League, Belliard cooled off as the season wore on but continued to be one of the year's best free agent acquisitions.

Casey Blake
(Third baseman and first baseman, 2003–2008)

Casey Blake, who sometimes moved from third to first base for defensive purposes in 2003, played first base in his first game in the big leagues in 2000. At the time he was playing for Minnesota in a game against the Indians at Jacobs Field and admittedly did not know all the inner workings of the position.

"I was holding Robbie Alomar on the bag," Blake said, "and he leaned over and whispered, 'Hey, you don't have to hold me. We've got a runner on second base.' When I looked at the Twins' dugout, everybody was laughing, which was pretty embarrassing."

In 2003, his first season with the Tribe, Blake recalled that his former Twins teammates kidded him after a game in Minnesota.

"I was having a good series, swinging the bat pretty good. After I went five for five in one of the games, [Twins third baseman] Corey Koskie, who is a good friend of mine, sent a ball over to our clubhouse for me to autograph. Koskie told our clubhouse manager, 'Tell Casey that I heard he's been telling people in Minneapolis that if he was still with the Twins, he could have a game like that every day and also that he is a much better player [than Koskie], all that kind of stuff.'

"Of course, I never said anything like that, and never would, but Corey wanted to yank my chain, which he did pretty good.

"So I took the ball that Corey sent over and wrote on it, 'To Corey Koskie, I owe it all to you, you are my idol,' and signed it.

"The very next day, after I had the clubhouse manager give it to Koskie, I popped up my first two at bats and went oh-fer [hitless]. After the game Corey said he was tempted to send the ball back, and I was glad he didn't."

Early in the 2004 season, Blake missed three games because of a strained right hamstring.

"I was examined and the doctor discovered that my right leg is slightly longer than the left," he said. "I was told that it might have caused the hamstring problem."

The solution was that a ⅜-inch pad was inserted in the heel of Blake's left shoe. When a reporter facetiously asked if Blake thought the doctor was "pulling his leg," Casey replied, "No, but maybe I should have had him pull my left leg."

Bert Blyleven
(Pitcher; 1981–1985)

"Sure, I knew I had a no-hitter going [in Toronto, May 6, 1981]," said Bert Blyleven. "Anytime you get through, oh, six innings without giving up a hit, you know you're working on one. And if you aren't aware of it, all you have to do is pay attention to your teammates. You get the silent treatment from them. Like Lenny [Barker] says, they treat you like you've got the plague, they don't want to do anything to jinx you."

Blyleven's near no-hitter was spoiled in the ninth when the first batter lined a "catchable" ball that was lost in the lights by left fielder Larry Littleton, who had entered the game that inning as a defensive replacement.

"My immediate reaction, of course, was dejection. The ball that Littleton missed hit him in the glove. He came in for it, and I could see by his reactions that he lost it in the lights. Remember, it was in the old ball park in Toronto, Exhibition Stadium, not Skydome. Maybe if Skydome had been built by then, it might have been different. But, hey, you can lose a ball in the sun, even in the roof at the Metrodome in Minneapolis. Besides, I wasn't the first guy to lose a no-hitter after going that far.

"Littleton apologized, and I told him not to worry about it, those things happen. What else could I say? I felt sorry for the guy. He tried.

Sometimes we as pitchers tend to forget all the great plays that are made behind us. You have to take the good with the bad.

"What really bothered me was that after I got the next two guys out, George Bell hit a pretty good curve ball for a base hit, so not only had I lost my no-hitter, I also lost my shutout, though we won the game, 4-1."

It would have been Blyleven's second no-hitter. When he pitched for the Texas Rangers in 1977, he hurled a no-hit, 6–0 victory over California on September 22.

Alva T. "Ted" Bonda
(Indians general partner/president, 1975–1978)

"I had to chuckle when I read that Larry Dolan bought the Indians [November 4, 1999 for a reported $323 million] because I'll never forget the day that Armond Arnson and I tried to give the franchise away.

"Yes, I said we 'tried' to give the franchise away. It happened during what you guys in the media like to call the "bad old days," which—though I hate to admit it—is very close to being accurate.

"It was during 1977 when things were going badly on the field and at the box office. Especially at the box office. We needed money to operate, to pay the bills, and Armond and I went to the bank and asked for a loan. Actually, a loan on top of the loan we already had with the bank.

"Before we went in, Armond, who was one of our partners, asked me for the keys to our offices at the Stadium. I asked him why, and he said, 'You'll see,' which I soon did.

"We met with the president of the bank, asked for more money, and were turned down. We already owed them too much, he said.

"With that, Armond said thanks and we got up to leave. Then, suddenly, he turned back and said, 'Oh, by the way, you're going to need these,' and tossed the keys to our offices on the desk. 'Now the bank owns the Indians,' he said.

"Which was all the banker needed. He invited us to sit down and talk some more. We did and, not surprisingly, the bank didn't want to take over ownership of the Indians, and we got the loan.

"That's why I had to chuckle when Dolan paid all that money for the club."

Frank Robinson became baseball's first black manager on October 3, 1975, when he was hired by the Indians, and exactly two years, eight months, and 19 days later—on June 19, 1977—he became baseball's first black manager to be fired.

"It [Robinson being fired] would have happened much sooner if [General Manager] Phil Seghi had his way," Bonda said. "I hired Robinson, because I thought it was the right thing to do. It was time [for an African-American to manage in the Major Leagues]. And when Phil wanted to replace him [in mid-May, 1977] I refused to do so, because I didn't think it was the right thing to do.

"I wanted to keep Frank, but eventually I caved in to too many pressures, from the media and the fans, as well as from my associates" [meaning Seghi].

Aaron Boone
(Third baseman, 2004–2006)

After the Indians signed Aaron Boone to a free agent contract in late June 2004, a story surfaced about the infielder's character. It was told by Hal McCoy, the Hall-of-Fame baseball writer for the *Dayton Daily News,* who covered Cincinnati when Boone played for the Reds from 1997 to 2003.

McCoy, the Reds beat writer for 32 years, had suffered optical strokes in both eyes and his vision had been reduced by 50 to 60 percent. The first day of Spring Training in 2002, McCoy had trouble recognizing the players because he couldn't see well enough. One of them was Boone.

"I was near tears," McCoy said. "Aaron came up to me, and I told him, 'You're seeing me for the last time. I can't see. I'm going to have to quit and go home.'"

Boone asked why, and McCoy explained what had happened to his eyesight.

"Aaron sat me down and said, 'I don't ever want to hear the word quit come out of your mouth again. What's happened to you is no reason to quit something you love doing.'

"I'll never forget what he said . . . what he did for me that day."

And every day after that in Spring Training Boone checked with McCoy to see how he was doing.

"He turned me around that day," added McCoy—who is still covering the Reds on a daily basis for the *Dayton Daily News*.

Ray Boone
(Shortstop/third baseman, 1948–1953)

As a minor league shortstop in the Indians farm system after being converted from a catcher in 1947, Ray Boone was promoted to Cleveland in the final month of the 1948 season. "That was a working man's team, a bunch of blue-collar guys," he said of the Indians. "Some [of the veterans] had a lot of mileage on them, but they were all pros. Nobody had an ego, not even the guys who should have, like [Ken] Keltner and [Joe] Gordon, not even [Bob] Feller, and certainly not [Bob] Lemon.

"Back then, in Spring Training [in 1948], not many guys— maybe not anybody—thought we could win the pennant for one simple reason: nobody knew Gene Bearden was going to be a 20-game winner."

Boone also remembered how the Indians celebrated after they won the playoff game for the pennant and would open the World Series two days later against the National League champion Braves in Boston.

"Oh, man! The party we had was really something. When we showed up for the workout the next day, you wouldn't believe how hungover some of the guys were. [Manager] Lou Boudreau came into the clubhouse and said, 'There are three cabs waiting outside . . . you, you, and you, get into one . . . you, you, and you get into another . . . and you, you, and you take the third one. Get over to the spa and sweat out the booze.'"

Dick Bosman
(Pitcher, 1973–1975)

Ted Williams was renowned as one of baseball's greatest hitters—perhaps *the greatest* in the game—but Dick Bosman said he learned more about pitching from Williams than from anyone else.

"Pitching for Williams, when I was a member of the Washington Senators in 1969 and he was our manager, was a very important part of my career," Bosman said. "That season was my first good year in the big leagues, and I give Williams credit for it and also for whatever success I had afterward.

"Because he was such a great hitter, Williams pretty much taught me the art of pitching, however strange that might sound. But think of it. Who should know better than the man who probably was the greatest hitter in the game? It made me a good pitcher then and a good coach now. I owe a great deal to Williams."

Bosman pitched a no-hitter for the Indians against Oakland on July 19, 1974, and hurled three one-hitters when he was with the Senators from 1956 to 1971 (and Texas Rangers in 1972 and part of 1973, after the Washington franchise moved to Dallas). One of those one-hitters was against the Indians in 1969 and was spoiled by Tony Horton, who singled in the second inning. Bosman also pitched a one-hitter in 1970 against Minnesota. He retired as an active player in 1976 after being traded to Oakland.

"I enjoyed my pitching career, but I enjoy coaching even more," Bosman said. "There is something about teaching that really turns me on. When I'm coaching—teaching—the words just come out. I don't always know where they come from, but they're there, and they're right. Many of them from Williams, I'm sure."

Lou Boudreau
(Shortstop, 1938–1950; manager, 1942–1950)

On November 24, 1941, at the age of 24 years, four months, and seven days, Lou Boudreau became Major League Baseball's youngest manager. He was given a two-year contract to play shortstop and pilot the team, replacing Roger Peckinpaugh, who moved into the front office as vice president of the Indians.

Boudreau's inexperience became evident almost immediately. On the first day of Spring Training, then at Ft. Myers, Florida, the "boy manager," as he was called, met with the writers covering the Indians and made an odd request.

"Fellows, I'd like to suggest that, in the future, you gentlemen show me your stories before they go into the papers, so that nothing will be written that might hurt our chances of winning."

Gordon Cobbledick, then the baseball writer for the Cleveland *Plain Dealer*, told Boudreau, "Lou, we work for our newspapers, not for you or the Indians. You can run the team, but don't try to tell us how to write our stories."

In 1947, Boudreau, who'd grown tired of the Indians losing to the Boston Red Sox because of Ted Williams, devised the unique "Boudreau Shift" (also called the "Williams Shift"). Only the third baseman covered the left side of the infield, with the left fielder virtually in center field. The object was to invite Williams to try to hit the ball to left.

"I knew Williams, and I knew his thoughts were on being the greatest hitter in the game of baseball," Boudreau explained. "I also knew Ted's disposition. It was important to him to face up to a challenge, and to beat it, when hitting was involved."

The shift was unveiled in the second game of a double header in Boston on July 14 (after Williams went 4-for-5 with three homers, all to right field, and drove in eight runs to help the Red Sox win the opener). When Williams saw how the Indians were deployed, he turned to umpire Bill Summers and said, "What the hell is going on? They can't do that."

But Summers told Williams, "As long as they have nine guys on the field, and eight of them are inside the foul lines, they can play anywhere they please."

Williams, as stubborn as he was good, seldom challenged the shift and, according to Boudreau at the end of the season, "Our charts showed that we were 37 percent more successful when we used the shift against Williams than when we didn't."

Several years later, after both were retired—and both enshrined in the Hall of Fame—Williams said of Boudreau: "He came the closest to being the most complete player of anyone I've ever seen in the game. Boudreau was a great hitter, a great shortstop, and a great manager."

An inspirational player-manager, partly because of his remarkable ability as a shortstop and hitter, Boudreau delivered what was one of the most important hits in the history of the franchise on August 8, 1948. It was in the opener of a crucial doubleheader against the New York Yankees. At the time, the Indians' record was 58–39, and they were in a virtual tie for first place with the Yankees and Philadelphia Athletics.

Boudreau had been sidelined, nursing an assortment of injuries— a contusion of the right shoulder, a bruised right knee, a sore right thumb, and a sprained left ankle—from a collision at second base three days earlier. The Indians were losing, 6–4, in the seventh inning, with the bases loaded, two outs, and Thurman Tucker, a left-handed batter, due to bat next. When Yankees Manager Bucky Harris brought his ace southpaw reliever, Joe Page, into the game, Boudreau put himself in as a pinch hitter.

"When I stepped out of the dugout with a bat in my hands and field announcer Jack Cresson intoned, 'Attention please. Batting for Tucker, No. 5, Lou Boudreau,' the fans went crazy. Their cheers were deafening and sent a chill up my spine. I forgot about how badly my ankle hurt, or that my back was stiff, or that my thumb was so sore I could hardly grip the bat."

Boudreau slashed a single to center, driving in two runs to tie the score, and the Indians went on to win, 8–6. They also beat the Yankees in the nightcap, taking over first place and eventually winning the pennant and World Series.

At the time Boudreau put himself in to bat for Tucker, Indians owner Bill Veeck, seated in the press box, told one of the writers, "Even if Boudreau doesn't get a hit, this is the most courageous thing I've ever seen in baseball."

When Boudreau was inducted into the Baseball Hall of Fame in 1970, Bowie Kuhn, then-commissioner of baseball, said in his introduction of the former shortstop-manager:

"The most remarkable thing about this remarkable man was the way he stretched the wonderful skills he had into superlative skills. As a shortstop, he was a human computer; he knew all the moves of the base runners, he knew what the pitcher was going to pitch. He had an instinct for where the ball would be hit, and from all of this he fashioned the wonderful ball player that we knew as Lou Boudreau.

"There are hitters in the Hall of Fame with higher lifetime batting averages, but I do not believe there is in the Hall of Fame a baseball man who brought more use of intellect and avocation of mind to the game than Lou Boudreau."

Before he died in 2001, Lou Boudreau reminisced on his career as a Hall-of-Fame player, player-manager, and broadcaster—as well as an All-American collegiate basketball player prior to his career in baseball.

"I have only one regret, and it's not that I was born too soon, before the big money came into baseball," he said. "My only regret, after a lifetime in sports, is that my teams won only one pennant [in 1948]. A player's—and a manager's—first World Series is like a child's first taste of ice cream. It's never enough."

Alva Bradley
(Owner, 1927–1946)

Shortly after Alva Bradley and two partners bought the Indians on November 17, 1927, he wrote a letter to Ed Barrow, owner of the New York Yankees. It was a bid by Bradley to purchase from the Yankees a rookie first baseman who was holding out for more money.

Bradleys initial offer for the player, $150,000, was rejected, after which the owner of the Indians raised his bid to $175,000, plus Indians first baseman George Burns, and subsequently to $250,000, but Barrow still said no.

The rookie first baseman was Lou Gehrig, who was elected to the Hall of Fame in 1939.

When Roger Peckinpaugh was fired as the Indians manager after the 1941 season, Bradley disclaimed any responsibility with the statement: "I hire the manager, but the fans fire him."

And of his decision to appoint Lou Boudreau as the team's player-manager, replacing Peckinpaugh, Bradley said, "The more I inspected the qualifications of various other candidates, the more I became convinced that we couldn't afford not to take advantage of [Boudreau's] natural gift of leadership.

"I didn't know of another man of whom I could be so certain that he would be thoroughly respected by the players, press, and public.

Lou is smart, he's a great ballplayer, a fine young man, a fighter, and a leader," Bradley said upon introducing Boudreau as the new manager of the Indians on November 25, 1941.

Milton Bradley
(Outfielder, 2001–2003)

"I live by a simple creed," said Milton Bradley early in his brief and tempestuous career with the Indians. "If you don't know me and I don't know you, don't approach me and I won't approach you. Don't insult me, and I won't insult you, because you don't know what I will or won't do.

"I want [opposing players] to hate my guts. That way when we beat them and when I get that [big] hit or make that [big] play, it hurts in their soul; it sticks with them and they have trouble sleeping.

"The energy you get when the crowd is booing you and cheering for the pitcher to get you when you're at the plate . . . I live for that. Then to be able to get a hit is something special."

★ ★ ★ ★ ★

Bradley also expressed disdain for his reputation as a problem player, saying, "I'm the reason why a lot of these people [clubhouse workers and members of the media] have got jobs. I know I am an interesting person. If I wasn't on this team, what would you be writing about?

"I don't just go with the flow. If I believe people are doing things to prove a point or abusing a position of power, I'm not going to sit back and take it. It might seem like I'm acting on the spur of the moment, or emotion, but I know every action has a reaction. I'm willing to accept the consequences to prove a point."

After incurring Manager Eric Wedge's wrath for not running out a pop fly in a March 31, 2004, Spring Training exhibition game and then being suspended for insubordination, Bradley was traded to Los Angeles for two minor leaguers. Upon reporting to the Dodgers, Bradley was quoted as asking God to "bless" Wedge because he "has a lot on his mind." Bradley's antics continued in Los Angeles, where he threw a plastic bottle at Dodgers fans and earned four ejections and two suspensions during the season.

Bobby Bragan
(Manager, 1958)

Recalling his managerial tenure with the Indians, Bobby Bragan said, "I was hired by Hank Greenberg, but shortly thereafter the Indians were sold, and the new owners brought in Frank Lane as the general manager. Knowing Lane and how he operated, I knew I wouldn't be around long—and I was right.

"Midway through the [1958] season we lost a game 2–1 to Boston, on a ninth-inning homer by Ted Williams. When I got into the clubhouse, there was a message from Lane for me to go up to his office. I knew what he wanted. I wasn't a virgin. I'd been fired before.

"Again, I was right. Lane told me, 'Bobby, I don't know how we're going to get along without you, but starting tomorrow we're going to try.' That was it. That's how he fired me."

Ben Broussard
(First baseman, 2002–2006)

When asked why he takes his guitar on every trip, Ben Broussard replied, "Sometimes when you have a bad day at the park, you can take things in a different direction with the guitar."

Jackie Brown
(Pitcher, 1975–1976)

"Cleveland is a great town, but when I was traded there, I have to admit there was no way I wanted to go," Jackie Brown admitted. "I didn't want to uproot my family, but the big reason why I wasn't sure about going to Cleveland was because of the prominent memory I had of the town. I was there on 'Beer Night' [as a member of the Texas Rangers in 1974] when the fans went crazy and rioted. It was the scariest thing I've ever seen.

"But the last few years [as a Major League pitching coach] I could not wait to go back to Cleveland. The new ballpark, the great fans—what a fantastic atmosphere. I'm happy for the people there. After that first bad memory of Cleveland, I found the fans to be just great. I'm glad to have been part of the Indians in a small way."

On being traded to Montreal for Andre Thornton in 1976: "That sure turned out to be a heck of a deal for Cleveland, so I guess it's fair to say that I did something good for the city and the Indians."

Larry Brown
(Shortstop and second baseman, 1963–1971)

In a 1963 game at the old Stadium in which the Indians beat California 9–5, Larry Brown hit the fourth of four consecutive home runs off Paul Foytack in the sixth inning. Previously, Woodie Held, Pedro Ramos, and Tito Francona delivered homers off the Angels right-hander.

Brown admitted to being—well, *suspicious* when he faced Foytack.

"When I went to the plate, I wasn't even thinking about hitting," he said. "I was getting ready to go down. Instead [Foytack] threw two fastballs down the middle for strikes, and I hit the next one out."

When Foytack was replaced on the mound by Jack Spring, Brown quipped, "They didn't take him out because he gave up four homers. They took him out because he gave up one to me."

(It was one of 47 homers Brown hit in his 12-year Major League career with the Indians, Oakland, Baltimore, and Texas.)

"I also well remember the day that Max Alvis tripped over third base in Chicago [in 1966]. The batter hit the weakest pop-up you ever saw, and, for crying out loud, you could have caught it in your teeth. Maxie went over to get it, stepped in front of the bag, then stepped backwards, tripped, fell, and missed the ball completely.

"I was standing there watching him and later [Manager] Birdie Tebbetts said to me, 'Brownie, you've got to catch that ball.' Believe it or not, by gosh, he was serious."

"I liked Birdie a lot. He was good. One time, when I went back to Cleveland for an old-timers game, I went up to Birdie and thanked him for all he did for me. He said to me, 'Don't thank me. . . . I want to thank you. You were the best shortstop I had.'

"I don't know if that was true or not, but I appreciated it a lot."

"We had started the 1966 season with 10 straight victories and won 13 of our first 14 games—though we still were only one game ahead of Baltimore—when we went into New York [May 4] for a series against the Yankees. Bob Friend pitched the opener for the Yankees, and I was playing shortstop, although, in all honesty, I don't remember playing the game. What I'm telling you is what people told me later.

"[Left fielder] Leon Wagner and I collided under a pop fly that Roger Maris hit in the fourth or fifth inning. The ball was headed for the left-field corner of Yankee Stadium, where the distance is about 300 feet [from the plate], but the wind was blowing from left to center and brought the ball back. I went out and Wags came in, and we ran together and hit head on. I don't know if he yelled or if I yelled. As I said, I really don't remember much about the whole thing.

"Anyway you know what people say, that all men are created equal? Well, I can tell you they're not. [In the collision] Wags took the skin off his nose, that's all, and I almost died, right there on the field. My skull was fractured above both eyes; I had two broken cheekbones, a broken nose, and was hemorrhaging from every cavity in my head. I was out, unconscious for something like three days.

"When my wife came to New York and went to the hospital, they told her I was in the intensive care unit. She went in but couldn't find me. She told the nurse, 'My husband's not here,' and the nurse said, 'Yes, he is. That's him over there.' I was such a mess she didn't recognize me. It was a pretty ugly thing, for her as well as me.

"I finally woke up after three days, and you know, with a bad head injury, you don't know what you're doing. One thing I do remember is that I kept hearing this beep, beep, beep, and it was really bothering me. I said to the nurse, 'What's that noise, that beeping noise?' and she told me it was a heart monitor for the man in the bed next to me. I said, 'Well, turn it off, it's bothering me,' and she said, 'We can't turn it off. If we do, he'll die.' And I said, 'I don't care. The noise is killing me.' That's how bad I was.

"I was in the hospital 18 days and didn't play again for six weeks, exactly 43 days after the collision. You know, when you're fighting for your job every year as I was, you want to get back out there as fast as you can, although I shouldn't have played as soon as I did. They flew me back to Cleveland for surgery, and I had lost about 10 pounds, lying around the hospital.

"When I did get back [in the lineup], ironically the first game I played was in Yankee Stadium where the collision had taken place. When I was introduced in the starting lineup, I got a standing ovation from the fans, right there in Yankee Stadium. It was really neat . . . probably was the only one I ever got.

"Don't try to tell me the fans in New York are all bad."

Dave Burba
(Pitcher, 1998–2001, 2002)

Dave Burba reluctantly recalled one of the longest home runs he ever relinquished.

"It was in 1998, when Charlie Manuel was the hitting coach of the Indians, and I was pitching in a game against the St. Louis Cardinals at Jacobs Field. I threw Mark McGwire a pretty good fastball, and he hit it a ton, a king-sized home run out of the ballpark into the left-field bleachers, away back. It almost went completely out of the park.

"After he hit it, I looked into our dugout and all my teammates were on their feet, looking at where the ball landed—and laughing. I thought to myself, 'Man, that's kind of disrespectful, that my own teammates are dogging me, teasing me.'

"When I went into the dugout at the end of the inning, I was kind of upset about it because even Manuel had a big grin on his face. He was actually giggling. I went up to him and said, 'Dammit, Charlie, what's so funny?' and he said to me, 'Oh, hell, Burb. I just like watching home runs. I don't care who hits 'em. And that one was a beauty.'

"Fortunately, we won the game, so I could laugh about it, too. Not right away, but later."

Ellis Burks
(Outfielder and designated hitter, 2001–2003)

Ellis Burks was the elder statesman among the Indians before he left as a free agent and enjoyed teasing his teammates, especially rookies.

"It was during our first home game in Spring Training [in 2003] and Ben [Broussard], a young first baseman who's a good kid and a pretty good player, hit a deep fly ball to the gap in left-center field. It was pretty deep and appeared it was going to be a home run, but the center fielder ran and caught the ball just as Ben, who was running with his head down, was making his turn at first base.

"When he approached second base he asked the umpire, 'What happened? Was it a homer?' and the umpire said it was. So Ben went into his home run trot around second and third, and everybody in the dugout wondered what the heck he was doing. We're all saying, 'No, no, noooo.'

"When Ben got home, he jumped on the plate and walked to the dugout with a big smile on his face, and all of us in the dugout started playing tricks on him, giving him high fives and all that, just as if he really had hit a home run.

"Then, all of a sudden, one of the guys said, 'Hey, Dude, it didn't go out,' and Ben said, 'What do you mean? The umpire said it did.'

"Finally Ben realized everybody—even the umpire—was putting him on and got all red faced and embarrassed, and we all laughed again. It was a fun time."

Cy Buynak
(Jacobs Field visiting clubhouse manager)

As the Indians clubhouse manager for 28 years (before switching to the visiting team clubhouse in 1990), Cy Buynak knew virtually everything that was going on behind the scenes with the players of his era.

"Max Alvis usually had a big chew of tobacco in his mouth, and one day during a game, he took a grounder off his chest and swallowed his chew. I turned to [then-Manager] Alvin Dark in the dugout and said, 'Skip, in a minute we're going to have a problem here.' Alvin asked why, and I told him, 'Because Alvis just swallowed his tobacco, and he's going to come running in here to the john to throw up.'

"With that, somebody on the field called time and Max came running into the dugout, just as I knew he would, and pretended he had to get his sunglasses, or something. Then he threw up.

"All Alvin said was, 'I hope that teaches him a lesson.'"

(It didn't.)

"Bert Blyleven was a great practical joker, but there were times I didn't think he was so funny. He used to pick me up and throw me into one of the big trash cans we kept in the clubhouse," said Buynak, who is slightly more than four feet tall.

"But I usually got even with him. Whenever he'd throw me into trash barrel, the next day I'd tie up his baseball uniform in knots. I guess he knew it was me because, after I did it, he'd come get me and throw me back in the trash can again."

"Probably the funniest guy we ever had on the team was Looie [Luis] Tiant. Everybody tried to pull pranks on him. One time Chuck Hinton put Looie's uniform on, and a reporter from out of town approached him for an interview, thinking he was talking to Tiant. Hinton answered the questions in broken English, and the reporter kept asking him what he was saying.

"I don't think the reporter ever found out that he really was interviewing Hinton, not Tiant, but it didn't matter because he couldn't understand half of what Hinton was saying anyway."

"One time we were going on a road trip in Spring Training and, in those days, everybody had to carry his own equipment bag. Gary Bell, who was one of the all-time funniest guys I ever knew, put two dead jackrabbits in Tiant's bag. You can imagine what happened when Looie opened his bag. The dead jackrabbits scared the hell out of him. Nobody ever told him it was Bell who did it, but I think Looie knew, because Bell was always doing things like that."

"After Albert Belle left and returned [to Jacobs Field] as a visiting player, he always was pretty nice, except one night [1999] when he was playing for Baltimore. He was mad because he was having a bad game. After every time he batted and didn't get a hit, he came into the clubhouse, took a cup of All-Sport [drink], sipped from it, and then threw the rest on the floor, all over the carpet.

"I don't know if he was trying to get on me or what, but I just let it go. I'd wipe it up and not say anything. When the season ended, the [Indians] ball club sent him a bill for cleaning the carpet. I don't know how much they charged him, but it was a lot. Probably about $500. I didn't know what to expect from him the following season. He never said anything to me about it, but he didn't spill any more All-Sport on the carpet."

"When Belle first came up with us, after he made an out, he'd take a bat—anybody's bat that was laying around—and swing it against the wall and break it. I told him, 'Albert, I don't mind if you break a bat, but one of these times you're going to hurt your hand and it'll be goodbye to your career.'

"After that he took my advice about not hitting the wall but, instead, went down where the john was located and started hitting the door on the partition.

"He did it so many times he broke the partition, not the bat he was swinging, and when the season ended Art Modell's company [that owned the Stadium] sent him a bill for repairing the john. That one cost him about $2,500, which he couldn't believe. As far as I know, he paid it."

Ernie Camacho
(Pitcher, 1983–1987)

As an Indians reliever from 1983–1987, Ernie Camacho enjoyed two splendid seasons as one of the American League's best closers in 1984 and 1986, when he was credited with 23 and 20 saves, respectively.

He also is "credited" with some verbal gems by the three beat writers who covered the Tribe during Camacho's tenure—Paul Hoynes of the Cleveland *Plain Dealer*, Jim Ingraham of the *Lake County News-Herald*, and Sheldon Ocker of the *Akron Beacon-Journal*.

According to the three scribes, the best of Camacho's malapropisms were:

"What states are Massachusetts and Oklahoma City in?" and "Were there any black catchers in the Negro leagues?"

And after he blew a crucial save during the 1987 season, Camacho explained, "My arm was tired because before the game I had to sign 100 baseballs at one time, while the other guys on the team signed them over three days."

Tom Candiotti
(Pitcher, 1986–1991)

"In 1986, when we were playing the Seattle Mariners in the last game of the season, I was all packed up and ready to go home because I'd pitched two days previously. At the time I was tied with Bert Blyleven [who then pitched for Minnesota] with 16 complete games, and I figured I'd just spend the day in the dugout watching the game, and leave as soon as it was over.

"But when I got to the clubhouse, [Manager] Pat Corrales came up to me and said, 'You're pitching today, and you're going to finish the game, no matter what.'

"Pat wanted to make sure that I wound up with the complete-game championship—one of the few things we [Indians] won that season—and we beat the Mariners, 4–2. But it wouldn't have mattered if I'd given up 14 or 15 runs, he would have left me out there.

"Blyleven had pitched for us [from 1981] until he was traded [August 1, 1985] to the Twins, which I think was Corrales' motivation for making sure that I finished ahead of Bert in complete games."

Rico Carty
(First baseman/designated hitter, 1974–1977)

It was a stunning acceptance speech delivered by Rico Carty upon his introduction at a banquet attended by 600 fans honoring him as the Indians "Man of the Year" for 1976.

With Manager Frank Robinson seated next to him at the head table, Carty criticized Robinson for a lack of leadership.

"They talk about the leader of the team. They mention this player and that player. But who is the best leader of the team? It's the manager. When he leads, we got a ball club. Believe me, I'm telling this with all my heart," said Carty, as Robinson winced. So did General Manager Phil Seghi, seated next to Robinson, and virtually all the players among the audience.

Carty ended his remarks by saying to Robinson, "We need your help, Frank. If you don't help us, we'll all be in trouble."

Two months later, on June 7, 1977, Carty was suspended by Robinson for 15 days for "insubordination."

And before Carty's suspension was lifted, Robinson was fired (June 19).

Joe Charboneau
(Outfielder, 1980–1982)

"It happened in 1980 and was the biggest thrill of my baseball career. We were in Yankee Stadium, and just being there was very exciting. Before the game, I went out to see the monuments in center field and I talked to Reggie Jackson [then a Yankee outfielder]. Somebody took a picture of us, which I still have hanging on my wall at home.

"Tom Underwood, a left hander, was pitching for the Yankees, and the first time I faced him I got ahead in the count, 3-and-1, and looked for a fastball in, which I got. I swung, and it was the best I ever hit a ball. It ended up in the third deck, and after the game they told me it was one of the three longest balls ever hit in Yankee Stadium. Imagine that! Yankee Stadium. The 'House that Ruth built.'

"I remember going around second base, and the crowd was totally silent. I looked up to where the ball landed and thought to myself that I'd never hit another ball like that one—and I never did. It was a once-in-a-lifetime swing. A perfect swing, and the pitch was right there. The whole thing was unbelievable. It seemed like the ball carried forever—which the memory of it does."

Allie Clark
(Outfielder/first baseman, 1948–1951)

Indians owner Bill Veeck and vice president Hank Greenberg were astonished—and, according to sources, infuriated—when player-manager Lou Boudreau assigned outfielder Allie Clark to play first base in the one-game playoff against the Boston Red Sox for the pennant in 1948.

The move also surprised Clark, who'd never previously played the position.

"I still don't have any idea why Boudreau decided to play me at first base, other than to get my [right-handed] bat in the lineup. After we'd lost that last game of the season [to Detroit, 7–1, in Cleveland], we showered, got dressed, went to the station, and rode the train all night to Boston.

"Lou never said anything to me, and when I got to the clubhouse [at Fenway Park] there was a first baseman's glove in my locker. I don't know whose it was. Maybe it was Boudreau's, because he could play any position. I took it and went into Boudreau's office and asked him, 'Lou, is this right?' He said, 'Yeah, you're playing first base.' That's all. So I did.

"Sure, I was scared. I'd never played first base before, and remember, the Red Sox had a guy named Ted Williams and a couple other pretty good left-handed hitters in their lineup. I didn't know anything about playing first base.

"I was the happiest guy in the world when Boudreau took me out and put in Eddie Robinson [after the Indians had taken a 5–1 lead in the fourth inning]. Actually, I guess I did OK. I went 0-for-2, but I fielded one grounder and took four throws without doing anything wrong.

"The amazing thing about it, if I had done something to lose the game, I wouldn't have been blamed. You know who would have taken the heat? Boudreau. That's the kind of manager he was. He'd play his hunches; he'd do anything he thought would help win a game. I thought he was a helluva manager and especially a helluva player."

Rocky Colavito
(Outfielder, 1955–1959, 1965–1967)

On June 10, 1959, Rocky Colavito became the sixth player in Major League history to hit four home runs in one game in the modern era (since 1901), and the third American Leaguer to do so. Since then, four players (all National Leaguers) have hit four, though only Colavito, Lou Gehrig in 1932, and Mike Schmidt in 1976 hit four in consecutive trips to the plate.

"My son Stevie remembers the night I did it [in Baltimore] better than anyone," said Colavito. "Every anniversary of that game he gets another picture of me made and framed that says, 'Happy 42nd,' or whatever year it is, which I think is a beautiful thing.

"Funny thing that night, early in the game, after I'd hit my first home run and as I caught a ball against the right-field wall, a guy in the stands threw a cup of beer in my face. I was livid and challenged him. I didn't think anybody should do something like that to a player who was trying to make a living.

"The next time up I hit my second home run, and when I got out to right field I told him that I'd meet him outside the stadium after the game.

"So then, when I hit my third home run, the fans in right field gave me a standing ovation and guess what? The guy who threw the beer in my face was one of them. He was standing there cheering with the rest of the fans.

"But after I hit the fourth home run, he was gone.

"Something else that's funny about that night. Before the game I was asked by a sportswriter, 'When are you going to start hitting?' He was being facetious, but I knew that he also was partly serious. I was only 3-for-28 going into that game. "I told him, 'You never know, maybe I'll get going tonight.' Which I did.

"I remember everything about that game. I walked my first time at-bat—Jerry Walker was the Baltimore starting pitcher—and I hit my first homer off him with a man on base in the third inning. The ball hugged the left-field foul line, and while I knew it was long enough, there was a question of whether it was high enough.

"Nobody was on base when I hit the second homer in the fifth off Arnold Portocarrero. It was the best of the four, and went deep into the [left-field] stands far from the foul line.

"I hit No. 3, also off Portocarrero, in the sixth with one man on. Both of them [off Portocarrero] were on good pitches, sliders that hit the outside part of the plate. I was able to reach over and get them.

"Before I went to the plate the fourth time in the ninth inning, my roomie, Herb Score, said to me, 'Go up there and hit the fourth one.' I remember telling him I'd be happy to get a single, and he said, 'Bull. Go up there and do it.'

"Ernie Johnson [the Orioles' ace reliever] was on the mound by then, and his first pitch was high and inside. I just raised my chin and the ball went under it. He probably thought I'd be looking away for the next pitch, so he came back up and in with another fastball. I was looking for it and connected. It also wound up in the left-field stands, and we won, 11–8.

"I was thrilled. I was aware that Gehrig was the only other player to hit four in a row, because he was my brother Vito's favorite player. Mine, too, until Joe DiMaggio came along. The crowd [15,883] gave me a standing ovation."

Just as thousands of Indians fans never forgave Frank Lane for trading Rocky Colavito to the Detroit Tigers (for Harvey Kuenn) in 1960, neither has the principal.

"Let me put it this way," Colavito said during a 2002 visit to Cleveland, "I never thought [Lane] was a good person, OK? And when you're not a good person when you're alive, you're not a good person when you're dead. By that I mean, when somebody dies a lot of people want to make that person out to have been an angel, but I don't believe in that baloney. That's a lot of . . . well, you know. It's a farce.

"And [Lane] was not a good person. I never thought he was a good human being, and that was very important to me. I also thought he was a terrible baseball man. He couldn't see; he had such bad eyesight, so how could he tell a good ballplayer?

"He also was an egomaniac. He had his secretary go through 35 newspapers a day to find references to his name. He knew if he made a deal of any magnitude, it would get his name on the front page. We should've won the pennant [in 1960], but he decimated the entire team with his crazy deals."

It was during that visit to Cleveland that, among the fans asking Colavito for his autograph, was a boy who called the former outfielder his "all-time favorite" player.

"I asked him, 'How can I be your favorite player when you weren't even born when I played here?' He said, 'Because my mother always talked about how good you were.'

"And if that doesn't warm your heart, as it did mine, nothing will."

Vince Colbert
(Pitcher, 1970–1972)

"When I came up with the Indians, they had a relief pitcher named Fred Lasher, and he and [Manager] Alvin Dark never seemed to see eye to eye about things, especially about how Lasher was being used," recalled Vince Colbert, also a relief pitcher.

"One night when Fred was pitching, Alvin walked out to the mound, stuck his hand out, and said, 'Fred, give me the ball.' But instead of handing the ball to Dark, Lasher slammed it to the ground and stalked off the mound. As Fred was walking to the dugout, the fans behind the dugout started booing him, and Fred got so pissed off, he threw his glove at the fans.

"Well, back then, those things weren't collector's items like they are now, and the fan who caught the glove threw it back at Fred. It was one of the funniest things I ever saw.

"After that, Fred didn't last long. Alvin told him to get out of here, and he was gone . . . never came back," Colbert said, though Lasher pitched briefly, appearing in two games for the California Angels in 1971 and then was out of baseball.

"I got along OK with Dark, but when Ken Aspromonte took over as manager [in 1972], he and [then-President-General Manager] Gabe Paul thought I would be more effective if I lost some weight. A lot of weight.

"I remember it as clearly as if it happened yesterday. Aspromonte called me in mid-January [1972] and said they wanted me to come to camp at 190 pounds. *One hundred-and-ninety pounds!* Geez, I hadn't been that light since I couldn't remember when. At the time I was pitching anywhere from 215 to 220.

"But in those days you did as you were told, and I went on a crash diet and lost more than 30 pounds. All I'd do, basically, was have a cup of black coffee and a piece of toast when I got up in the morning. For lunch I'd have another cup of black coffee and maybe a piece of fruit. Something like that. That was it. I was determined to get down to what they wanted. I finally did. I got down to 190.

"The trouble was, in addition to losing all that weight, I also lost a lot of strength—and the steam on my fastball. I couldn't throw hard at all. Until then my fastball ranged in the low 90s. But not after I got down to 190. It was awful. People who knew me asked if I had been sick because I was so thin, so gaunt looking. In fact, when I got to Spring Training, they ran tests on me because they thought I might have sickle cell anemia or something.

"I didn't realize at the time what I did to myself, going on that crash diet, but it wound up costing me my career. It took me more than two years to regain my weight and my strength, but by then it was too late. The Indians just gave up on me. They told me I didn't have it anymore. And it didn't help to gain back the weight because, to do so, I ate the wrong things. I got my weight back, but not my strength.

"As I said, things were different then. A lot different.

"I like to believe that if the Indians had left me alone, if they had not told me to lose weight—for my own good, they said— everything would have turned out differently, and I would have had a better career, certainly a longer career. But that's my only real regret."

Pat Corrales
(Manager, 1983–1987)

"Gabe Paul was getting up in his years [73] when I came in to manage the Indians [in 1983]. Dave Garcia, who'd managed the team before I got to Cleveland, warned me that sometimes Gabe had trouble staying awake.

"Dave told me he used to put a paperback book in his pocket and would read it as soon as Gabe dozed off. He said he got in a lot of reading that way.

"But I came up with a different strategy, because I didn't want to waste that much time. As soon as Gabe dropped off, I would slap his desk and say, 'Gotta go now, Gabe.' He'd wake up and, not realizing how long he'd slept, he'd be too embarrassed to ask me to stay any longer."

Del Crandall
(Catcher, 1966)

Prior to joining the Indians, Del Crandall played 15 seasons in the National League for the Boston/Milwaukee Braves, San Francisco Giants, and Pittsburgh Pirates, during which he caught Hall-of-Fame pitchers Warren Spahn and Juan Marichal, as well as Lew Burdette and Bob Veale.

It gave him unique insight in comparing them with Sam McDowell, who in 1970 was at the peak of what should also have been a Hall-of-Fame career.

"Sam McDowell's fastball, slider, curve, and change-up—all four of his pitches—were as good as any guy I ever caught."

Coco Crisp
(Outfielder, 2002–2005)

It would seem that Coco Crisp has an easy time of it, signing autographs, because his name contains only nine letters—four in his nickname and five in his surname. But that's not necessarily so, he said. "It's no big deal, but when someone asks for my autograph, I usually sign my full name," which is *Cavelli* Crisp.

He was nicknamed Coco by his grandmother when he was an infant.

"A lot of people ask me why I always look so serious, but I'm not really a serious guy," he said. "I clown around a lot, except when I step on the field, and especially not when I'm up to bat. Then I'm very serious. I know baseball is a game, but it's my job, and I know I have to focus when I'm on the field. I'll clown around in the clubhouse and off the field, but not on the field."

When he dropped a routine fly ball for an error in the Tribe's 2004 season opener against Minnesota, Crisp explained, "It was textbook. I saw the ball all the way as it was coming down. I held up my glove. The ball is supposed to go into my glove. I close my glove, and the ball stays there. But that time, I did my job. The ball didn't do its job."

Another time later that season, in a game against the New York Yankees, Crisp slapped a grounder down the first-base line that pitcher Orlando Hernandez fielded. Instead of tossing the ball to the first baseman, Hernandez straddled the line and waited with his arms folded to tag Crisp.

But Coco had other ideas. He faked a move to the left and then another to the right, but still Hernandez didn't bite, just held his ground, waiting for Crisp.

Finally the umpire called Coco out for leaving the baseline.

"I tried to juke him, but he wouldn't fall for it," said Crisp—who enjoyed the failed maneuver as much as the fans did.

Alvin Dark
(Manager, 1968–1971)

"My first year in the big leagues was 1948 [as a shortstop for the Boston Braves], and the way we won the pennant, how easy it was, I thought, 'Man, we are going to play in the World Series every year.' I never realized until later how tough it was and what a big thing it is to win the pennant and get to the World Series.

"I found out in a hurry. When we lost to Cleveland and their great pitching staff, that's when I knew how really tough it is.

"We were lucky to win the first game of the Series, and probably wouldn't have if it hadn't been for [umpire] Bill Stewart's call [in the eighth inning when Bob Feller tried to pick off pinch runner Phil Masi at second base]. Stewart was a great [NL] umpire, but he called that play wrong, and everybody in the ballpark knew he blew it. Masi was out, or should have been called out.

"We knew the Indians had the play and that Feller and [shortstop Lou] Boudreau worked it good, but it just so happened that . . . uh, well, Masi was out.

"I was kneeling in the on-deck circle, because I was up next [following Tommy Holmes] and naturally, as soon as Feller turned [to throw to Boudreau] I stood up to see the play. When Stewart called

Masi safe, I almost clapped my hands. I'm standing there thinking, 'Man, he was out, how in the world did the umpire call him safe?'

"Then Holmes singled to score Masi and we won, 1–0. But the man was out and everybody in our dugout—heck, everybody in Braves Field—knew it. I believe Stewart knew it too, that after he called it, he knew he called it wrong.

"But then, as Feller once told me, if Stewart had called Masi out, its still a 0–0 game, and we might still be playing."

"When I managed the Indians [1968–1971] all kinds of things were happening with Sam McDowell, who was one of my favorite guys and should have been a great, great pitcher. I loved Sam McDowell, I really did, but he was his own worst enemy.

"One time, when we were on a road trip in California, I was checking up on some of the players. Not all of them, but some of them, because I liked to have them in their rooms at a decent hour and it already was past the curfew. That's when I saw Sam walking down the hall in his undershorts.

"When he saw me he took off running out the back door of the hotel, jumped in the swimming pool, and clung real close to the edge of the pool [in the water]. He didn't think I could see him, and he just stayed there, hiding until I left. I was dying laughing, but I wouldn't do anything because if I did I'd get Jack Sanford, my pitching coach, mad at me."

Jeff Datz
(Coach, 2002–2009)

"One night during a game, [then-Manager] Charlie Manuel made a call that something was going to happen, and it was one of the damndest things I ever saw," Jeff Datz recalled from the 2002 season.

"Jim Thome was batting, and when the other team's pitching coach—I don't want to say who it was—started to the mound, Charlie tapped me on the shoulder and said, 'Watch this, Big Daddy,' which is what he sometimes called me, 'Jimmy is good for a home run, right now.'

"When the coach finished talking to his pitcher, he walked back to the dugout and Charlie tapped me on the arm again. 'I'm telling you, Big Daddy,' he said, 'watch this. After that conversation we're good for a home run. Jimmy is going deep right here.' And damned if it didn't happen just like that. Thome hit the first pitch into the right-field seats. Wow! I couldn't believe it."

After pitching batting practice before a game during a hot spell in July 2004, Datz remarked, "It's so hot out there I saw a dog chasing a cat and they were both walking."

Jason Davis
(Pitcher, 2002–2007)

After getting his first look at the Big Apple during the Indians' first series in New York in 2003, Jason Davis, who was born and raised in Chattanooga, Tennessee, said, "I bet there are more people in this town than there are in all of Tennessee."

(For the record, the population of Tennessee in 2002 was 5,797,289 people; New York City recorded 8,008,278 residents in 2002.)

Bob DiBiasio
(Vice president/public relations, 1979–1986, 1987–)

"The press box at the old Stadium was remodeled in the late 1970s and one of the features—as then Indians President Gabe Paul liked to point out—was that shatterproof and unbreakable glass panels were installed to protect the working media.

"However, one night in 1979 when we were playing California, [Angels second baseman] Bobby Grich fouled off a pitch that flew up and hit one of the supposedly unbreakable glass panels in front of Dick Svoboda, who was covering for *United Press International*.

"Well, the unbreakable glass broke, the ball went right through the panel, and hit Svoboda in the head, which in itself was bad enough.

"But then to make matters worse, a couple of pitches later, after Svoboda changed his seat, Grich fouled off another one that hit the panel in front of Svoboda's new seat, and it also broke the glass.

"Except for a couple of scratches and bruises, Svoboda was OK, although his pride was seriously shattered, along with the window panels.

"So much for the unbreakable glass windows at the old Stadium."

Larry Doby
(Outfielder, 1947–1955, 1958)

"Winning the World Series was the highlight of my career, and I'll always cherish the memory of Steve Gromek hugging me. It was completely, totally spontaneous; we just grabbed each other because we were so happy to win [Game 4, 2–1, when Doby hit a home run and Gromek scattered seven hits to beat the Boston Braves and Johnny Sain].

"As they say, God works in mysterious ways. Here was a white guy and an African-American guy who are put together and win a game, and when it's over they don't wonder, 'Should I not do this because I'm white and he's black? Or because 'I'm black and he's white?'

"No, they just do it, they just hug each other because they're happy, which made up for everything I went through. I would always relate back to that whenever I was insulted or rejected by hotels. I'd always think back to that picture of Gromek and me. It would take away all the negatives."

"I roomed with Satchel Paige, but I can't say we were close. It wasn't so much that Satch was a loner. It was how he dealt with people, those he knew, and he knew an awful lot of people because he'd pitched in all the towns that we played in.

"He'd been in those towns long, long ago. Not just like two or three years . . . it was more like 10 or 12 years previously. So all the black hotels that we lived in, he knew all the people, he was comfortable with them.

"Another reason I wasn't really close to Satch, I abided by the rules, and he didn't. Not always. You can't have different rules for different people. Everybody has to go by the same rules. Everybody has the same curfew, or should. That's the way it is, or should be."

Al Rosen, who was Doby's teammate from 1947–1955, said of the former outfielder: "This is not to denigrate Jackie Robinson, but Jackie was a college-educated man who had been an officer in the service and who played at the Triple-A level. Jackie was brought in by Branch Rickey specifically to be the first black player in Major League Baseball.

"Larry Doby came up as a second baseman who didn't have time to get his full college education, and who was forced to play a different position in his first Major League season. I think, because of those circumstances, he had a more difficult time than Jackie Robinson. I don't think he has gotten the credit he deserves.

"I saw Larry get knocked down on four straight pitches by Dizzy Trout [of the Detroit Tigers], but Larry just got up, brushed himself off, and walked to first base. I've always admired him."

Before he died in 2003, Larry Doby talked about how he had wanted to coach and manage in the Major Leagues after he retired as a player with the Chicago White Sox and Montreal, in addition to the Indians, but that he knew because of the way baseball had changed that the game had "passed me by."

"The discipline that was in place when I played doesn't seem to be there anymore. I couldn't see myself saying to a player, 'I am going to sit you down and fine you, blah, blah, blah,' and then have him go upstairs and complain to the front office or for the players union to tell me I couldn't do this or that, even though I was the manager of the team.

"Because of the money the players are making today, and the rules that are in effect, you can't fine a guy enough to make it meaningful, which is a shame."

Larry Dolan
(Owner, 2000–)

Upon purchasing the Indians on November 4, 1990, Larry Dolan said: "Dick [Jacobs] is my greatest asset and my greatest liability. He's an asset because of all the outstanding things he's done for this organization and this city. But he's a liability, because he's going to be a tough act to follow."

And, "My idol was always Lou Boudreau. It never occurred to me to be Bill Veeck."

Frank Duffy
(Shortstop, 1972–1977)

"I liked being an Indian, and I really enjoyed my time in Cleveland [1972–1977], even though the old Stadium was a tough ball park to play in. I think my [batting] average was better on the road than at home, one of the reasons being that Gaylord [Perry] loved long grass in the infield so that ground balls he threw didn't get through. But I hit a lot of ground balls, and a lot of mine didn't get through, either. So, statistically, offensively, the Stadium hurt me, and it was cold, like a big cavern sometimes.

"But, talking about the whole thing, living in Cleveland and playing for Frank [Robinson] was my best time in baseball. One of my favorite memories, maybe the best of all, was the Opening Day game in 1975 when Frank hit a home run [off the New York Yankees' Doc Medich]. What a way to start [his career] as Major League Baseball's first black manager!

"I wasn't in the lineup that day because I'd pulled a rib cage muscle in the last Spring Training game and missed the first 10 or 12 games. I was in the dugout and remember what it was like when Frank came around the bases. There were about 75,000 fans in the Stadium that day, and 7,500 the next day. That's how it always was in April in Cleveland, with the weather and school still going on.

"I thought playing for Frank was great, though some of the guys on that club had a little problem with him. I don't think it was ever racially motivated, at least not that I knew of. It's just that Frank came in and was still more like a player than a manager. He was still too close to being only a player. Everything came so easy for him as a player, unlike the way it was for most of the rest of us."

"Being traded to Cleveland [November 29, 1971] was a big break for me. I'd been at Cincinnati [1970–1971], where I didn't play much because they had Dave Concepcion. Then I got traded to the Giants where Chris Speier was the shortstop, and I was just basically sitting. We had a young club in Cleveland, with a lot of good talent coming up—Jack Brohamer and Buddy Bell and Rick Manning and Dennis Eckersley—and we were really a team of equals, socially speaking.

"It was different when I was traded to Boston [March 24,1978] where everything was stratified. The Red Sox had their superstars—Yaz [Carl Yastrzemski] and Jim Rice and Fred Lynn—a bunch of middle-echelon players, and then the bench guys, of which I was one, and it wasn't much fun.

"I wasn't really shocked when the Indians traded me, because I could see the handwriting, but I was disappointed, really disappointed. [General Manager] Phil Seghi called me into his office and said, 'Hey, you should be happy. You're going to a strong club,' which the Red Sox were. But I knew I wasn't going to play much. Rick Burleson was their shortstop, and I didn't want to be a utility player, which I was all of 1978 and part of 1979, before I was released in the second year of a two-year contract. That was it for me, so I just said goodbye and made the transition."

Though his highest batting average was only .263 (in 1973) and his 10-year Major League record was only .232, Frank Duffy was considered one of baseball's best shortstops and probably could have extended his career instead of retiring in 1979 after he'd been traded to Boston the previous season. But he had no regrets about leaving the game at the age of 32.

"When I retired I actually had a feeling of relief," he said. "I knew it was time for me to go. I had other objectives. I wanted to find out what it was like to live in the real world. I was tired of the whole routine [of Major League Baseball], the regimentation.

"It got to be like the military—you have to be on the bus at a certain time, at the airport at a certain time, at the ballpark at a certain time—it was more than I wanted to live with. I still wake up some mornings and think how glad I am that I don't have to catch a bus, or be at an airport, or get to the game.

"Sure, baseball was good to me. I made some money that helped me get started in the real estate business, and I'm grateful for what baseball did for me. But that part of my life is behind me. I'm facing new challenges now."

Dave Duncan
(Catcher, 1973–1974)

Since leaving the Indians, Dave Duncan has become one of baseball's most highly respected pitching coaches (under Manager Tony La Russa with Oakland from 1986 to 1995 and St. Louis from 1996 to 2011).

He also played for the Kansas City/Oakland Athletics (1964–1972) and Baltimore (1975–1976), and despite his brief tenure with the Indians, Duncan has the highest regard for Cleveland and its fans.

"Cleveland is the only place I played where you can drive 100 miles away from the city, walk into a store, and have somebody ask you about the team. The fans in Cleveland are tremendous."

Steve Dunning
(Pitcher, 1970–1973)

"It was overwhelming to be drafted No. 1 in the country [in 1970] and then to be given the opportunity to pitch in the big leagues immediately—and to win," said Steve Dunning, who started and hurled five innings in a 9–2 victory over the Milwaukee Brewers on June 14, 1970.

"It was almost beyond comprehension—a dream come true, something I'll never forget as long as I live. And if I could play my [seven-year Major League] career over again, the only part I'd change would be the middle and end, certainly not the beginning."

After beating the Brewers in his first professional baseball game fresh out of Stanford University, Dunning said, "I'm so excited and jubilant and happy. This is the greatest thrill of my life. It is a magnificent moment, a fairy tale. I'm not even sure it is real."

Dennis Eckersley
(Pitcher, 1975–1977)

"It was the most humbling experience of my career [1975–1998] and happened as we were being introduced on Opening Day in 1976. I was really pumped and went charging out of the dugout onto the field at the old Stadium. But I missed the top step and took a headlong dive, flat on my face. It was terrible, humiliating, because in those days in Cleveland, the opener usually was the only time that everybody got jazzed up for the Indians and the stands were packed [with 58,478 fans].

"Fortunately, I didn't hurt myself—physically, that is—although my ego was shattered. Really shattered. Nobody said anything, because I think they were as embarrassed as I was."

★ ★ ★ ★ ★

A year later, on May 30, 1977, Eckersley pitched a no-hitter, beating California, 1–0, at the Stadium, fully restoring his shattered ego.

"[In that game against the Angels] I remember being on the mound in the ninth inning, all fired up, and then noticing that Jim Kern and Dave LaRoche were throwing bullets in the bull pen. I was thinking, 'Here I am, pitching my ass off, and they've got two guys throwing fire in the bull pen. I've got a no-hitter going, and if I give up a hit, I'm probably gone.' Of course, it was a 1–0 game . . . we scored in the first inning, but got nothing after that against Frank Tanana.

"Something else I recall is that I was yelling at Tanana most of the game. I guess I was doing it because [Manager] Frank Robinson didn't like Tanana, for whatever reason. I did whatever made Robbie happy, and whatever he did. If he yelled at somebody, I did, too.

"But nobody in our dugout said [bleep] to me. They all stayed away from me. Every inning, same thing. It was like a ritual.

"When I got the second out in the ninth, I looked over to Buddy [Bell] at third base and yelled, 'One more out!' I was pretty cocky then, but Buddy didn't say anyhing. I think he was too nervous, because the pressure is on the fielders as much as the pitcher. Nobody wants to screw it up.

"In those days I was young and stupid to think that I could throw a no-hitter every time I pitched. And then, every time I'd give up my first hit I'd curse to myself and get mad, which sounds kind of crazy, I know, but that's how I felt back then."

"I can still pitch, I just can't get anybody out," quipped Dennis Eckersley upon his annual return to Cleveland in 2003 for a fundraiser on behalf of his late agent, Ed Keating.

Eckersley sure could pitch—and get batters out—when he broke in as a starter with the Indians in 1975 and pitched a no-hitter against the California Angels on May 30, 1977. He was traded to Boston in 1978, then to the Chicago Cubs in 1984, and in 1987 to Oakland where he launched his Hall-of-Fame career as one of the greatest relief pitchers in baseball history under Manager Tony La Russa. He pitched for St. Louis in 1996–1997 and ended his outstanding career back in Boston in 1998.

Eckersley, with a 197–171 won-lost record and 390 saves in 1,071 games, was inducted into the Hall of Fame in 2004, in his first year of eligibility.

Eckersley's reformation as a pitcher—from starter to ace reliever—virtually coincided with his reformation as an alcoholic.

"I am an alcoholic and was out of control," he said. "It began when I was in Cleveland and continued until I hit bottom in January 1987, when I finally went into rehab, which saved my life. If I hadn't gotten a second chance, I probably would have wound up the same as my brother Wallace. He's in prison serving a 40-year sentence for attempted kidnapping and attempted murder. That's what drugs and alcohol did to him."

It's the reason Eckersley returns to Cleveland every year to raise money for Keating's project, the Freedom House, a rehab center for young men trying to break loose from drug and alcohol addiction.

"I enjoyed my time with the Indians. I didn't want to leave. When I was traded [to Boston] I cried like a baby. I loved being a member of the Indians. But I guess it was only natural for me to feel that way. The first time you get traded is huge, because you are so close to so many players. I was close to Buddy Bell and quite a few guys. I didn't want to go. It's like college or something. You build such closeness to your teammates. It doesn't matter if you're on a .500 team, you want to stay right there.

"Little did I know that there were a lot of great things ahead for me."

Doc Edwards
(Catcher, 1962–1963; coach, 1985–1987; manager, 1987–1989)

"One day in 1986, when Pat Corrales was the manager [1984–1987] and I was a coach, we were playing Baltimore at the Stadium. I was in our bullpen in left field and noticed something that [Orioles shortstop] Cal Ripken was doing. He was relaying the catcher's signals to the outfielders so they'd know what pitch was coming. Ripken put his right [bare] hand behind his back before every pitch and, when the catcher called for a curve ball he'd close his fist, or leave it open for a fastball.

"We arranged for me to relay the information to our guy who was on deck [to bat next] and he would yell something to the batter to let him know what pitch to expect. The way we'd do it, I'd lean against the fence in front of the bullpen with my right arm up if it was a fastball, and drop my hand to my hip if it was a breaking ball.

"We scored ten runs—ten runs!—that game, but here's how bad we were: we still lost, 11–10, because we had so many pitching problems. We had them all year.

"Ripken is a pretty smart guy, and the next day he stopped using his hand signals, probably because he either figured out what was happening—or maybe one of our players leaked to him what we were doing, though I hate to think any of our guys would do something like that.

"Stealing the other team's signals is all part of the game. Like [Bob] Feller always said, 'All's fair in love and war—and in baseball, when you're trying to win a pennant.'"

"When I played in Cleveland [1962–1963], I roomed with Sam McDowell, who was only 19 or 20 then and was as pure as the driven snow. Duke Sims and Joe Azcue also caught Sam, and we all agreed on one thing, that McDowell had the four greatest pitches of any one man in the history of the game. I don't know of any pitcher who could throw all four pitches—fastball, curve ball, slider, and change-up—as good as McDowell.

"After I left the Indians and then got traded to the Yankees from Kansas City, we were in a ball game against Cleveland, and Sam had punched [struck] me out three times in a row. The fourth time I batted against him, in the bottom of the ninth, there were two outs and we were losing, 1–0. I was behind in the count, 0-and-2, and I knew I couldn't hit his fastball, or curve, or slider. I knew if he threw me one of those three pitches, I'd go down for the fourth time, and the game would be over.

"But instead of a fastball, curve, or slider, Sam threw me a change up, and I hit a dying quail over second base. You've seen on TV, when birds get shot and they just kind of flutter down to the ground. That's the way my ball looked when I hit Sam's change up. Don't ask me why he threw me a change-up. Probably just to fool me, have some fun at my expense.

"So now, instead of the game being over, I was on first and Elston Howard pinch hit for the pitcher. He swung late at one of Sam's fastballs and hit it into the right field seats to win the game.

"But the reason we won wasn't because Howard hit the home run, it was because McDowell threw me a change up instead of a fastball, curve, or slider. I never said anything to him about it, because I was afraid I'd make him mad and, next time I'd bat against him, he'd hit me in the neck with a 110 mph fastball."

Harry Eisenstat
(Pitcher, 1939–1942)

"As long as people talk about Bob Feller's career, how it started and how great he was, fans should remember me. I'm the guy who was the winning pitcher in 1938 [October 2] when Feller set the Major League record [since broken] by striking out 18 batters in one game."

Eisenstat, who was with the Indians from 1939–1942, pitched for Detroit in that 1938 game against Feller and had a no-hitter going until the eighth inning. He wound up with a four-hitter and a complete game, 4–1, victory, though Feller got all the accolades because he struck out 18 batters.

"Only one time in my Major League career [1935–1942] did I ever intentionally try to hit a batter, and I was under orders [by Detroit catcher-Manager Mickey Cochrane] to do so.

"It was in 1938, right after Hitler had come to power in Germany. I was pitching against Chicago and heard a bench jockey yelling from the White Sox dugout, 'Hey, Eisenstat. Hitler is looking for you and Greenberg.' At that time there were not many Jewish players in the Major Leagues.

"Cochrane also heard what the guy was yelling and came out to the mound. He told me, 'When that sonofabitch comes to the plate, if you don't hit him right between the eyes with your first pitch, you'll be on a bus to Toledo [and the minor leagues] tomorrow.

"And if he starts to come out after you, I'll toss you the ball, and you hit him with it again.'

"So I did. I threw at him and he ducked, but the ball hit the peak of his cap. When he got to first base I saw Greenberg [then the Tigers first baseman] talking to the guy and pounding his finger on his chest. The minute the game ended Greenberg ran into the White Sox clubhouse, chasing the guy who'd been yelling at me, and had to be restrained by [Chicago Manager] Jimmy Dykes, otherwise he'd have killed him."

"When I was with the Indians in 1940 and we were having all that trouble with the manager [Oscar Vitt], we were in Detroit, fighting for the pennant late in the season, trying to hold on to first place. We'd just lost a tough game to the Tigers, and that night in the Booke-Cadillac Hotel—my room was on the 21st or 22nd floor—and my roommate [pitcher] Bill Zuber and I, left the window open because it was very warm and there was no air conditioning in those days.

"I had to get up during the night to go to the bathroom, and while I was there, Zuber woke up and noticed that I wasn't in bed, and that the window was wide open. He started yelling, 'Eisie, Eisie,' and ran to the open window thinking I'd jumped because I was depressed that we had lost the game that day.

"When I heard him yelling, I ran out of the bathroom and saw him at the open window, and then I thought *he* was going to jump, so I started yelling, 'No, no, Bill, don't do it, it's not worth it.'

"He'd just put a deposit on a farm and was planning to pay it off with our World Series checks, and all he could think about was, there goes the farm. When he saw me, he said, 'Why the hell didn't you tell me you were going to the bathroom?'

"I said to him, 'What do you want me to do, wake you up every time I take a leak?'"

In 1937, when he pitched for Detroit, Eisenstat was the winning (relief) pitcher in both games of a double header, in which future Hall of Famer Hank Greenberg hit three home runs to provide all the offensive support the Tigers needed. "After the games," said Eisenstat, "[Manager] Mickey Cochrane told everybody, 'Fellas, lock yourselves in your rooms tonight. The Jews in Detroit will be going crazy.'"

"Once, when Greenberg and I went to the synagogue for Yom Kippur, the congregation saw Hank and started to applaud. The rabbi didn't know why . . . he thought they were clapping for him."

Ed Farmer
(Pitcher, 1971–1973)

When he first came up with the Indians as a 21-year-old pitcher, Ed Farmer admitted, "I was kind of embarrassed because my father had filled out my [publicity] bio for me. In it he wrote that I had said my goal was to win both the Cy Young Award and the Most Valuable Player award in the same year—in my first year in the big leagues.

"He meant well and did it to motivate me, but you can imagine what the veterans on the team thought when they read what I was supposed to have said. And then, when one of the writers read it and wrote it in the paper, it got picked up by other papers around the league, and I really got kidded a lot. Chuck Hinton was on my back about it for a long time."

After Farmer was traded by the Indians on June 17, 1973, he went on to pitch for Detroit, Philadelphia, Baltimore, Milwaukee, Texas, Chicago White Sox, and Philadelphia again and Oakland through 1983 and for the last several years has been a broadcaster for the White Sox.

"I went to arbitration in the winter of 1980–1981 after I appeared in 64 games for the White Sox, had a 7–9 record with a 3.34 earned run average, and saved 30 games, which was then a club record. I did all that with a team that won only 70 games all season. Not only did I save 30, I pitched 99 innings, and nowadays if you are a short man and you pitch maybe 40 or 42 innings or something like that, you're doing good.

"My 30 saves were second most in the American League to Goose Gossage and Dan Quisenberry, who each had 33, but their teams [the New York Yankees and Kansas City Royals] both won the ALCS for the pennant. I asked for a $495,000 salary, which was $365,000 more than I made in 1980, and $145,000 more than the White Sox were offering.

"The arbitrator was a man named Theodore J. St. Antoine, who was the chairman of the law school at the University of Michigan. He listened to the presentations by my agent, Steve Greenberg, and by the ball club, which took about two and a half hours. The arbitrator compared my record to the other guys' numbers, which is the way those things go, and finally the hearing ended and he said he would consider the arguments and make a decision in a few days.

"But then, as my agent and I got up and walked to the door to leave the room, we were called back by St. Antoine. He said, 'I have a question. I'm just not clear on one thing.' My agent said, 'OK, what is it?' And he said, 'Tell me . . . what is a save?' We couldn't believe our ears.

"I told him, 'Well, it's like when a war is going on and the enemy is closing in to capture the city, and I'm the only guy out there and keep them from capturing the city. That's a save.'

"He said, 'Oh, and that's it? That's a save? And you had 30 of them?' I said, 'Yes, that's it. So help me.' That's the way it went.

"A couple days later I was getting ready to fly with my family from California to Florida, and I called my agent. He wasn't in, and his secretary said she wasn't supposed to tell me if we won or lost. I told her, 'All I want to know is if this is going to be a happy flight or a sad flight.'

"She said, 'Well, let me tell you this. We have champagne here in the office, and it's open.' That's how I found out that we won.

"Here's a sidebar to that story. After I won the arbitration case, I got paid over 12 months, instead of six, as had been the case previously, and when I got my first big paycheck—it was for $39,000 after taxes and other stuff—I showed it to my wife, Barbara. She said, 'I thought you were making a half million dollars. That check doesn't look like much more than you brought home last year.'

"I said, 'No, Barbara. Look again. Now the comma is *behind* the nine, not in front of it, as it was the year before when I was getting, like, $3,900 every two weeks, after deductions.'"

In 1991, eight years after his pitching career ended, Farmer was diagnosed with terminal kidney disease. He underwent a successful kidney transplantation—Farmer's donor was his younger brother Tom—and since then has been active in the Kidney Foundation.

Because of his celebrity status as one of baseball's premier relief pitchers and now as a Major League broadcaster and Kidney Foundation spokesman, Farmer said he often uses an alias when he registers in a hotel on the road.

Among the names he said he used were, "Chuck Roast, Dakota Smith, and Cheyenne Bailey, although I have others that I'll keep to myself."

"We were going to be on the 'Game of the Week' one time in 1972, and Curt Gowdy, who did the game on television, came to our early workout. Gowdy was a good friend of Warren Spahn, our pitching coach, who was throwing batting practice. In those days pitchers hit for themselves, and I took [hit] one of Spahnie's pitches to the upper deck at the old Stadium. Gowdy saw it and yelled, 'Spahnie, I never saw anyone hit a pitch from you that far.'

"Well, anyone who knows Spahnie knows how competitive he is, and when Gowdy said what he did, that was the end of batting practice. Spahn started throwing curve balls, sinkers, screwballs, and change-ups, and even though he was then in his 50s, the old guy could still pitch.

"I said to him, 'What the hell is this?' and he said, 'Sometimes batting practice becomes pitching practice,' which it was for him—and all because Gowdy got on him for the ball I hit.

"I said to Spahnie, 'You retired 20 years ago, can we hit now?' and he said no, which was the end of it—but not until after he threw a fastball behind me."

"One of the first things I learned in the big leagues was in a game against the Giants when I was pitching to Willie McCovey. I threw a pitch that was about two inches—at least—wide of the plate and Ed Runge, who was umpiring, called it a strike.

"McCovey turned around and said something to Runge, and my next pitch was three or four inches wide, but Runge called it strike two. Now McCovey started raving and ranting, and when he went back to the bat rack to get some pine tar, [catcher] Ray Fosse came out to the mound and said, 'Runge just told me, throw it anywhere in the ball park, it'll be strike three, no matter where it is.'

"I asked Ray, 'Does he do that a lot?' and Ray said, 'No, just in certain instances.' And when my next pitch wasn't even close, Runge called it strike three. McCovey just shook his head and walked away. I think he learned a lesson. I know I did."

Bob Feller
(Pitcher, 1936–1941, 1945–1956)

During the 1948 season, when the Indians fought the Boston Red Sox and two other teams (New York and Philadelphia) for the pennant, a high-powered telescope from Bob Feller's World War II ship, the USS Alabama, was hidden in the center-field scoreboard at the old

Cleveland Municipal Stadium. It was used to steal opposing catchers' signals.

"All's fair in love and war—and in baseball, when you're trying to win a pennant," Feller said. "The way I felt about it, it was like in the war, you had to decipher a code, break it down, which we did against the Germans and the Japanese, and we won [World War II], right?"

And the Indians won the 1948 American League pennant and World Series.

Feller struggled through most of the 1948 season, finishing with a sub-par (for him) 19–15 won-lost record. It resulted in speculation that his career as one of baseball's greatest pitchers was near the end, to which he quipped: "I must've been the cleanest guy in the game because the writers kept saying I was all washed up."

"The 1948 season was not one of my best, though it certainly was for the Indians. We had a bunch of great guys, and some pretty tough guys, too. Al Rosen, who came up late in the season, was one of them. A real tough guy.

"After we won the playoff game [for the pennant], Rosen, Joe Gordon, and a couple other teammates and I were sitting at the bar in the Kenmore Hotel. Two guys who looked like lumberjacks came along and started harassing us, especially Rosen. One of them tapped Al on the shoulder and said, 'Hey, Rosen, what are you doing here?' Rosen asked him, 'What do you mean, what am I doing here?'

"The guy was very offensive and abusive, and finally Rosen said, 'Tell me, are we bothering you?' And he said, 'No, you're not bothering me,' and Rosen said, 'Well, you're bothering the hell out of me' and hit him right on the button, knocked him on his butt. It was a terrible mess.

"The guy didn't know that Rosen had been the heavyweight boxing champion of Florida when he went to the University of Miami.

"If something like that happened today it'd be in all the papers, Al probably would get sued, the commissioner would come down on him, and it probably would cost him a nice piece of change. But things were different then."

"If it hadn't been for baseball, I probably would have spent my life picking corn in Iowa, and I've got my father to thank for that. He taught me how to play baseball instead of how to shoot a rifle—and to not cause trouble, which more fathers ought to do with their sons now."

Bob Feller's autograph is one of the most sought after and one of the easiest to get because he makes himself readily available to fans everywhere, which led to the following quip: "A guy came up to me and wanted me to sign a picture. I told him, 'I thought everybody in the United States already had my autograph or didn't want it.'"

The outspoken Hall-of-Fame pitcher often is asked about one of his few disappointments in baseball—that he never won a World Series game.

"In 1954, after we lost the first three games, Al Lopez came back with Bob Lemon instead of starting me. I guess he thought Lemon had a better chance to win the fourth game because he'd had a great year, won over 20 games [23]. He pitched real well in the opener even though we lost 5–2 on a 10th-inning bloop home run by Dusty Rhodes that only went about 250 feet, maybe 251, down the right-field foul line. Rhodes hit the ball on the handle of his bat and [right–fielder] Dave Pope almost caught it.

"I was just spot starting that particular year. I wasn't throwing as hard in 1954 as I did in my prime, even though I still won 13 games mainly with curves and sliders—and with smoke and mirrors. Leo Durocher said to me later that he'd told his ball club that I was the only pitcher they might not be able to beat, and several players confirmed it to me. But the Giants were hot. [Johnny] Antonelli pitched well, they got some very timely hitting, and Durocher did a good job of managing.

"Lopez never talked to me about not starting a game in the Series, and I never asked him about it, so I have no idea what his strategy was or why he didn't let me pitch. But Lemon never could pitch with only two days' rest. Everybody in the league knew it and Bob knew it himself. Al probably thought, well, maybe our luck would change [in the fourth game].

"I don't bear any resentment toward Lopez. I just think it was bad strategy. There was nothing personal about it. I don't care if he had pitched me or not, but he never should have pitched Lemon in my opinion.

"As for my losing [1–0] the opening game of the 1948 World Series [against the then-Boston Braves], when people ask me about the pickoff play that was screwed up by National League umpire Bill Stewart in the eighth inning, I remind them that it cost me a tie game, not a victory.

"The Braves won because I made the mistake of walking the leadoff batter, Bill Salkeld. And it was Phil Masi [Salkeld's pinch runner] who was called safe on the pickoff play, which enabled him to score the only run [on a single by Tommy Holmes].

"When you walk the leadoff batter in an inning, he's going to score 80 or 90 percent of the time. That was the mistake that hurt me as much—maybe more—than the mistake the umpire made, which everybody knew was a mistake.

"Boudreau had planned to tell the umpires and alert them to our pickoff play so they wouldn't also get picked off. But when Boudreau met with them in the commissioner's meeting the day before the Series began, he didn't say anything because [Boston Braves Manager] Billy Southworth was there and he didn't want to alert him as well as the umpires.

"We won the Series, which was more important than the disappointment I felt [in losing Game 1 and also Game 5 11–5]."

"One winter when I was nine or 10 years old, I went to see Lou Gehrig and Babe Ruth play an exhibition game on their barnstorming tour. Their teams were named the 'Larrupin' Lous' and 'Bustin' Babes,' and I got both of them to autograph a ball that I'd bought for five dollars. I raised the money to buy the ball by catching 50 gophers, which were overrunning the farms in the area.

"Those gophers would burrow into the ground and ruin the crops, so the county put out a bounty of 10 cents for each pair of claws we turned in. We'd catch them and kill them by putting them in a bag connected to the exhaust system of our old Dodge truck, then cut their claws off, and take them to the treasurer's office and collect our money.

"Ruth retired [from the Boston Bees] in 1935, one year before I got to the big leagues with the Indians. But I did get to pitch against Gehrig for two and a half seasons. Lou was a big, strong guy, and even though he was not a real good curveball hitter, he could hit a fastball a mile. Especially if you got the ball up.

"I used to throw him a lot of overhand curve balls and kind of wasted my fastball. And, when I did throw him a fastball, I tried to keep it down and in. He was so strong; he had a lot of power and could hit the ball out of any park, in any direction, even though he was basically a pull hitter. He also was a very good first baseman, a very quiet fellow who smoked quite a bit.

"The Babe was different. He was kind of a blunt guy who smoked big cigars and was known to take a drink now and then—even more than now and then—which Gehrig did not.

When someone called Feller a "hero" because he enlisted in the navy two days after the start of World War II and then spent 44 months aboard the battleship USS *Alabama* during the prime of his career, he said: "I wasn't a hero. I was a survivor. The heroes didn't come back. The survivors returned."

And, as for his 266 victories in his 18-year Major League career, Feller said, "There's only one win that was worth it to me . . . and that was World War II."

In the press box one night, a visiting scribe asked Feller about the then-ongoing scandal involving players' uses of steroids and growth hormones.

"Did the players in your day take anything to make themselves bigger, stronger, faster?" the reporter wanted to know.

Feller's deadpan response: "Yes—it was called Wheaties."

Ray Fosse
(Catcher, 1967–1972, 1976–1977)

"Sam McDowell and I were on the American League All-Star team in 1970, and the night before the game the two of us and our wives were having dinner in the hotel dining room," said Ray Fosse as he recalled one of the most significant incidents of his 12-year Major League career.

"Pete Rose came into the hotel dining room and asked Sam and me if we were doing anything special. We weren't, so he invited us—Sam and his wife and me and my wife—over to his house.

"Later, about midnight or 1 a.m.—it was no later than 1 a.m.—Pete took us back to the hotel. We had a nice time. There was no drinking, nothing like that; it was just a nice visit.

"But a funny thing happened—though, in retrospect, it really wasn't so funny. Pete's story changed over the years, which is amazing, maybe because Pete has amnesia or something. What bothers me and has for a long time is that the man keeps telling a different story. If he would just tell the truth about everything, I'd feel a lot different.

"He doesn't mention that we were all together and that we were back at 1 a.m., not 4 a.m. as he has told the story; he also fails to say that we weren't drinking, and that Sam and I were not alone, that we had our wives with us, which he has never said. Those are the things that bother me."

It was in the 12th inning of the 1970 All-Star Game the next day that Pete crashed into Fosse, scoring the National League's winning run for a 5–4 victory and causing an injury to the catcher that hampered him the rest of his career.

"When the play [the collision with Rose] began, Pete was on second base and the batter was Jim Hickman, who hit the pitch to center field. Amos Otis [the AL center fielder] charged the ball and, as Pete was coming around third, I positioned myself to where I thought Otis's throw would come, which happened to be up the line.

"If I had stayed on home plate, I would have missed the ball by three or four feet. I was looking straight out to center field and all of a sudden [Rose] hit me. I never saw him coming. It was total shock. I wasn't braced. All I wanted to do was catch the ball, and he smoked me.

"I knew I was hurt because I couldn't move my left shoulder. But I told everybody it was OK.

"Our first game after the All-Star Game was in Kansas City, it was a doubleheader, and when I caught the first game, Sam was on the mound throwing 100 miles an hour. I couldn't lift my left arm above my shoulder; it was so sore, but I went on playing through the end of the season. It wasn't until the following April that I realized I had fractured and separated my left shoulder.

"Remember, that was [34 years] ago, and things were different then. I was making 12 grand, and in those days, if a bone wasn't sticking out of your body they'd say, 'You're OK . . . go ahead and play.'

"It's different now. Players are really protected. But then, hey, in our day, you played. Period. Pete says he missed two or three games afterward because of the collision, but it was his thigh that was bruised. That's all.

"Sure, it hurt my career. Definitely. I had 16 home runs at the time of the All-Star Game, and when I took batting practice in Kansas City the first day we were back, I could hardly swing the bat. Everything was a swing with my right arm. Every time I think about it, I wonder, could I have been a 30-home run hitter? And could I continue to hit 30 to 35 home runs a year?

"Yeah, I think I could have—but I didn't. I still think, if things back then were the way they are now, the way they take care of guys, it all might have been different for me."

On catching Sam McDowell, Fosse said, "Sam had four of the greatest pitches of any pitcher I ever caught. I mean, he had a helluva fastball, hard-breaking curve, quick slider, and a real good change-up, and he was consistent with all of them.

"Sam was funny about some things, one of them was that he wanted to call his own pitches, so we let him most of the time. He'd do it by adding or subtracting from the numbers I'd put down, by brushing up or down with his glove against his uniform shirt.

"But sometimes it would get to be a problem, especially when I first started catching Sam. I'd signal for a pitch—we usually used two and five [fingers] for a fastball, one for a curve, three for a slider, and four for a change-up. Then Sam could add or subtract from my numbers to change the call.

"Here's how we did it. Say, I'd put down two fingers for a fastball, and he'd add three by brushing his glove three times, which would be his signal for a fastball, same as mine when I put two fingers down. I'd look out at him and wonder, 'What are you doing?' I had just called for a fastball. Basically, I think he just wanted everyone to know that he was calling his own game.

"Everybody talked about how hard he threw, which he did, but he also had a great change-up and loved to fool batters with it. He liked to do it so much that sometimes he'd throw the change-up without even telling me. I'd be looking for a fastball and he'd change up on me.

"Now, as a catcher, I don't care if you throw a change-up off a fastball signal. But when there was a runner on first base, I had to be ready in case he tried to steal, and I didn't want to be looking fastball and have the hitter hit me in the back of the head with his bat because Sam threw a change-up. When he'd do that, when Sam would throw me a change-up when I was looking for a fastball, I'd tell him, 'Hey, I'm on your side, don't try to fool me.'

"After we were together a few years, I figured out that he was tipping off his pitches—every time he was going to throw a fastball he'd take his glove over his head, and when he'd throw a change-up, his glove would go straight up. Because I learned to recognize what was coming, I'd catch his change-up without any trouble, and he'd look at me like, 'How'd you catch that?' He was really a piece of work."

After his retirement as a player in 1979, Fosse returned to Cleveland often as a broadcaster for the Oakland Athletics. And although he hadn't played for the Indians since 1977, there was one occasion in 2004 when he was walking in the downtown area and was surprised to be recognized and greeted by an old fan.

"He was a cop and said to me, 'Hey, you're Ray Fosse, aren't you?' I told him I was and he said, 'I watched you play for the Indians,' and I said, 'You must have been two or three years old.'"

Julio Franco
(Shortstop and second baseman, 1983–1988, 1996–1997)

"I'm ageless," said Julio Franco, who initially came to the Indians as a rookie shortstop in a trade with Philadelphia in 1983.

Since an aborted comeback with the Tribe in 1997, he has played baseball all over the world, including Japan in 1998, Mexico in 1999, Korea in 2000, and Mexico again in 2001.

Franco signed with Atlanta at the tail end of 2001 and has been a key member of the Braves the last three seasons, extending his Major League service to nine teams—Texas, the Chicago White Sox, Milwaukee, and Tampa Bay, in addition to the Phillies, Indians, and Braves—in a professional career that now spans 27 years and counting.

As he said during the 2004 season, "I want to play five more years. Why not? Age doesn't mean you're old. Your body will tell you when you're old. My body tells me, 'Julio, you were born to play baseball, so keep playing.' God gave me the gift to play for a long time, and I am honoring Him. If you can keep playing, why not? If you are 21 and hit a double or if you're 40 and hit a double, it's still a double."

As for Franco's official chronological age, the Indians' and Braves' media guides, as well as *The Baseball Encyclopedia,* say he was born August 23, 1958, which would have made him 46 in 2004.

Franco evaded a direct answer when pointedly asked how old he was in the winter of 2003–2004.

"I'm 51, no, 43 . . . and [the Braves] say, 45. When they took our pictures, they asked us questions [for the media guide] and one of them was, 'Can you tell us something about you that nobody else knows?'

"I wrote down, 'My age,'" Franco told the Braves and left it at that. So be it.

Tito Francona
(Outfielder/first baseman, 1959–1964)

"I know a lot of guys had trouble with Frank Lane, but I didn't. The fact is, I kind of liked the guy. After I joined the Indians in 1959, in my first time at bat as a pinch hitter, I got a single that drove in the game-winning run. Lane came down to the clubhouse and gave me a check for $250.

"A week later I got another key hit, and this time Lane gave me $500, which was pretty good because my salary was $10,000 for the season.

"At the end of the season, after I hit .363, Lane called me up to his office and gave me a contract for 1960 for $20,000, a $10,000 raise. I didn't waste any time signing, and went down to the clubhouse to pack up my stuff to go home for the winter. [Manager] Joe Gordon asked me how much of a raise I got, and I told him, '$10,000.'

"Joe didn't say anything except to tell me to not leave the clubhouse. He went over to the phone and made a call. I didn't know who he called, but when he got off the phone, he told me to go back upstairs, that Lane wanted to see me again. I did and Lane had another contract already made out for me. It was for $2,500 more, for a total of $22,500.

"So, no, I don't dislike Lane . . . and I liked Joe Gordon a helluva lot, too."

"My relationship with John McHale was not as good as it was with Frank Lane when McHale ran the Tigers and I was with Detroit [in 1958], before I was traded to Cleveland. The previous winter [1957–1958], I tried to get a $1,000 raise, but McHale flat-out refused, wouldn't even consider it, so I had no choice but to sign for what he was offering.

"But I got even with him a few years later . . . well, several years later when my son Terry graduated from the University of Arizona.

"Terry had been a big star in college and was picked by Montreal in the first round of the [1980] amateur draft. McHale was then the general manager of the Expos, so when it came time for them to sign Terry, I told him, 'Let me do it [the negotiations], I know John McHale very well.' Boy, did I ever.

"A few days later McHale called with an offer, and Terry gave me the phone. Right off I asked McHale, 'Do you remember that $1,000 raise you wouldn't give me when we both were with Detroit?' McHale said he didn't remember, so I told him, 'Well I do, and if you want to sign my son, it's going to cost you a $300,000 signing bonus.'

"Terry was listening in the other room and almost fainted when he heard what I said. But it set the stage for a real good contract for Terry—a signing bonus of $100,000, which at that time was very good."

Vern Fuller
(Second baseman, 1964, 1966–1970)

"One night, we were in the middle innings of a game and I looked in at the plate and saw Joe Azcue, who was catching, leaving the field and going into the dugout even though there were only two outs.

"Then I realized why. Joe forgot his mask. He caught for the first two batters without a mask! It was crazy. I said to Brownie [shortstop Larry Brown], 'Look, Joe wasn't wearing a mask.' Brownie laughed and said, 'With a puss like Joe's, it wouldn't matter if they fouled a pitch off his face or not.'

"After the inning Joe told us that he just forgot his mask, and nobody reminded him. Imagine that. Neither the umpire nor either of the two guys who batted asked him why he wasn't wearing his mask. Joe said, 'All of a sudden I realized I didn't have it on, so I just called time and went in and got it.'

"Then he said, 'But that was the only time I ever did that,' although, knowing Joe, I wouldn't bet on it."

Richie Garcia
(Supervisor of umpires, 2002–2010)

"In 1974, my first season as an American League umpire, I had a little problem with the Indians and even bigger problems with them in 1976," recalled Richie Garcia, who had a reputation for being strong willed—OK, *hot-headed*—before he was promoted to a supervisory position in 2003.

"I think I had 14 ejections in 1976, and out of those 14, a lot of them were Indians players. I had a little bit of a feud going with Rocky Colavito [then the Tribe's first base coach under Manager Frank Robinson], and I ran him a couple of times, once because he bumped me—or I bumped him, whatever.

"Anyway, Rocky and I had a mutual friend, Frank Cozza, who lived in Anaheim and owned a restaurant. I was in town and so were the Indians, and my friend Cozza called me and said, 'C'mon over after the game and I'll fix something for you and some of the guys to eat.' So I did. No problem. I had [fellow umpire] Ron Luciano with me, and we went to Frank's house.

"But unbeknownst to me, he also invited Rocky, Herb Score [then a Tribe broadcaster], and a couple of Indians players.

"So we went to Cozza's place, and he's got this big table set up with food, and I walk in the room and there's Rocky Colavito. I'm like, oh, my God!

"But you know what? It probably was the best thing that could have happened because Rocky and I talked about the things that had happened between us, why they happened, how they happened, and we patched things up. Our feud was over, and we became good friends, which was the reason Frank Cozza set it all up. Frank was a good friend to both Rocky and me—and still is."

Wayne Garland
(Pitcher, 1977–1981)

As one of baseball's first free agents in the winter of 1975–1976, Wayne Garland signed with the Indians for what was then the largest contract in the game—$2.3 million over 10 years. At the time, the minimum salary in the Major Leagues was $19,000, and the average salary the preceding season was $51,500.

"I was coming off a pretty good season, 20–7 with Baltimore, and my agent, Jerry Kapstein, was collecting offers," said Garland. The contract called for him to receive a $300,000 signing bonus, and he was guaranteed annual salaries of $200,000 through 1986. "Thirteen clubs wanted to sign me, and Los Angeles offered a five-year deal for something like $1.2 million, which is what we were basing our negotiations on. Basically, a million dollars.

"Then, one night Kapstein called and said, 'Wayne, I've got you a real good contract, though I didn't get you a million dollars.' I said, 'Jerry, I understand that [the Dodgers' offer] was just what we were looking at, that it was the high scale, so whatever you got, I'm sure you did a helluva job.' Then he said, 'Well, I got you over two million . . . a 10-year contract for $2.3 million—all of it guaranteed, no cut, no trade—from the Indians.'

"I almost dropped the phone. I said, 'No way,' and Kapstein said, 'Yes.'"

However, in his second season with the Indians, Garland suffered a rotator cuff injury and subsequently underwent surgery. He attempted several comebacks, but never was able to live up to expectations and eventually was released, during the winter of 1981–1982, despite his guaranteed contract.

"Right after the strike [in 1981] ended and we went back to finish the season, we [the Indians] were in the backup game on Monday night television, and I was scheduled to pitch. But Gabe Paul called up [Manager] Dave Garcia and told him not to start me. He said he didn't want me to pitch on national TV and maybe embarrass the club.

"Things got progressively worse after that. I had to be in the bullpen even though I couldn't pitch. If I went out and pitched two innings or nine, my arm felt dead for three or four days afterwards, but they still wanted me to go to the bullpen and pitch in relief.

"They told me they were paying me a lot of money and that I should start earning it. I told them there was nothing I could do, because my arm wouldn't come back. It's not like I went out and hurt myself on purpose. It seemed like everyone held a grudge against me, because I was making what was big money then.

"But I didn't ask for it . . . they offered it. And who wouldn't have taken it?"

In his nine seasons as a Major League pitcher, Garland won 55 games and lost 66 (his five-year record with the Indians was 28–48) before quitting the game at the end of 1981, although he coached at the minor league level for a few years after hanging up his glove.

Jody Gerut
(Outfielder, 2003–2005)

After playing right field against New York for the first time in Yankee Stadium, Jody Gerut said, "It's like a college crowd. They have an ugly chant that ends with 'Jody, you're ugly.' I also heard a lot of 'mother' comments, too."

Pedro Gonzalez
(Second baseman, 1965–1967)

As a good fielding but light-hitting second baseman from 1965–1967, Pedro Gonzalez was once called a "Smiling Volcano," for reasons that often became obvious.

Once, in 1966, the Smiling Volcano erupted when the box score in the *Plain Dealer* did not credit him with a hit. However, it was a mistake in the newspaper as the line after his name read "4–1–0–1," for four at-bats, one run scored, no hits, and one run batted in, but should have been "4–1–1–1."

Gonzalez confronted the official scorer and demanded to know why he was not credited with a hit. The scorer tried to tell Gonzalez, "It was a typographical error," to which the now (un) Smiling Volcano responded, "Error! Error! How could it be an error? [The fielder]never touched the ball!"

Joe Gordon
(Second baseman, 1947–1950)

During the clubhouse meeting following the final regular-season game in 1948 when the Indians finished in a tie with Boston, Manager Lou Boudreau announced that Gene Bearden would pitch the playoff game against the Red Sox.

Several players were surprised, and some openly expressed their objection because Bearden would be taking the mound with only one day's rest. Johnny Berardino was the most vocal of the critics.

But second baseman Joe Gordon said, "Lou, we went along with your choice for 154 games and finished in a tie. There's not a man in this room who, two weeks ago, wouldn't have settled for a tie. I'm sure we can go along with you for another game."

And, after Boudreau hit two homers and Bearden pitched a five hitter to beat the Red Sox, 8–3, Gordon toasted his manager and double-play partner: "To the greatest leatherman I ever saw; to the damnedest clutch hitter that ever lived; to a doggone good manager, Lou."

In June of 1958, Frank Lane asked Gordon if he'd like to manage the Indians. Gordon replied, "Hell yes." Then Lane asked when he could come to Cleveland to take over the team, Gordon said, "Yesterday." And what about (contract) terms? "The hell with terms," Gordon said, ending the "negotiations."

Johnny Goryl
(Coach, 1982–1988)

"A lot of unusual things happened during my 50 years in professional baseball, and one I remember best was in 1986 [May 27] during a game at the old Stadium against Boston. The Red Sox had just gone ahead, 1–0, in the top of the sixth inning when fog started rolling in off the lake. Mike Brown was on the mound for the Red Sox, and Dwight Evans, the Red Sox right fielder, complained to the second base umpire that he couldn't see the hitter or the pitch to the plate because of the fog.

"So the umpires stopped the game and got Bobby Bonds, then one of our coaches, to hit fungoes—fly balls—to Evans in right field, to see if he really couldn't see the ball. We were sitting in the dugout and watched the balls go out there. We could see them pretty good, though Evans made like he couldn't. Naturally, he wanted the umpires to call the game, which they finally did, because the fog never lifted. And because five innings had been played, it counted as a regulation game, a victory for the Red Sox.

"It would have been very bad if that one loss had cost us the pennant, or even a higher place in the standings, though it didn't. We weren't very good and finished in fifth place.

"After the game was called off, Oil Can Boyd, a pitcher for the Red Sox, said in all seriousness, 'That's what they get for building this stadium next to the ocean,' which capped a crazy day."

Jim "Mudcat" Grant
(Pitcher, 1958–1964)

"Years back they used to use pitchers for pinch runners, and one time, early in the 1962 season, we were in Kansas City and Mel McGaha was the manager. That's smart Mel McGaha, and our first base coach was Ray Katt.

"We'd lost the front end of a double header and late in the second game [Jim] Piersall got a single and McGaha put me in to run. Piersall had a sore leg or something, and I was pretty fast then, and we needed the run. When I got to first base Katt told me, 'Mudcat, if this guy hits a 'tweener, I want you to run like you done stole two watermelons and the farmer is chasing you with a shotgun.'

"Well, I was pretty level then, but somehow what he said hit me wrong. I said, 'To hell with you,' which is making what I really said sound pretty good, and I walked off the field. Katt yelled, 'No, no, come back, come back,' but I wouldn't. He knew he was in trouble for what he'd said, but I wouldn't go back.

"I went across the infield [to the Indians dugout on the third base side] because, that way I knew it would hold up the game. When I got to our dugout McGaha said, 'Get your ass back out there,' and I said to him, 'To hell with you, too,' and finally they had to put somebody else in to run.

"Normally, when you're African-American and raised as a southern kid, you learn to handle comments like what Katt said. But back then, I was young and, remember, it wasn't all that long after Jackie Robinson [broke the color barrier in baseball], so that's probably the reason I reacted the way I did."

"Another time, when we were in Cooperstown to play in the Hall-of-Fame game, Vic Power and I were on the field working out and we saw Ty Cobb in the other team's dugout. I said to Vic, 'That's Ty Cobb, let's go and shake his hand.'

"Well, even though we'd heard all those rumors that Cobb was a bad-ass racist, he was still Ty Cobb, and we wanted to shake his hand. So we went over and Vic said, 'Hi, Mr. Cobb. I'm Vic Power and this here is Mudcat Grant. He's a pitcher and I'm a first baseman and we want to shake your hand.'

Cobb looked at us and said, 'Hey, how you two nigger boys doin'? OK, I hope.'

"Well, me being from the south, and being just a boy, I thought, I don't care if he's Ty Cobb or who, but he's got a lot of nerve, though I didn't say anything.

"But Vic, who's Puerto Rican, went crazy. He said, 'You old soma-nabeech, how can you say something like that, you somanabeech.' I guess it kind of shook up Cobb because, next thing we know, we saw him kind of sneaking out of the ball park."

When Grant returned to Cleveland as one of the Indians' "100 Greatest Players," he was interviewed on the radio and told a few stories from his days as a pitcher for the Indians. The trouble was, a veteran sportswriter recognized several of the tales as not being totally factual, which didn't faze Mudcat one iota.

"Oh, that's what makes this so much fun," he said. "There ain't no fun telling a boring story."

Hank Greenberg
(Vice president/general manager, 1948–1957)

Hall-of-Fame outfielder/first baseman Hank Greenberg, who came to the Indians as farm director under Bill Veeck in 1948, then served as general manager from 1950–1957, had a stormy relationship with the media in Cleveland.

It prompted Greenberg to remark, "The only way to get along with newspapermen is to be like Dizzy Dean. Say something one minute and something different the next."

★ ★ ★ ★ ★

Before his death in 1986, Greenberg was invited to return to Cleveland for a reunion of the 1954 team. He declined, saying, "The closest I ever want to get to Cleveland is 30,000 feet in the air, on my way somewhere else."

Alfredo Griffin
(Shortstop, 1976–1978)

"When I played in Cleveland, I couldn't speak much English—I had trouble even ordering food in a restaurant—and Rico Carty was the one who helped me most. He was like a father to me, telling me how I was supposed to be on the field, and how to behave off the field. I liked him a lot.

"He also was a very funny guy, although not everybody saw that side of him. Once in 1979 when Rico and I were with the Blue Jays, Nolan Ryan, who was in his prime then, was going to pitch against us, and Ryan said in the paper that he was going to strike out 20 of us.

"Rico said, 'No he won't . . . maybe 17 or 18, but not 20,' which was pretty funny, because even if he didn't strike out 20, 17 or 18 were a lot. I don't know how many he did strike out, something like 14, but he won the game—and struck out Rico a couple of times, too.

"After Rico retired he wanted to become a politician in the Dominican Republic, but it didn't work. He didn't have the character to do that."

Steve Gromek
(Pitcher, 1941–1953)

"A game I remember so well, one of my favorites, although the result wasn't as good, was the first one I pitched in the big leagues," Steve Gromek remembered. "The Indians brought me up from Flint [of the Class C Michigan State League] when I was only 21 years old. I went out to the mound for my first game, and I was shaking like a leaf. Rollie Hemsley was supposed to catch me, but he told [Manager] Roger Peckinpaugh, 'I'm not going to catch that kid. . . . He's too wild. He's going to be all over the place.'

"After Gene Bearden pitched [and won] Game 3 of the 1948 World Series, giving us a 2–1 lead against the Boston Braves, Lou Boudreau called a team meeting and said that he'd decided to pitch me in the fourth game and save Bob Feller for the fifth.

"The way Boudreau explained it was, 'Instead of Feller, I'm willing to sacrifice and pitch Gromek, then come back with Feller.' The key word was 'sacrifice.' I didn't know what to think, although I knew it wasn't a compliment. What it did was motivate me, and I beat the Braves, 2–1, on Larry Doby's homer [off Johnny Sain] in front of the largest crowd [81,897] in baseball history at that time. It was the best game I'd pitched in a long time, so what Boudreau did was great for me and my career.

"A few years ago [in 1998 when the Indians celebrated the 50th anniversary of the 1948 team] I called Boudreau on the telephone and told him, 'I never thanked you for what you did, but I am thanking you now.' It turned out to be a big break for me. A lot of people remember me because of that game."

After Gromek's victory over the Braves in Game 4 of the World Series, he and outfielder Larry Doby, whose homer was the winning run, were photographed embracing in the Indians clubhouse. "I can talk about it now because the people involved are gone and times are different," recalled Gromek during the team's reunion in 1998.

"I'll never forget the reception I got from the pastor of my church when I returned home to Hamtramck [Michigan], after that picture of Doby and me appeared in the newspaper. I guess just about every newspaper in the country used the photo. The assistant pastor, who's also gone now, told me what happened.

"The two priests were having breakfast and reading about the game. When the pastor saw the picture of me hugging Larry, he said to the assistant pastor, 'Oh, my goodness, look at this. Steve is hugging a black man. How could he do something like that?'

"The assistant pastor said he looked at the photograph, read about Doby's game-winning home run, and replied, 'Father, if I were pitching in the World Series and a black guy hit a home run to win a game for me, I'd hug him, too.

"'In fact,' the assistant pastor said," according to Gromek, "'Father, if it had been me, I'd be so happy I wouldn't have just hugged him . . . I would've kissed his black ass.'

"Actually, I didn't kiss Larry, though I probably would have if the photographer had asked. What would be wrong about that? We had just won a big game and we both were as happy as could be."

"So Peckinpaugh put in Gene Desautels, and after I pitched good, even though I lost to Washington 4–2, Hemsley came over and apologized. He told me he'd said what he did to Peckinpaugh for my benefit, to motivate me—but I'm not sure he was right about that."

Travis Hafner
(First baseman and designated hitter, 2003–)

Travis Hafner was holding a base runner, Armando Rios, on first base with Danys Baez on the mound against Chicago and with Joe Crede at bat during a game on June 1, 2003. Crede hit a liner that Baez caught while lunging in the direction of first base.

Although Rios was only about two or three steps off the base, Baez, in full adrenaline rush—and only about 20 feet from Hafner—wound up and fired a fastball to the first baseman, attempting to double Rios off the base.

"When I saw him wind up, I thought to myself, 'Oh, no!' Hafner said. "Luckily, the ball hit me in the chest, not in the face or somewhere else that it could have really hurt and rolled down into my glove. After the game Omar [Vizquel] suggested that I play first base wearing a [catcher's] mask."

After he hit for the cycle against Minnesota on August 14, 2003, becoming the first member of an Indians team in 25 years to hit a homer, triple, double, and single in the same game, Hafner said, "I'm trying to think of something clever to say."

Then, when kidded about how he lumbered around the bases on his triple, Hafner said, "I felt like I was flying, until I saw the replay on TV. Geez, I might be the slowest person in baseball."

How did Hafner come to be nicknamed "Pronk"?

"It started in Spring Training my first year with the Indians. It's supposed to mean I'm part project and part donkey because, first, Bill Selby called me 'The Project,' then other guys started calling me 'Big Donkey.'

"So, one day Selby put the two together. 'Pronk.' That simple."

When someone suggested that he drop the project part of his nickname, considering the fact that, at the time during the 2004 season Hafner was batting .324 with 21 homers, he thought for a minute and said, 'But then I'd just be Donk. No, 'Pronk' is good enough."

"My high school [in Jamestown, North Dakota] was so small we didn't have a baseball team, so in the spring I competed in track, even though I was bad in everything. At track meets the top six finishers would place [earn points], but sometimes there weren't even six in an event, and if there were less than six, I'd enter. I'd go from event to event seeing if they had enough people entered. If they didn't, I'd enter. I'd run the two mile, the 110 hurdles, triple jump—anything to try to get some points for my school."

When his high school counselor asked Hafner—who was one of only eight students in his senior class—what his career aspiration was upon graduation, Hafner said he wanted to be a professional baseball player.

"When the counselor asked if I had a No. 2 choice, I said baseball was my No. 1 choice and my No. 2 choice. He didn't ask if I had a third choice, but it would have been the same."

When he was on the online fan ballot for the 2004 American League All-Star team (along with Lew Ford of the Minnesota Twins, Hideki Matsui of the New York Yankees, and Frank Thomas and Paul Konerko of the Chicago White Sox) to be chosen for the 32nd and final place on the team, Hafner politicked for votes.

"I brought my laptop computer to the clubhouse so my teammates could vote for me," and said his slogan was, "Vote Pronk."

It helped, but not enough. Matsui won, and Hafner finished last.

On another occasion Hafner wore a T-shirt that was lettered on the front: "I may not be very smart, but I can lift heavy things."

Sammy "Bad News" Hale
(Second baseman/third baseman, 1931, 1933–1940)

"I sure used my head on that one," Sammy Hale said after a game against Boston at Fenway Park on September 7, 1935. His comment was made after a line drive off the bat of Joe Cronin with the bases loaded tore through Hale's glove at third base. The ball ricocheted off Hale's forehead to shortstop Bill Knickerbocker, who caught it for one out, tossed to second baseman Roy Hughes for the second out, who then tossed to first baseman Hal Trosky to complete what has to be one of the rarest triple plays in baseball history.

Mel Harder
(Pitcher, 1928–1947; coach, 1948–1963)

"In all the years I was in baseball—from 1928–1947 as a pitcher for the Indians, and from 1948–1969 as a pitching coach for the Indians, New York Mets, Chicago Cubs, Cincinnati Reds, and Kansas City Royals—one of the funniest things I ever saw took place during a game at League Park in the early 1930s.

"Smead Jolley, who was a good hitter but not a real good outfielder, was playing right field for Chicago this particular day, and one of our guys hit a liner that Jolley backed up to catch, but the ball went right through his glove for an error [No. 1].

"Jolley turned around to play the ball off the wall, but it caromed off the concrete part, and before Jolley could get his glove down, it went through his legs for another error [No. 2].

"By now the batter was heading to second with Jolley chasing the ball as it rolled toward the infield, and by the time he got to it, our guy was going to third. Jolley picked up the ball and threw to third base, but it was wild and went into the stands for another error [No. 3], all on one play I swear I never saw anything like it."

Harder was a member of the Indians in 1940 when they staged a rebellion against then-Manager Oscar Vitt, which subsequently caused them to be called the "Cleveland Cry Babies."

"We had a good ball club—Bob Feller, Hal Trosky, Jeff Heath, Lou Boudreau, Ken Keltner and a lot more—and they all thought we had a good chance to win the pennant. But they didn't feel we could do it with Vitt managing," said Harder. "It was the way Vitt operated. He would pat you on the back one minute and criticize you behind your back the next. He was two-faced, and it finally got to some of the guys."

On June 13, 1940, they petitioned then-owner Alva Bradley to replace Vitt, though he refused to do so, and the Indians lost the pennant to Detroit on the final weekend of the season. Nine days after the season ended, Bradley fired Vitt.

Mike Hargrove
(First baseman, 1979–1985; coach, 1990–1991; manager, 1991–1999)

It was February 1999, and Mike Hargrove was starting his ninth season as manager of the Indians, who were seeking their fifth consecutive American League Central Division championship. On the first day of Spring Training, Hargrove distributed tee shirts upon which the following message was printed, "Go hard or go home."

Eight months later Hargrove himself went "home," replaced as manager by Charlie Manuel, after the Indians won another division title but failed to reach the World Series.

Ken "The Hawk" Harrelson
(First baseman and outfielder, 1969–1971)

When he was traded to the Indians on April 19, 1969, Ken Harrelson initially refused to report to Cleveland, insisting he would retire.

"It was quite an experience," he said, "I held out for a week, although I wasn't holding out just for money. There were a couple of issues involved. Money was a non-issue at the time. I either got it, the salary I wanted [and a couple other concessions he was unwilling to specify], or I wasn't going to go to Cleveland.

"I finally got what I wanted and signed. Actually, the big reason I agreed was because of [then-Tribe Manager] Alvin Dark and [catcher] Duke Sims. They were great friends of mine. I played for Alvin in Kansas City, and he always treated me great and gave me good advice. And Duke and I used to run together. We had a lot of fun. That's when we were young.

"I moved into the Winton Place when I got to Cleveland, and my apartment, which was on the top floor, overlooked the lake. It was beautiful. Art Modell had a place in the building, and so did Vernon Stouffer, and my place was nicer than theirs. My late sister Iris, who had an IQ of about 170, decorated the apartment, and it was unbelievable what she did.

"*Sports Illustrated* did a big layout on it. It was what you'd call the *consummate bachelor pad* because it had everything a bachelor could want in an apartment. A lot of mirrors, a lot of zebra skin, even a swing from the ceiling, although that was just for show.

"Every now and then, if I got hung up and it wasn't comfortable to go where I wanted to go, I could call up a helicopter to come and land on the roof of the building, and to get to it, all I had to do was walk up one flight of stairs.

"And, yes, I used it quite often.

"Now I look back on those days and just shake my head because it was—well, I'm a lot older and about 180 degrees different now than I was then. Actually, I don't think about those days unless somebody asks me, and it's hard for me to believe that I really did some of the things I did back then. I had fun, don't get me wrong, and it was all innocent fun, but I can't believe some of the things I did.

"Older conservative people didn't like me; I know that because I used to get mail all the time saying I should cut my hair, that I was a bad influence on kids. Occasionally I'd write back and say, 'Look, if your kid had a nose as big as mine and ears as big as mine, you'd let him wear long hair, too.'"

John Hart
(Vice president/general manager, 1991–2001)

"I'll never forget my first game as [interim] manager of the Indians. I had always aspired to manage in the Major Leagues, and spent my whole career in baseball until then working for that position. I finally did [become a Major League manager] if only on an interim basis in 1989, late in the season, when I replaced Doc Edwards for the final month of the season.

"We were playing Detroit, and Bud Black was my starting pitcher against Frank Tanana. For six innings it's a nothing-nothing game, and I had Doug Jones sitting in the bullpen. When we went ahead, 1–0, in the seventh, I wanted to bring Jones in. Actually, I started asking Black in the sixth inning, and I kept asking him in the seventh and eighth how he was feeling, if he was getting tired. I really wanted to win, not only because it was my first game, it also was against a future Hall of Famer, Sparky Anderson, which made it even bigger to me.

"But Buddy kept telling me, 'John, I'll tell you when I get tired. Stop worrying. I'm feeling so good I want you to go and sit down at the end of the dugout and be quiet. I'm going to get you your first win. Just let me go back out there and don't worry about me.'

"So I didn't. I sat down at the end of the dugout and left him alone, and he got the Tigers out one-two-three in the ninth for my first win. I'll never forget it.

"It was something that only a few men have the opportunity to do . . . become a Major League manager. Even though I was only an interim manager and I knew it would be for only a short time, it was very important to me, a guy who had fought through the minor leagues, managed all the way through them and finally had achieved a lifelong goal. I'd won my first game, and it was against a Hall of Famer. And so, yes, I was a little nervous. But Bud Black got it for me, just as he said he would—and we've been buddies ever since."

"Another time during a game I was managing, we were really struggling and had runners on first and second with nobody out. The batter was Joe Carter, whose statistics at the time were terrible . . . he was hitting under a hundred. I saw that the third baseman was playing all the way back, so I gave Joe the bunt sign, thinking we could surprise the third baseman.

"Well, what I did was surprise Joe. He stepped out of the batter's box and looked into the dugout at me with such a look on his face, I took off the bunt.

"But I shouldn't have . . . he hit into a double play."

Ron Hassey
(Catcher, 1978–1984)

Although he is the only player in the history of baseball to catch two perfect games in the Major Leagues, Ron Hassey said that the "highlight" of his career was "just being called up to the big leagues and to get my first hit off Dennis Eckersley in my first game. You don't forget things like that.

"Of course, I'll never forget catching those perfect games [by Lenny Barker in 1981] and Dennis Martinez [in 1991], but the highlight was just getting to the big leagues."

Von Hayes
(Outfielder, 1981–1982)

"Before the Indians traded me [to the Philadelphia Phillies] in 1983, there were a lot of rumors that I'd be going somewhere, but I was still absolutely shocked when it actually happened.

"A lot of friends had been calling me up, teasing me by pretending they were Phil Seghi or Gabe Paul, and telling me I was traded. So, when the call did come from Seghi, I didn't believe him. I said, 'OK, who is this? I'm getting tired of this crap.' It took some doing for him to convince me it really was Seghi. He told me [the trade] was going to be good for me, that with Philadelphia I'd have an opportunity to play for a team that could win it right then and there. Which we [the Phillies] did.

"But, looking back on it, I kind of regret I didn't get the opportunity to stay with the Indians. Who knows? I might have been with Cleveland long enough to play in this beautiful ball park [Jacobs Field].

"I also wonder if my Major League career would have lasted longer in Cleveland. My last season [1991 with the Phillies], I broke my arm when I was hit by a pitch from Tom Browning. And, yes, I think he was intentionally throwing at me, and I was finished. I tried to make a comeback with California [in 1992], but it was no good."

Jim Hegan
(Catcher, 1941–1942, 1946–1957)

Though Jim Hegan's batting average never was anything to rave about, there's no doubt about the high esteem in which he was held by his peers as a catcher, as Birdie Tebbetts once said:

"You start and end any discussion of catchers with Jim Hegan. Add all the things a catcher has to do—catch, throw, call a game—and Jim Hegan was the best I ever saw."

Woodie Held
(Shortstop/second baseman/outfielder/third baseman, 1958–1964)

"Playing with Gary Bell and Tito Francona in Cleveland was like a comedy hour every day. Guys were laughing all the time. It was a fun clubhouse, although we didn't win too many games until 1959. That was a good year for us. We should have won the pennant.

"Gary, especially, kept everybody loose. He's one of the funniest men I've ever known. I used to tell him, the way you pitch, you should have been a comedian, though he knew I was only kidding. He was a very good pitcher. We were roommates for five years. I guess that's why we're both crazy, or at least why people think we're crazy.

"But [Bell] also has a temper. Especially the way he'd get mad at an umpire if he wasn't calling pitches the way Gary thought they should be called. When he'd get mad, [Manager] Joe Gordon used to tell me to go talk to Gary and calm him down. But just about every time I'd get to the mound Gary would say, 'What the hell are you doing here? Get your ass back to shortstop and leave me alone.' So I would. Like I said. He was a funny guy—most of the time."

"I was in Cleveland when Frank Lane traded managers, Gordon [to Detroit] for Jimmy Dykes [in 1960]. Everybody on the team was shocked. We couldn't believe what he'd done, but that's the way Frank was. You never knew what to expect from him, which is the way he liked it. We also were shocked when he traded Rocky [Colavito] for Harvey Kuenn [in 1960], and a couple days later traded Herb Score for Barry Latman. I think Lane did a lot of that crazy stuff because he liked to see his name in the newspapers.

"Like most guys, I had trouble getting any money out of Lane. After I had a good year in 1959—I hit 29 home runs—he wanted to give me only a thousand dollar raise. Finally he went up to $2,000, and I told him I'd stay home before I'd play for what he was offering. Hell, 29 home runs for a shortstop was very good. I was OK in the field, too. I think I made 21 errors, but that wasn't bad. If you don't make any errors it means you never got to any balls.

"The way we wound up [contract negotiations], Lane agreed that if I was hitting .275 by the All-Star break, I'd get a brand new station wagon, which is what happened. I got a station wagon, which represented the raise I'd wanted, although I didn't get it in actual dollars."

"I was with the Yankees in Cleveland the night [May 7, 1957] that Gil McDougald's line drive hit Herb Score in the eye. I was in the bullpen and could hear the crack of the ball hitting Score all the way out there. It was awful. Poor Herb—but also, poor Gil. He was crying, couldn't stop crying, he felt so bad. Gil was the type of guy that things like that hurt him. He was very sensitive. I know a lot of guys think that [hitting Score with that line drive] hurt Gil's career. I don't know, maybe it did. As I said, he was very sensitive."

George Hendrick
(Outfielder, 1973–1976)

During his 18 seasons in the Major Leagues from 1971 to 1988—with Oakland (1971–1972), the Indians, San Diego (1977–1978), St. Louis (1978–1984), Pittsburgh (1985), and California (1985–1988)—George

Hendrick earned the nickname, "Silent George," because of his unwillingness to be interviewed by the media.

Yet Hendrick realizes he was wrong.

"I guess part of the problem was that I was very young and didn't know how to handle it, the attention and all that stuff," Hendrick said during a return to Cleveland for a reunion with his former teammates.

"I decided then that I wouldn't trust anybody in the media, and the way I handled it was to not speak, not even to say hello. I was rude . . . and I'm sorry now."

Hendrick is now the first base coach for the Tampa Bay Rays, where he has been since 2005.

Orel Hershiser
(Pitcher, 1995–1997)

Cleveland, in 1995, was an unbelievable year, and while everybody tells you what happened on the field, let me tell you something that happened off the field.

"In the super [field] boxes around the [backstop] of the playing field they serve dessert to the high roller fans in the fourth or fifth inning. One day, during a game, I walked past the double doors that connect the dugout with those super boxes and saw the dessert cart between the crack in the doors, so I knocked.

"A girl came to the door and asked what I wanted. I told her I wanted some carrot cake. She gave me a piece and from then on, because I knew the dessert cart always came down there at the same time, between the fourth and fifth innings, I'd get dessert and go back behind the dugout and have coffee and cake—except when I was pitching.

"The manager [Mike Hargrove] never found out, and other guys probably are doing it now—and now it's going to be in your book and I'll be in trouble. So will the guys who are doing it since I left."

"That season [1995] was awesome. The biggest thing I remember about that team was how loose we were. I came from the Dodgers, a team that was a lot more professional—and by that I don't mean in a positive or negative way, where the Indians are concerned. That was the year of the bubblegum bubbles on caps, and the hot foots and things like that. Wayne Kirby and [Alvaro] Espinoza were doing all kinds of pranks to keep people loose in the dugout and in the clubhouse.

"We had great players, and it's too bad we didn't win the World Series after getting so close (losing in six games). I lost the opener to Greg Maddux when I let the team down by walking two hitters in a row, Fred McGriff and Ryan Klesko, in the seventh inning on eight straight pitches. I know it really disappointed the team. The score was 1–1 at the time, and we ended up losing a tough game, 3–2, and I felt really bad.

"Between that game and the next one I pitched [Game 5], I kept my mouth shut and took the heat from the press and different people, then came back and beat Maddux on three days rest. It was the best I pitched since my career-threatening surgery, my shoulder reconstruction, so I was very proud of the way I responded there."

Chuck Hinton
(Outfielder/first baseman/third baseman/second baseman, 1965–1967, 1969–1971)

As a part-time infielder-outfielder for the Indians from 1965–1967, Chuck Hinton often served as an "advisor" to teammate Leon "Daddy Wags" Wagner, which he did one day as the two players took batting practice before a Saturday afternoon game.

"I don't know what I'm doing wrong," lamented Wagner. "I keep popping up."

"Here's what you're doing wrong," said Hinton with a straight face. "You're hitting the bottom half of the ball. Try putting two extra pairs of inner soles in your shoes. That will raise you up so that you meet the ball square, instead of hitting under it."

"Hey, that sounds good. I'll try it," said Wagner.

Of his career in Cleveland, when the Indians played at the old Municipal Stadium, Chuck Hinton said, recalling a bad game he played against the Minnesota Twins in 1966, "You've never heard boo-ing until you've been booed by 66,000 fans, although it was seldom that we had that many in the old Stadium.

"Then again, you've never heard cheering like when it comes from 66,000 fans, so I guess that evens it out, although, again, more times— *many more* times—than not, we didn't have 66,000 fans in the Stadium cheering or booing us."

Harold "Gomer" Hodge
(First, second, and third baseman, 1971)

He signed for a $1,000 bonus in 1963 and, when he made it with the Indians in 1971, after eight years in the minor leagues, his sal-ary was all of $13,500 which, to Harold Hodge—better known as "Gomer"—was a lot of money.

"I spent 39 years in professional baseball. It has meant everything to me. I want to stay in the game, but it is very hard to get a job," he said after his contract wasn't renewed as batting coach for Boston's Class AAA farm club, Pawtucket of the International League in 2001.

"I loved the game and the people in it, but it's all changed. Now it's all about money."

The "secret" to the minimal success he enjoyed with the Tribe in 1971, when he batted .205 with one homer in 80 games, Hodge said:

"I asked the good Lord for help every time I went to the plate, and He helped me."

After he delivered four straight hits, three as a pinch hitter in his first four at-bats for the Indians in 1971, Gomer Hodge proudly announced to reporters interviewing him: "Gollee, fellas, I'm batting 4.000!"

Willis Hudlin
(Pitcher, 1926–1940)

In 1936, at the height of his pitching career with the Indians, Willis Hudlin suffered a sore arm.

"In those days if you had a sore arm, the first thing doctors would tell you were to have your tonsils taken out," said Hudlin, who died in 2002. "They figured that tonsils absorbed poison and then the poison would get distributed to the part of your body you used the most, which for a pitcher was his arm.

"So, that winter [1936–1937] I had my tonsils removed and, sure enough, my arm was better in 1937. Was it because I had my tonsils taken out? I don't know. I was just glad that my arm felt better, never mind why."

He compiled a 158–156 won-lost record during his 16-year Major League career, all but one season with the Tribe.

Early in Hudlin's career, on August 11, 1929, he made a pitch that wound up flying high and far over the right-field wall at League Park, which then was the Indians home field, after it was hit.

"In my mind I can still see the ball flying over that damned fence," Hudlin said in an interview many years later.

The ball that flew over that "damned fence" was hit by Babe Ruth and was the Bambino's 500th career homer, then the most hit by any player in baseball.

"My best pitch was a sinker, and that's what the Babe hit, although I guess that sinker didn't sink the way it was supposed to sink."

Luis Isaac
(Coach, 1987–1991, 1994–2008)

"The funniest man I ever knew was Looie [Luis] Tiant. One time when he was pitching, somebody hit a long fly to center field. Looie started yelling, 'Go foul! Go foul!' even though the ball was hit dead away to center and went for a home run.

"Another time we were playing in Detroit and, in the ninth inning, Bill Freehan was hitting, and Looie got two strikes on him, then he hung a breaking ball. Freehan hit a high fly to left field, and by the time the ball landed over the fence to win the game for Detroit, Looie was in the dugout and yelling, 'OK guys, let's go, the bus is leaving in 45 minutes.'"

Brook Jacoby
(Third baseman, 1984–1991, 1992)

"When *Sports Illustrated* put us on the cover [March 1987] and said the Indians were the coming team in the American League, we all were kind of surprised—and at the end it was very embarrassing, because we finished in seventh [last] place. We had some very good young players, but we didn't have the pitching to go with our offense. Rick Sutcliffe and Bert Blyleven had been traded to get the nucleus of some young hitters, and when you look at what they [Sutcliffe and Blyleven] did after they left Cleveland . . . well, they had pretty good careers. So we had a good ball club, but we were young. We weren't quite ready.

"Most of the guys knew that if we put a winner on the field, the fans would come out, which they did at times. One year [1986], we were only one game out, behind Boston in August, when we came home from a trip and the Stadium was packed that whole weekend. It was a lot of fun playing there then.

"I think Andy Thornton said it best, that [at that time, early 1980s] there was no solid ownership [of the Indians], and by doing what we did on the field helped keep the ball club in Cleveland. I like to think that what we did back then helped make it possible for what's happening in Cleveland now, because that was a pivotal time, whether there was going to continue to be a team playing in Cleveland or not."

David Jacobs
(Co-owner with brother Richard Jacobs, 1986–1992)

During their negotiations to buy the Indians in 1986 and after the purchase was finalized, the Jacobs brothers seldom met with or spoke to the media, staunchly maintaining a strict code of privacy, especially the younger brother, Richard.

However, on one occasion during the winter of 1986–1987, David (who died in 1992), upon being congratulated during a social gathering by a man he had not yet met, spoke eloquently of the brothers' plans to build a winning team.

Upon the conclusion of David's remarks, the man to whom he'd been talking introduced himself as a reporter for the *Plain Dealer*.

Jacobs stammered, "Oh, my goodness . . . everything I told you is off the record . . . off the record . . . absolutely off the record, do you understand?"

The reporter acquiesced, albeit reluctantly—and several years later David Jacobs's "off the record" prophecy became true because the Indians won five consecutive division championships from 1995 to 1999, another in 2001, and pennants in 1995 and 1997.

Charley Jamieson
(Outfielder, 1919–1932)

After Charley Jamieson was honored with a "day" in 1929 and given a purse of $3,200, he grounded out to end the game as the

Indians lost to future Hall of Famer Lefty Grove and the Philadelphia Athletics.

Jamieson, who died in 1969, sought Alva Bradley, then-owner of the Indians, and reportedly told him, "Mr. Bradley, I'm Scotch and I like money as well as the next guy. But I'd have given this whole $3,200 for one more hit off that big monkey."

Tommy John
(Pitcher, 1963–1964)

A southpaw whose career began with the Indians, Tommy John was traded after winning just two games (and losing 11) in 1963 and 1964, though he became one of baseball's most consistent pitchers with the Chicago White Sox (1965–1971) and Los Angeles Dodgers (1972–1974) before suffering arm trouble.

He underwent ligament transplant surgery—which has subsequently been called a "Tommy John operation" and resumed his career with the Dodgers (1976–1978), New York Yankees (1979–1982), California Angels (1982–1985), Oakland (1985), and the Yankees again (1986–1989), retiring after the 1989 season.

"When they operated I told the doctor to put a Koufax fastball in my arm," said John. "They did—but it was a Mrs. Koufax fastball."

Maybe so. But in the 14 seasons after his surgery, John won 164 games, for a career total of 288 (with 231 losses).

Alex Johnson
(Outfielder, 1972)

During his one season with the Indians, outfielder Alex Johnson had few friends among the media. He seldom consented to be interviewed, usually greeting reporters with profane remarks. Most of the time, after games, he sat facing in toward his locker, reading the same soft-cover book that he tried to keep out of the sight of others.

However, a player whose locker was adjacent to Johnsons, was able to see the book and once revealed, "It was an electronics book and, funny thing, every time I looked, Alex was on the same page . . . I don't remember seeing him ever turn a page."

Mike Kekich
(Pitcher, 1973)

Mike Kekich, who was notorious for trading wives, families, and homes (even dogs) with Fritz Peterson in 1972, before both players were acquired in separate transactions by the Indians, didn't last long, nor did he do well for the Tribe. After one season in Cleveland, Kekich was jettisoned to Texas and, subsequently, elsewhere, later claiming he was "blackballed" by Major League teams.

Whether it was true or not, Kekich—who was once called "another Sandy Koufax" when he was a rookie with Los Angeles in 1965— wound up pitching in the Mexican League.

When asked what it was like to play south of the border for Nuevo Laredo, Kekich described it this way: "We had 18- to 24-hour bus rides. There were spiders, cockroaches, and no air-conditioning in our motel rooms, the bed sheets just split from your weight, and the towels shredded when you touched them.

"When guys go to Mexico or Japan, they're usually never heard from again."

And Kekich never was.

Bob Kennedy
(Outfielder, 1948–1954)

It was called "a helluva story" by Bob Kennedy, one that never came out at the time it happened, in 1948, after the Indians lost the final game of the season. The loss dropped them into a tie with Boston, forcing a one-game playoff for the pennant.

"We were on the train, going to Boston to play the Red Sox the next afternoon, and I got into my berth and tried to go to sleep. After a while [second baseman] Joe Gordon came by and asked if I was asleep. I said, 'Well, yeah, I was until now.' He said, 'I thought you'd want to know . . . you're playing tomorrow.'

"I said, 'That's great. I'm glad to hear that.' He said, 'I'm gonna take a sleeping pill, you want one?' I said I'd never had one, but since I was awake, I thought it would help me get back to sleep, so I told him to give me one.

"Next thing I know it's morning and it's quiet, real quiet. I pulled the curtain back and leaned out of my berth, but didn't see anybody. I looked down the aisle and there was Gordon, and a little farther down I saw (Bob) Feller. But nobody else. I looked at my watch and it was eleven o'clock. Eleven o'clock in the morning, and the game was at one o'clock! The train was parked in the yard and everybody was gone. Everybody but Gordon, Feller, and me.

"So, Judas Priest, we got dressed, ran like a son of a gun, and caught a cab to Fenway Park. On the way, Joe told the cabbie to stop at one of those little lunch stands.

"He ran in, got three milkshakes with a couple of eggs in each of them, and jumped back in the cab. When we got to the park and walked in the clubhouse [Manager Lou] Boudreau looked at us and started to say something, but Joe put his hand over [Boudreau's] mouth and said to Lou, 'Not now . . . later.'

"Can you believe I almost missed the greatest game . . . the most important game of my career? Gordon and Feller, too."

Talking about Satchel Paige, Kennedy said, "Don't let anybody tell you that Satch was a clown, or that he wasn't a good pitcher, because he was. A very good pitcher. Most of the time he'd come to the ball park in a big limousine accompanied by a lady, and when we asked who she was, he'd say, 'That's my wife.'

"Well, I'll tell you, there sure were a lot of Mrs. Paiges in the American League that year."

Kennedy played for the Chicago White Sox before he was traded to the Indians in 1948, and later for Baltimore, the White Sox again, Detroit, and Brooklyn, but said his seven seasons with Cleveland were the best of his 16-year Major League career.

"My wife used to say that, when we were in Cleveland, it was like being in Camelot. She was right. Especially in 1948."

Jim Kern
(Pitcher, 1974–1978, 1986)

When he attempted to make a comeback with the Indians in 1986 at the age of 37, Jim Kern, who, because of his appearance was nicknamed by his teammates, "The Emu," was quoted as saying, "My game is power. . . . I'm strictly a one-trick pony."

However, Kern's comeback as a one-trick pony didn't last long. He was released 10 weeks into the season with a 1–1 won-lost record and 7.90 earned run average (with 11 strikeouts in 27⅓ innings on a yield of 34 hits, 28 runs, one homer, and 23 walks).

"I'm totally embarrassed by my statistics," he said when the end came. "I feel like somebody has been sticking needles in a voodoo doll of me. This is my fourth pink slip in the last three years, but I'm going to stick around long enough to get a whole deck.

"There's only one problem. I'm still throwing good, but I'm running out of teams."

Ralph Kiner
(Outfielder, 1955)

In 1955, upon joining the Indians after hitting .285 with 22 homers for the Chicago Cubs the preceding season, Ralph Kiner insisted that his salary be cut 40 percent, instead of 25 percent, the maximum allowed by Major League rule. "Maybe I should go to a psychiatrist [but] this is not a grandstand play. I simply want my performance with the Indians to determine my future salary," he said.

Wayne Kirby
(Outfielder, 1991–1996)

When the Indians vacated Municipal Stadium at the end of the 1994 season and moved into Jacobs Field, Wayne Kirby had the perfect description for the switch.

"We went from the outhouse to the penthouse," he said.

Duane Kuiper
(Second baseman, 1974–1981)

"Mark Fidrych [of the Detroit Tigers] didn't last long, only a few years [actually six], but I swear he was one of the goofiest guys I ever saw. But, goofy or not, he could really pitch, especially his first season [1976] for the Tigers.

"He used to talk to the ball . . . hold it up in front of him, look at it, and talk to it, before he pitched it. This one night, during a game at the old Stadium, a couple of our guys got one of the balls between innings, and wrote on it, something like, 'You're a jerk,' and some profanity stuff like that, hoping he would see it. We were just trying to get into his head, you know, hoping it would rile him up. But it didn't. He held the ball up in front of him, like he always did, looked at it, and then pitched it. It didn't have any effect on him, not that we could tell. And the pitch he made, as I recall, the batter didn't swing at it, and then the umpire threw the ball out. That's all there was to it. Fidrych didn't care."

★ ★ ★ ★ ★

"Most people don't remember the game in 1977 that I hit my home run—my only home run [in 3,378 at-bats]—and that Al Michaels was doing it on national television. Michaels, you know, was famous for what he said during the 1980 Olympics. When the US hockey game team beat Russia, Michaels said, 'Do you believe in miracles?'

"Well, he used that same line—'Do you believe in miracles?'—when I hit my home run, and that was three years before he said it in the Olympics.

"When I hit it, I probably was even more surprised than Michaels. It was in the first inning. Paul Dade had just struck out and I was the second batter. I got ahead, 1-and-0 on the count and, in all honesty, I almost didn't swing at the next pitch, the one I hit out. It was either a high fastball or a hanging slider, and I was more of a low ball hitter in those days. So, when I swung—and you've got to remember, before that I never experienced watching a right fielder turn around and go back—and when I saw the number on the back of the right fielder's shirt, I thought to myself, 'Wow! This might have a chance to go off the wall,' but it did better than that. It sailed out of the ball park.

"Buddy Bell was waiting for me at the plate and half the guys came out of the dugout to greet me. Then, when I got up to hit for the second time, Bill Melton was standing nearby in the on-deck circle and said, 'You're not going to use that bat again, are you?' I said, 'Yeah, why not.' And he said, 'You better put it away, save it, because you might never hit another one,' which I didn't.

"Somebody retrieved the [home run] ball, and they threw it in for me to keep. I have it somewhere in my attic, though I don't exactly know where."

Frank LaBono
(Visiting team batboy, 1938–1941)

"I got my job as the batboy for visiting teams at League Park and the old Stadium when I was 13 years old, and it's an experience I'll never forget as long as I live.

"It was during that season [on October 2] that Bob Feller struck out 18 batters against Detroit [setting a then-Major League record]. He got Chet Laabs five times, and when Laabs came back to the dugout after the fifth strikeout, he broke every one of his bats—five or six of them, even a couple of other guys' bats—he was so mad. Finally Hank Greenberg and a couple other guys grabbed him before he could do any more damage, although he'd already done plenty."

"A lot of players played cards in the clubhouse before and after games, but Luke Sewell, who managed the [St. Louis] Browns and Bucky Harris [Washington Senators] wouldn't allow it. I think that was pretty wise, because I'd see guys get mad at each other during a card game.

"Connie Mack was a real gentleman. Everyone called him 'Mr. Mack.' During double headers he would not allow anybody to eat anything except ice cream. That's all he allowed. Just ice cream. And no food could be brought in, even after the game. Mr. Mack was a very nice man and always wore a high collar and a tie. I remember one day it was so hot my shirt was soaked with sweat in the first inning, but Mr. Mack still had that high collar, shirt, and tie with a straw hat. I went to him and asked, 'Mr. Mack, aren't you hot?' and he laughed and said, 'No, young man, I'm always cool.'"

"My favorite player was Mickey Vernon, who played for Washington [1939–1948] and then the Indians [1949–1950]. He was such a gentleman, probably the most gentlemanly visiting player I knew. We still write to each other, and I see him if he comes into town. Of all the players my mother had me invite for dinner, Vernon was the only one who ever brought her a gift, a box of chocolates once. She liked him, too.

"I also liked Joe DiMaggio, maybe because we're both Italian. I know there's a book that came out recently that made him look pretty bad, but to me he was a good guy.

"In those days the players didn't tip a lot, because they didn't make a lot of money. Not like today. But some of them were very generous to me. Back then, brown and white, and black and white dress shoes—saddle shoes, I guess they call them—were very popular. Guys used to ask me to clean them up before they left the clubhouse, and when I did, they'd give me a couple of bucks."

"I was there in 1940 when somebody dropped a basket of rotten fruit and vegetables on Birdie Tebbetts' head. Birdie went into the stands after the guy and gave him a helluva going over. Old Birdie [who became the Indians manager in 1963] was as tough as they make them, until he got old.

"The Tigers went crazy the day [September 27] they beat Bob Feller and the Indians [2–0] to win the pennant in 1940. After the game I went into the clubhouse and they gave me three brand-new balls. My pay in those days usually was two brand-new balls and a couple of dollars each game. But that day they gave me three. I couldn't wait until I got back to the clubhouse and got everybody's name on them, and then I went out and sold the balls for 25 bucks apiece. Twenty-five bucks in those days was real big money. Don't forget, that was 1940. You wouldn't get 25 bucks in a week if you worked a regular job.

"It was the following year [1941] that DiMaggio's [consecutive game hitting] streak was stopped [at 56 on July 17] at the old Stadium. When DiMaggio came back to the dugout after he grounded out [to shortstop Lou Boudreau] in the eighth inning to go 0-for-4, he said he hoped the Indians would tie the game so he'd get another chance. They didn't, although they did score twice in the bottom of the ninth and cut the Yankees' lead to 4–3. That's the way it ended.

"Nobody, including Joe, said much afterward. Everybody just left him alone, stayed away from him, not because he was mad or anything, but just to give him a little privacy, respect. Even when he went into the shower, nobody showered with him. Finally, when he came out and was getting dressed, I heard him tell Lefty Gomez that he was glad it was over. I guess because of all the pressure that had been on him."

"It was in 1938, when I was 14 years old, that I played catch with Lou Gehrig at League Park. Here's how it happened: many of the New York players were arguing about something, and doing a lot of swearing in the dugout before a game one day. Lou didn't like to hear it, and he didn't want me to hear, so he said to me, 'C'mon, Frankie, get a glove and play some catch with me . . . let's get out of here. You shouldn't hear that kind of talk.' I said to him, 'OK, Mr. Gehrig,' and he said, 'I'm Lou to you, Frankie. Not Mr. Gehrig.' Imagine that! Me, Frank LaBono, playing catch with the great Lou Gehrig."

"When World War II started, I went into the Navy and served aboard the USS Lexington, an aircraft carrier, until we got torpedoed on May 6, 1942, in the battle of the Coral Sea and the ship went down. I swam away from it as far as I could and saw a rubber raft with 13 other men on it, and was able to get on it. We were on that raft five days and four nights before a submarine came and picked us up.

"I was in the Navy a total of 39 months, and was discharged in May 1946, but I didn't go back to work at the ball park. By then I guess I was too old to be a batboy."

Napoleon Lajoie
(Second baseman, 1902–1914; manager, 1905–1909)

It was during Spring Training in 1908 that Napoleon Lajoie, then the player-manager of the Indians, was hit in the head during batting practice by a pitch thrown by an erratic rookie southpaw named Jack Graney.

That night Lajoie summoned Graney to his hotel room and told the pitcher, "They tell me that the place for wild men is out west. So, you're going west, kid, so far that, if you go any farther, your hat would float. Here's your railroad ticket [to the Indians farm team in Portland, Oregon]."

Graney switched to the outfield that season and two years later made it back to the Indians as their regular left fielder until his retirement at the end of the 1922 season. Nine years later, in 1931, Graney became the radio voice of the Indians, a job he held for the next 22 years.

Frank Lane
(General manager, 1957–1961)

Because of his penchant for wheeling and dealing, Frank Lane was not a very popular man among Indians players. However, one who liked him a lot was Hal Naragon, who caught for the Indians in 1951 and again from 1954 to 1959, before he also was traded to Washington by Lane.

"During Spring Training in 1959, when my daughter Pam was about two years old, my wife, Joanne, often brought her to the ballpark to pick me up after a workout or exhibition game," Naragon recalled. "Somebody on the team that year had a big boxer dog, and my daughter loved to play with it. She loved dogs, still does.

"Lane really took a liking to Pam, and one day he came into the clubhouse and told me, 'Hal, since your daughter likes that dog so much, you go out and buy her one and I'll pay for it. Just send me the bill.' I told him, 'Frank, my wife travels so much with a two-year-old, and I don't think she could also handle a dog.' He said, 'Well, whenever the time comes that she can, you buy your daughter a dog and send me the bill.'

"So what happened? Lane traded me [on May 25, 1959], to Washington, and shortly after I left the Indians he sent me a letter. It said, 'I'm still waiting for that bill, because I still want to buy your daughter a dog.'

"A couple of months later I did. I paid $100 for a little poodle, and I sent him the bill, not really expecting I'd hear from him, but I did. He sent me a check for $100 with a nice little note.

"I know most guys didn't have good things to say about Lane, but I'm not one of them."

They called him "Trader Lane" and "Frantic Frank" because of the 49 deals involving 108 players he made while serving as general manager of the Indians for three-plus seasons. Lane's justification for his incessant wheeling and dealing, and scorn for holding special promotions to attract larger crowds: "If the team doesn't do well, the fans won't give a damn about Bugs Bunny. The only promotion I care about is getting one more run than the other team."

Neither would he admit to regretting any of his transactions. "The only deals that irked me are the ones I didn't make," he said.

Longtime Indians pitcher Mel Harder, who was the team's pitching coach from 1948–1963, during Lane's tenure, said of the former general manager: "Lane was a wild man. He couldn't go to sleep at night without dreaming up a trade. He was always up to something, and we never knew what it was until after he did it. I can't say what kind of an effect Lane had on the team, except that I know the players didn't like him."

Matt Lawton
(Outfielder, 2002–2004)

"I was really scared when I got drafted by Minnesota [in 1991] and [Twins scout] Cal Ermer came to sign me," Matt Lawton reminisced about his start in professional baseball. "I didn't know if I wanted to go to college or what, so I didn't sign right away. South Alabama [University] was close to home, and I really didn't want to leave home, so I kept telling Mr. Ermer that I didn't think I wanted to play professional baseball."

But Ermer was persistent.

"I remember the last time he came to visit me, he brought his wife along and she got to talking to my mother. As it turned out, Mrs.

Ermer persuaded my mother that, if I signed with the Twins, every-thing would be OK—which it turned out to be. And now, every time I see Mr. Ermer I thank him for giving me the opportunity, although I should thank his wife, too.

"I don't know what she said to my mother. You know women kind of bond together, and if she hadn't convinced my mother to let me sign, who knows what I'd be doing today, instead of working on my 10th year in the Major Leagues. My brother Marcus also played [10 games] in the Major Leagues for the New York Yankees."

The highlight of Lawton's amateur baseball career, he said, was in 1984 when he played second base and his double-play partner was shortstop Brett Favre, who went on to become an All-Pro NFL quar-terback for the Green Bay Packers.

During the 2003 season when the Indians' roster was loaded with rookies, Lawton was not in the starting line-up.

"It's hard to say you get left out on a team as bad as ours," he said then. "I mean, if you can't play for a team this bad, who can you play for?"

Lawton made a "comeback" with the Indians in 2004 and became a very popular player in Cleveland. He was particularly upset midway through the 2003 season when, prior to a game at Jacobs Field as mem-bers of the Indians greeted fans as they entered the park, Lawton was approached by a little old lady.

"She must have been 100," Lawton said, "and she told me, 'I boo you every time you come to the plate, and I hope you start hitting so they can get rid of you.'"

So how did Lawton respond?

"What could I say to her. I just stood there, speechless, while she walked away. It was not a good time for me."

He was traded to Pittsburgh in the winter of 2004–2005.

Hal Lebovitz
(*Cleveland* Plain Dealer *sportswriter*)

"I liked Dale Mitchell a lot, though I didn't especially like the way he played ball. He was a slap hitter and didn't have a very good throwing arm, although he always hit for a high average. One day he put it all together—all the negative things. He didn't pull the ball when he should have and made a couple of weak throws from left field, so I ripped him—well, criticized him—in the paper.

"Several players told me the next day that I shouldn't go near Mitchell, because he was angry at me. But I felt it was important that I give him a shot at me, as I always did after I criticized a player. So I went up to him in the clubhouse and he seemed to be as nice as could be.

"He asked me, 'How are you, Hal?' I told him I was fine. Then he asked, 'Do you have a brother?' I was pleased that he wasn't mad anymore, and said, 'Thanks for asking, and, yes, I do have a brother.' Then he said, 'Well, he can go to hell, too.'"

Bob Lemon
(*Outfielder, third baseman, and pitcher, 1941–1942, 1946–1958*)

Before he became a full-time starting pitcher, Bob Lemon—who was elected in 1976 to the Hall of Fame—was hanging on with the Indians as an outfielder-third baseman who also made 32 pitching appearances, mostly in mop-up relief assignments in 1946.

In fact, in the 1946 opening game, Lemon made a sensational game-saving catch in center field to preserve Bob Feller's 1–0 victory over the Chicago White Sox, although it was the only high point of his outfield career. In 55 games that season Lemon batted .180 (16 for 89) and was 4–5 in 94 innings on the mound.

A year later, still without a regular position or even a defined role on the team, Lemon almost was lost in a waiver deal with the then-Washington Senators in a story related by Al Lopez, who was then a backup catcher for the Tribe.

"A lot of people probably find this hard to believe, but Bill Veeck tried to get rid of Lemon," Lopez said. "Veeck thought that Lemon would never hit enough to play either the outfield or third base, which probably was accurate, and until then nobody gave much thought to making him a starting pitcher.

"Midway through 1947, Veeck requested waivers on Lemon, and he was claimed by Washington. The day it happened I was playing golf with Lemon, Ken Keltner, and Joe Gordon, and when we got to the turn [the tee on the 10th hole], there was a message for Lem to call home. He did, and when he came back to us he said, 'It looks like I'll be leaving you guys. . . . I'm going to Washington.' He was happy about the deal because he wanted to play and knew he wouldn't get much of a chance with us because we had Keltner at third and a veteran outfield. We finished the golf game, and he went home to pack.

"But what happened was that Veeck got mad at [Senators owner] Clark Griffith because [Griffith] prematurely announced the sale in the evening papers in Washington. Veeck said he owed Cleveland's morning paper [the *Plain Dealer*] the release, and called off the deal [before it was officially filed with the league office]. Imagine if the deal had gone through. The Indians would have missed a helluva pitcher.

"A few days later Bill McKechnie, who was one of [Tribe Manager] Lou Boudreau's coaches, came to me and asked if I thought we should give Lemon a chance to concentrate on pitching?

"I told him, '[Lemon] is a good athlete, he's got a good arm and a helluva live fastball, but he's got to concentrate on his control, on getting the ball over the plate, and to develop a curve ball and slider.' Actually, Lemon already had a pretty good slider that was better than most pitchers' curve balls because it broke so much . . . almost, in fact, too big [a break] for a slider."

Boudreau agreed to give the strong-armed outfielder a shot as a full-time starting pitcher through the second half of the 1947 season. And with Lopez and Pitching Coach Mel Harder working with Lemon, he went on to post an 11–5 record and 3.44 earned run average, with six complete games in 37 appearances—15 as a starter. And in 1948, when the Indians won the pennant and World Series, Lemon became a 20-game winner (20–14) and went on to win 20 in six of the next eight seasons.

"That's how lucky the Indians were," Lopez said. "There they were, on the verge of giving Lemon away for the waiver price. And if he'd gone to Washington, he would have ended up being an outfielder, just a mediocre outfielder at best."

Instead he became a Hall-of-Fame pitcher.

When asked if he took any bad games home with him, Lemon replied, "Never. I always left them in a bar along the way."

And these Lemonisms:

"The two most important things to a pitcher are good friends and a strong bullpen, and not necessarily in that order."

"Baseball was made for kids. . . . Grownups only screw it up."

Eddie Leon
(Shortstop/second baseman, 1968–1972)

"It was either 1969 or 1970 when one day Sam McDowell came into the locker room and everybody knew he'd had a problem—a typical Sam McDowell problem—the night before. He had a little chunk of hair missing in the back of his head . . . there might even have been stitches, though I'm not sure.

"Anyway, Sam walked past Larry Brown, who could be very sarcastic in a kidding way, and Brownie said, 'Sam, would you please replace your divots?'"

"It's great to see the Indians doing so well now. What a difference—in both the team and the ball park—from when I played. Like

I told Looie Tiant, 'I'm embarrassed when people talk about how bad we were in 1969.' He said, 'Yeah, but you can't blame it all on me,' and I said, 'I was only there for half of the season, so nobody can blame it all on me either."

Johnny Lipon
(Coach, 1968–1971; interim manager, 1971)

In 1969, when Johnny Lipon was a coach for the Indians, a Japanese team, the Hiroshima Carp, shared the Tribe's Spring Training facilities in Tucson, Arizona.

Early one morning that spring, Lipon went to the clubhouse at Hi Corbett Field before the players were scheduled to report and was shocked at what he saw going on in the trainer's room.

There, with five or six members of the Japanese team surrounding him on the treatment table, was Sam McDowell with several needles sticking out of his back and shoulder. Lipon screamed, "What the hell is going on in there! Leave that guy alone and get the hell out of here!"

The Japanese were administering an acupuncture treatment for McDowell, who had complained of a sore shoulder—but Lipon said later he thought the pitcher was being harmed, maybe even tortured.

Joe Lis
(Outfielder, 1974–1976)

It was mid-April, 1974, and the Indians were playing in Milwaukee when rain halted the game in the fourth inning, delaying it for nearly an hour. Rusty Torres, an Indians outfielder, was in the bullpen beyond the right-field fence when the storm hit, and remained there for about a half an hour waiting for the weather to clear.

Also waiting for the rain to stop was Joe Lis in the dugout with several teammates and members of the Brewers grounds crew, when a fan, who'd had too much to drink, jumped out of the field boxes and ran onto the tarpaulin covering the infield. The grounds crew raced out of the dugout like a pack of police dogs to apprehend the inter-loper, which motivated several other fans to do the same—and for the grounds crew again to react accordingly.

Finally, when order was restored and, as the rain continued to fall, Torres decided to leave the bullpen and join his teammates. He climbed over the outfield fence and, carrying a bat, trotted across the field toward the dugout.

Lis, seeing Torres running in, prodded the grounds crew to "go after him like you did those fans" who'd invaded the field.

"Oh, no . . . he's got a bat in his hands, and he might swing it at us," the grounds crew chief said.

Lis told him, "Well, go after him like a curve ball and he'll miss you."

"Now that I have my pension [vested], I can go to heaven or hell and Joey, [my son], and Susie, my wife, will still be taken care of," said Joe Lis, who never was a fan of Frank Robinson, who managed the Indians from 1975 to 1977.

"Superstars never make good managers, and maybe I'm fortunate because I've never been in that class. I've been up and down. I've gone through success and failure. When a guy did something wrong, Frank couldn't understand it because he always did things right.

"Not me. I've done a lot of things wrong."

Al Lopez
(Catcher and manager, 1947, 1951–1956)

"For me, 1954 was the greatest season in the world, but the way it turned out it also was my greatest disappointment," said Al Lopez, who turned 97 on August 20, 2005, died October 30, 2005, and was the oldest living member of the Baseball Hall of Fame.

When asked why the Indians, who'd won a then-American League-record 111 games under Lopez, were swept by the then-New York

Giants in the 1954 World Series, Lopez said, "I still don't understand. I still believe we were the better team. In fact, I believe that team was one of the best in the history of baseball, primarily because of our pitching staff."

That pitching staff featured a starting rotation of Early Wynn, Bob Lemon, Mike Garcia, and Art Houtteman. Bob Feller, nearing the end of his career, was the fifth starter, and the bullpen was headed by Ray Narleski and Don Mossi, and included Hal Newhouser, who also was nearing the end of his career.

Wynn and Lemon, each of whom won 23 games in 1954; Feller (13–3); and Newhouser (7–2 in relief) are in the Hall of Fame.

"If the Series had opened in Cleveland, we would have done better. We would have won the first game, maybe the first two games, because those two home runs that Dusty Rhodes hit were just little pop flies down the right-field line that wouldn't have gone out of the Cleveland Stadium," Lopez continued.

And as for the "greatest ever" catch Willie Mays made in the opener of the Series, robbing Vic Wertz of what would have been a homer in any Major League ballpark other than the Polo Grounds, Lopez laughed and said: "It was a great catch, but the greatest? Willie made it more difficult than it actually was. He overran the ball and let it get over his head. He could have caught the ball to the side a lot easier than he did."

★ ★ ★ ★ ★

When Lopez managed the Chicago White Sox (from 1957–1965 and 1968–1969), he admitted he didn't appreciate the promotions that then-owner Bill Veeck staged to bolster attendance.

"My job was to manage the club and win ball games. I guess some of Bill's promotions did some good, but a winning team was the best promotion."

One promotion in particular upset Lopez.

"Veeck had what he called a 'Circus Day' and had a bunch of elephants and clowns running around the ballpark, along with caged animals, lions and tigers, the whole damned circus. We must have lost the day before because I wasn't in real good humor, and one of the elephants laid one—you know, call it a 'pie,' or whatever—about this big," Lopez said, holding his hands a couple of feet apart. "There were flies swarming around it, and I'll be damned if I didn't almost step right in it when I went out of the dugout. It was awful.

"Another time Veeck hired a helicopter that was going to land on the pitcher's mound. I didn't like that either, but Veeck had advertised it would happen and couldn't call it off. As the helicopter was getting ready to come down, the phone in the dugout rang and it was Eddie Short [then the White Sox publicity director]. He said, 'Al, you know who's going to land in that helicopter?' I told him I didn't, and he said, 'It's Satchel Paige.'

"But that part of it was a joke. Eddie knew I wouldn't take Paige even if I got fired. So I said to Short, 'You tell the guy who's flying that helicopter to be ready to get the hell out of there because if Satchel Paige gets out, I'm going to leave and not come back.

"Short laughed and when the helicopter landed, guess who got out? It was the midget, Eddie Gaedel, the guy Veeck hired to pinch hit when he owned the St. Louis Browns [in 1951]."

Would Lopez want to manage again?

"Sure, I would, if I were 30 years younger," he said. "But if I were 30 years younger there are a lot of things I'd like to be doing again.

"Could I [manage today's players]? Sure. It's all a matter of doing with what you've got."

"I played against and with so many great hitters; it's hard for me to pick one or two over the others. But I have to say that Ted Williams was one of the most complete hitters I ever saw, although I would say that Babe Ruth was the best overall player.

"You've got to figure [Ruth] was a great hitter, a home run hitter, and at the same time he was a great pitcher. He would have made it to the Hall of Fame as a pitcher. I don't say he was the greatest hitter, but I am saying he was the greatest player, all around. I'd have to rate Joe DiMaggio high up there, too, along with Rogers Hornsby—remember, he hit .440 and .420 a couple of times, and Ty Cobb, although I saw only a little of him.

"But this I know, it'd be hard for anybody to pick one of those guys as the best."

Lopez, a National League catcher for 18 seasons before joining the Indians as a backup receiver in 1947, said he didn't have many occasions to talk with Ruth, except when they played Spring Training exhibition games.

"Babe was one of those guys who'd show up, take batting practice, play the game, and never had much to do with other guys.

"Lou Gehrig was different. He was a very friendly guy. A nice guy. Everybody liked him. I remember a time we played the Yankees in Bradenton, [Florida], in 1939 when I was with the [Boston] Braves. Gehrig came up to the plate and said to me, Al, you've caught against me a lot of times. . . . What do you think I'm doing wrong? I'm having a lot of trouble.' I told him, 'Lou, you're not snapping the bat the way you did. You're kind of just pushing at the ball, feeling for it,' and he said, 'That's the way it feels to me, too, but I don't know why.'

"What he didn't know at the time—nobody did—[was] that he had something wrong with him. It was just coming on him then. When the Yankees got back to New York for the opening of the season, they had him examined and that's when they found out what was wrong."

Gehrig was diagnosed with amyotrophic lateral sclerosis (ALS)—a.k.a. Lou Gehrig disease—and played only eight games in 1939, ending his then-record streak of playing 2,130 consecutive games. He died on June 2, 1941.

Lopez's memories of Rocky Colavito and Herb Score also are vivid.

"I'll never forget one of the first games Rocky played for us in 1956," he recalled. "Somebody, I don't remember who it was, hit a grounder that went through [second baseman] Bobby Avila's legs. Rocky got the ball in right field, and when the base runner rounded second, Rocky cut loose and fired it to third base, but overthrew the third baseman. It hit the wall behind third base and bounced all the way back to the field and damned if it didn't go right through Avila's legs again. Now Rocky picked up the ball and started to throw it home and we're yelling from the dugout, 'Hold the ball, Rocky. Hold it!' It was the damnedest thing I ever saw."

As for Score, Lopez recalled, "I was the manager when the Indians signed Herb in 1952 out of high school in Lake Worth, [Florida], and brought him to Cleveland for a workout before he went to the minors. Mike McNally, who was the Indians' farm director, told Herb, 'Don't throw hard, just get good and loose. Lopez will come out in a few minutes, and we want him to see how you throw.'

"So when I got out on the field, Herb had been throwing to Birdie Tebbetts. I stood behind Score and asked him, 'Herb, do you want to cut loose?' and he said, 'Yes, that's what I've been waiting to do.' I told him, 'Go ahead, but don't hurt yourself. If you want to wait until tomorrow or the next day, it'll be OK.' But he said he was ready.

"With that he said to Birdie, 'Mr. Tebbetts, I'm going to let it out,' and Birdie said, 'You mean you haven't thrown hard yet?' Herb said he hadn't and with that, Tebbetts yelled over to [catcher] Joe Tipton, 'Hey, Joe, c'mon over here and catch this kid. I'm the next hitter [in batting practice].'

"So Tipton came over, picked up Birdie's glove, and yelled, 'OK, kid, let it come.' Herb fired his first pitch, and it went right over Tipton's head. He didn't even get a glove on it, and the ball hit the backstop. Joe turned pale. If it had hit him, it would have hit him right between the eyes and maybe killed him.

"Tipton yelled to Birdie, 'Tebbetts, you son of a bitch, you almost got me killed,' which he did, and Tebbetts started laughing like hell. Then Tipton got down in a catcher's crouch and told Score to throw another pitch. Herb did, and it hit Tipton right on the instep of his left foot. Now Tipton was jumping around in pain and was really mad at Tebbetts. Finally Jim Hegan came out and caught Score."

John Lowenstein
(Outfielder/infielder, 1970–1977)

Early in John Lowenstein's career with the Indians, he was asked if he'd like to see a banner in his honor hung at the old Stadium. Lowenstein reacted as if he'd been shot. "Basically, I'm against all banners. If somebody puts up a sign about me, I'd immediately disqualify myself from the game. Signs have no ethereal value."

And when it was suggested that a fans club be formed in his honor, Lowenstein instead created what he called an "apathy club" about which, he said, "Nobody knows how many members it has, because nobody is interested enough to show up for meetings."

When asked what he planned to do after he retired from baseball, Lowenstein said, "I'm going to be a [players'] agent and go to Taiwan and sign up all the Little League champions."

He didn't.

Reviewing his Major League career, Lowenstein said, "I went from playing a lot, to playing a little, to being used sometimes, and to playing on a platoon basis, although instead of being called a *platoon player*, I preferred being called a *situation player*."

Ditto Lucarelli
(Indians publicity/public relations director, 1967–1975)

"John Lowenstein was one of my favorite players, even though he wasn't always the easiest guy to work with. Every year we'd send out questionnaires, and every year his would come back different. One year he said he was born in Great Falls, Montana, the next year he was born in Las Vegas, and so on. Every year it was something else.

"So was his nationality. One year he was Jewish, another year he was German-American. We never did know exactly what it was, though I never bothered to pressure him, because I probably wouldn't have gotten a straight answer anyway.

"Then, too, one year he would tell us his name should be pronounced Lowensteen, and the next it was Lowenstine. He drove the field announcers crazy, because he'd go up to one of them during a game and say, 'You're pronouncing my name wrong. It's not Lowensteen, it's Lowenstine. So the guy would change, and the next time we'd come to town he'd go to the field announcer and say, you are mispronouncing my name, and say just the opposite from what he had previously.

"And this one, which was a classic. One year [General Manager] Phil Seghi set it up for Lowenstein to go to Venezuela to play winter ball. But we hadn't heard from him, and the general manager in Venezuela told Seghi that John never reported. We tried to reach him by phone and telegraph, but never could. Finally, I got a postcard from him. It said, 'Dear Dino. Here I am trying to hit the old apple in Venezuela. The Chinese people here are great, but the Chinese food isn't so hot. John.'

"That was it. I took it in to Seghi . . . which is how we found out that he finally reported."

Another Lowenstein story: "One night we were on the road, and Lowenstein had a single room next to Buddy Bell and Jack Brohamer, who shared a room. Buddy and Brohamer were watching a movie on TV, and when there was a commercial break they went down the hall to the pop machine, leaving the door to their room open. While they were gone, Lowenstein sneaked into their room and hid in the closet. He stood there like a zombie and closed the door. When Bell and Brohamer come back, they sat down to watch the rest of the movie, and then went to bed. Bell opened the closet door, and there was Lowenstein standing there, his eyes closed and arms folded across his chest. Buddy screamed . . . he was scared to death. Lowenstein laughed and laughed."

Another character—and because he was, he also was a favorite of Lucarelli—was Joe Lis, who also was a favorite of then-Manager Ken Aspromonte, even though Lis was only a substitute. "One time we were getting beat, like, 7–0, in the seventh inning," recalled Lucarelli, "and Aspromonte, who especially appreciated Lis for his rah-rah spirit in the locker room, hollered down the bench to Lis, 'Joe, do something. Get these guys worked up when they come off the field.' So, as the players came in, Lis knelt down on the top step of the dugout, took off his hat and started making the sign of the cross."

"Here's how bad things were back then. One night we were getting beat bad, something like 11–0 going into the bottom of the seventh inning. Johnny Singer, who was the leader of the band that played between innings, got on the microphone and said to the fans, 'C'mon, everybody, let's sing 'Take Me Out To the Ball Game.' But instead of singing, the crowd, which was unusually large for those days, started booing.

"Another time we were playing Baltimore and, when Ken Singleton struck out, the organist played, 'Bye, Bye, Blackbird.' Gabe Paul went crazy. He called down and had the organist fired, then and there, right on the spot."

"One year Gabe had a new Cadillac and, when he got to 1,000 miles, he told [handyman] Joe Botta to take the car back to the dealer for a checkup. So Joe did. But while he was driving to the dealer, he lit a cigar, wasn't paying attention, and went through a caution light. He got broadsided, and Gabe's new Cadillac was demolished. Totaled. It was a miracle that Joe wasn't killed, though Gabe probably wished he had been.

"At the time it happened, Gabe was holding court in the Wigwam [media dining room] after lunch, with five or six reporters, when Joe called him on the phone to tell him the car was demolished. Gabe sat there in front of all of us and, as nice as he could be—which was very nice when the media was watching—was saying into the phone, 'Uh, huh . . . yes . . . OK,' and then, still sweetly, 'Thank you, and good bye.'

"He hung up the phone and, totally unruffled, continued to tell his favorite stories, reminiscing about all the guys he knew in the old days. Finally, one by one, all the reporters left and, as they were leaving, Gabe gave me one of his looks that meant I was supposed to stay put. Then, as soon as the last guy left and he heard the elevator door close, he looked around the corner to make sure nobody was there, and started pounding his fist on the table and yelling, 'That no good son of a bitch . . .' and more, for five minutes, before I knew what was wrong.

"Finally he said what happened, and I had to be careful not to laugh. But it was funny as hell."

"Then there was the famous Jimmy Dudley-Bob Neal story. They were broadcast partners on the air, but hated each other and didn't speak to each other off the air. When Dudley suffered a heart attack in the mid-1960s, Neal was asked if he went to visit his partner in the hospital. Neal reportedly said, 'I tried to get in his room to pull the plug on him, but they wouldn't let me in.'"

Candy Maldonado
(Outfielder, 1990, 1993–1994)

"People started calling me 'Candy' in 1978 when I was playing rookie ball in Leftwich, Alberta, Canada, for the Dodgers. Everybody was having a rough time pronouncing my first name—which is Candido—so I just cut it in half and let them call me Candy. That's how I got the name. But then, later, I told people it was because my mother thought I was so sweet."

"When I played for John McNamara in Cleveland [in 1990]—I guess because I was a veteran—he allowed me to, sort of, initiate the rookies . . . make them dress up in weird clothes on road trips.

"So, one time when we were in Baltimore, I went to the Salvation Army and bought a bunch of old clothes for the rookies to wear. The funniest of them all was Alex Cole. We made him go through the airport terminal dressed in women's clothes—high heels with pink pants and a yellow suit coat, and a sanitary sock tied around his waist as a belt.

"The best part of it—for us but not for Alex—was that there were about a hundred people, family and fans of his from his home in West Virginia, and he had to walk out the front of Memorial Stadium in Baltimore to our bus in front of all those people. If he didn't, it would have cost him a $500 fine—and he also would have had to go to the bus in his underwear because we had taken all of his regular clothes."

Rick Manning
(Outfielder, 1975–1983)

"I'll never forget Lenny Barker's perfect game against Toronto [May 15, 1981]. As a no-hitter goes on, the anticipation doesn't really start building until the fifth or sixth inning. But in this case Lenny was getting better the longer he went. He didn't have a strikeout the first three innings, but wound up with 11, all of them from the fourth inning on. The slider he was throwing was vicious. Standing behind him in center field, as I was, I could see how it was breaking, and by the sixth inning I sensed the real possibility that he would throw a no-hitter.

"The funny thing is, in the dugout, when a guy is pitching a no-hitter, nobody wants to talk to him, and definitely not say anything about a no-no. But not with Lenny. I remember [third baseman] Toby Harrah and I were telling him along about the eighth inning, 'C'mon, you can do this.' We came right out and said it. He was very laid back about it and just kept going. Everybody could sense something was going to happen.

"I think he made only one mistake pitch the whole game, to Lloyd Moseby, in the middle innings. Moseby ended up hitting a rocket that went foul by about three feet, and then Barker got him.

"Normally there are some great plays made in a no-hitter, but not really in this one, which also proves how dominating Lenny was. Harrah went into the stands to catch a foul ball [in the fifth inning] and [second baseman Duane] Kuiper made a good back-handed play in the sixth, but otherwise there was nothing close to a hit.

"By the time the Blue Jays sent Ernie Whitt up as a pinch hitter, with two out in the ninth—I don't remember how the first two batters were retired—I'm thinking, 'I want this baseball.' It could be in right field or left field; I was going to catch that ball no matter where it went.

"Lenny went to a l-and-2 count on Whitt, and I'm saying to myself, 'C'mon, let's go, either strike him out or make him hit the ball to me.' Whitt swung and hit the ball in the air and I was calling for it before it even went out of the infield. It was a very easy catch.

"People have asked me, was I nervous? You don't have time to be nervous. I mean, your awareness is so much more heightened because it was a perfect game. Imagine that! A perfecto! Only the eleventh in the history of baseball [at that time]."

Rick Manning remembered how it was in the "bad old days" of Cleveland baseball.

"A lot of guys on the team wanted to be traded because they thought the Indians would never be a winning team," Manning said. "Not me. I was one of the few players who lived here year round. I wanted to stay here. I actually thought that one day we'd turn it around and win a pennant.

"In fact, most Spring Trainings I believed we had a chance to win the division. How dumb was that? We were playing in the East Division with Baltimore, New York, and Boston, and the truth be told, I had no clue back then.

"Something else I remember is how hard the game is to play, and that the further you get from it, the easier it looks."

Asked to comment on Sammy Sosa's use of a corked bat in 2003, Manning admitted that he used a corked bat a few times during his playing career.

"It didn't do me any good," said the lifetime .257 hitter. "Instead of blooping a single in front of an outfielder, the few times I tried [a corked bat] all it probably did was help me fly out to an outfielder."

After he was appointed the Tribe's base running and outfield coach (in addition to broadcasting games on television), Manning spent time in the batting cage in Spring Training learning to hit with a fungo bat.

"Buddy Bell was giving me lessons," he said. "It was embarrassing because I kept hitting the ball over the center-field fence."

He didn't do that too often against live pitching. In his 13-year playing career Manning hit 56 homers in 5,248 at-bats.

"When I was playing [for the Indians and Milwaukee Brewers from 1975–1987] and I'd see all those old guys in uniform, I'd say to myself, 'I'm not listening to that coach. What does he know?'

"Now I'm one of those old guys. I guess it's true, what goes around comes around."

Jeff Manto
(Outfielder, 1990–1991, 1997–1999)

The Indians never seemed to get enough of Jeff Manto—although it also seemed they could never make up their mind about the first baseman-third baseman-outfielder. He spent five tours of duty with the organization from 1990 to 1999.

Manto joined the Indians initially in a deal with the California Angels; was released in November 1991; was reacquired in a trade with Toronto in 1997; was released in April 1998; was re-signed as a free agent in June 1998; was released after the end of the 1998 season; was re-signed and recalled in June 1999; was let go in July 1999; and finally was re-signed as a minor league free agent in August 1999 and released at the end of the 1999 season.

"I never had a bad day in the Major Leagues, although I never had many of them [days in the Major Leagues]," he said. "I just appreciate the game, and I know it owes me nothing."

Charlie Manuel
(Coach, 1988–1989, 1994–1999; manager, 2000–2002)

"During the 2000 season, when we were having so many injury problems and had to use 32 pitchers [a Major League record], I went out to the mound to make a change. I said to the pitcher, 'OK, Bill . . .'" and he looked at me real funny and said, 'My name isn't Bill, it's Mike, Mike Mohler.' I said, 'OK, Mike, I'm glad to meet you, but I'm still going to make a change.'"

"I was playing in Japan one year and hit a line drive that hit the pitcher and broke his shoulder. The next year that same pitcher hit me. I went out after him, and he ran into my dugout and hid behind the manager. I couldn't get at him, but I was yelling at him, and finally my interpreter came along and said, 'Charlie, let him go. You've already scared him enough.' So I did.

"In Japan, if the Japanese sportswriters saw a blond woman in the stands, they'd write that it was my girlfriend. I'd tell them, 'She's not my girl- friend, but I'd like to meet her. Why don't you guys introduce me to her?' "

Manuel was the Indians' batting instructor before becoming the team's 37th manager in 2000. He played in the Major Leagues for Minnesota and the Los Angeles Dodgers, from 1969–1975, and in Japan from 1976–1981, then managed in the minor leagues the next six seasons, before joining the Indians' coaching staff.

In his 38-year professional baseball career, Manuel played with and against many great hitters. One in particular stands out, as he said upon taking over as manager of the Indians: "The more I see of Manny Ramirez, the more I believe he is the best right-handed hitter I've ever seen.

"Ramirez is such a good hitter because he is tension free. A couple of years ago, when we were coming out of Spring Training, Manny lost his suitcase. He was real upset because he had his gold necklaces in the suitcase and asked [Clubhouse Manager] Ted Walsh if he knew where his bag was. Walsh tracked it down and it turned out that Manny had left three or four paychecks in there. We're talking about big money, too. But Manny didn't care about that. He was just glad he had his gold necklaces back. That's why he can hit .400. He's tension free."

These are some Manuel-isms, a la Yogi Berra.

"We'll tackle that bridge when we get to it."

"If I'm going to use Wil [Cordero], I've got to start using him."

"When Russell [Branyan] is striking out, he's missing the ball a lot."

"I'm just going to let the chips fall where they lay."

"Sometimes people don't see what they are looking at."

"C.C.'s [Sabathia] problem is that he always has to throw a strike."

"Were just getting beat too early. It's like getting beat late or getting beat in the middle of the game. There are a whole lot of different ways to lose a game."

"I have two children and they both have degrees in English. After hearing their old man speak, I guess they figured they better learn English the right way."

Tom McCraw
(First baseman, 1972, 1974–1975; coach, 1975, 1979–1982)

Tom McCraw was a close-up observer of Frank Robinson when the latter was named Major League Baseball's first black manager. McCraw also was a close friend and admirer of Robinson.

"Frank's Opening Day home run in 1975 was one of the most amazing things I've ever seen in baseball," McCraw said. "I felt it was destiny. . . . I mean, here's a guy who's a player-manager, and he hits a home run in his first at-bat as baseball's first black manager. How can that be? That's what you call answering the call. It was like something scripted in Hollywood.

"I was coaching at first base when Frank connected off [New York Yankees right-hander] Doc Medich. I thought, 'How can you do anything better than that?' If somebody had bet me that he'd hit the ball out of the park in his first at bat, I'd have lost everything I own, because I would have bet it all that he couldn't do it. Who would have bet otherwise? Even a single or a double. But no. He hits a home run. The most glorified hit in the game. It's one of my favorite days in baseball."

It also was early in the 1975 season that Phil Seghi, then general manager of the Indians, was quoted as saying the team had a chance to win the pennant.

"I didn't say anything at the time, but I wondered what Phil was smoking in his pipe when he made that statement," McCraw recalled.

(The 1975 Indians finished fourth with a 79–80 record, 15½ games behind the Boston Red Sox.)

"One of the amazing things that happened when I was a coach here—and I'm still amazed when I think about it—was that one night

Frank Robinson was in a full-blown argument with one of the umpires. I mean, the veins were popping in his neck, and all the profanity was coming out. Then the darnedest thing happened.

"While all this profanity and arguing is coming out of Frank's mouth, at the same time he is giving signs to his third base coach Dave Garcia, as to what he wanted the hitter to do.

"It also was almost as amazing to me that Garcia picked up the signs from Robinson as Frank was arguing with the umpire.

"When Frank finished arguing, I asked myself, 'What the heck did I just see?' I could hardly believe it, though I know it was true, because Garcia told me that what I saw was what was happening.

"I never saw anything like that in baseball before or since."

"Speaking of Robinson, he was very mentally tough and fought for what he wanted, what he thought was right. Now, when I see him in his job as vice president of on-field operations for the commissioner and dishing out all those fines, I call him the 'Hanging Judge,' because he's fining and suspending guys for doing the same things he always did as a player and manager.

"He was tough on umpires, but only if an umpire slacked off in his job. He expected everybody to do his job the way he tried to do his. And if you slacked off, whether you were an umpire or a coach or a player, he let you know about it."

Sam McDowell
(Pitcher, 1961–1971)

"I think everybody in the ball park was shocked, including everybody on my team—though I wasn't—when Alvin Dark moved me from the mound to second base against the old Washington Senators [July 6, 1970, Cleveland Stadium]. It didn't surprise me, because Alvin told me before the game that he might do it.

"We had a meeting and talked about what had happened in the previous game I pitched against the Senators. In that one, Frank Howard hit two home runs off me, and two other balls that should have been home runs, that almost killed our outfielders. I think Frank hit about .800 off me. I probably kept him in the big leagues for five or ten extra years.

"Alvin told me, 'Sam, I know you're a pretty good athlete, so this is what I'm going to do if you're pitching against Washington and the right situation presents itself. If Frank Howard comes up any time after the seventh inning and we're either winning the game or one run behind, I'm going to take you out, bring somebody in to pitch to Howard, and then bring you back to close out the game.'

"I said, 'Fine, no problem.' But that's because I assumed he meant he'd put me in right field or first base, which I had played. If you recall, I was signed by the Indians as an outfielder and a pitcher.

"But this time, with Howard coming up with runners on second and third and two out, and we were ahead by two runs [4–2], Alvin came to the mound and said, 'Sam, you go to second base.' Then he switched [second baseman] Eddie Leon to third [replacing Graig Nettles], and brought Dean Chance in to pitch.

"Dark's plan was for Chance, a right-hander, to intentionally walk Howard, which would load the bases and bring another right-handed batter, Rick Reichardt, to the plate. That way, if the Senators substituted a left-handed pinch hitter for Reichardt, Dark could counter it by putting me back in to pitch.

"What happened was that Reichardt, with the bases loaded, batted against Chance and hit a sharp grounder to Leon, who—I guess, without thinking—scooped it up and fired it to second to me. His throw was a little low, and I dropped to my knees because I wasn't about to miss it, and it beat Howard as he came roaring into second for the third out.

"I went back to pitch the ninth inning and got them out [three strikeouts], and we won, 4–2 [giving him a 12–4 record].

"What's really interesting to me is that the rules state that a pitcher gets credit for a complete game if he's responsible for all 27 outs. Well,

I made the out at second base, which means I was responsible for all 27, but I didn't get credit for a complete game, and I still want to know why not."

On September 18,1966, McDowell was pitching what he later called "the game of my life" against the Tigers in Detroit. "I often wonder if I could have struck out 18 [and tied what was then the Major League record] if I could have gone all the way . . . if I hadn't said anything to [Interim Manager] George Strickland . . . if he hadn't taken me out of the game.

"One thing I do know, I had everything that night. My fastball was as good as it ever was, and my control was nearly perfect. I got 14 strikeouts in only six innings. No matter what pitch I threw, I could put it anywhere I wanted. I was at my all-time best, and I don't think I was ever that good after that night.

"I went back to the dugout at the end of the sixth inning and told Strickland my arm was beginning to tighten. I only said it because I wanted him to have somebody ready, just in case. We were winning [5–1], and I didn't want to take any chances.

"I remember telling George, 'I'm OK, and I want to stay in there. But maybe you should keep somebody ready just in case.' Just like that, he took me out. I'd had some shoulder trouble early that season, and Strickland probably wanted to be sure I didn't hurt myself again.

"Nobody will ever know for sure what might have happened. But I only needed four more strikeouts to tie the record [then shared by Bob Feller and Sandy Koufax] and five to break it, and I had three innings to get them. That's why, of all the games I pitched, it's one I'll never forget."

By his own admission, McDowell was the biggest drunk in the Major Leagues during his too-brief pitching career with the Indians (1961–1971), San Francisco (1972–1973), New York Yankees (1973–1974), and Pittsburgh (1975).

Sam McDowell is the first to admit that he drank himself out of baseball and that he ruined what most observers believe would have been a Hall-of-Fame career.

Instead, his career ended in 1975, four years and three teams (San Francisco, New York Yankees, Pittsburgh) after being traded to the Giants for Gaylord Perry on November 29, 1971.

"Sudden Sam," as McDowell was nicknamed during his pitching career, has been sober for 16-plus years. But he also is the first to admit that his sobriety and his recovery from alcoholism is an ongoing day-to-day project.

"I am still an alcoholic. I always will be one; it's something that never changes," he said.

"I was a jerk, and I know it. But I also know it was alcoholism that made me a jerk. I don't like to talk about my career because I truly believe in my recovery. I live one day at a time, and I don't give a [bleep] about the past. I think about today and what I can do today to better myself as a person, what I can do today to help somebody else, what I can do today to try to do things the right way, that's all I care about. And if people don't like it, tough [bleep]."

When asked if he regrets not making it to the Hall of Fame and that his credentials—a 141–134 lifetime record for 15 Major League seasons—fell far short of what so many had anticipated when he signed his first professional contract with the Indians in 1961, McDowell said:

"I would love to be in the Hall of Fame, but I know I would not be here today if it were not for my alcoholism and my subsequent recovery. . . . I know I would not be here if I had not gone through the alcoholism and the recovery process. And I know, too, that I would not be in the position I'm in, or have the respect of my peers that I know I have, and the satisfaction of helping others who need the help that I can give but couldn't get during my career in baseball.

"But that said, there also is absolutely no doubt in my mind that I would be in the Hall of Fame if I had not been a drunk, if I had not been kicked out of baseball because of my drinking. If I'd had the kind of help that I can provide players now, Nolan Ryan might not be baseball's leading strikeout pitcher."

Of his aborted career—aborted because of his drinking—McDowell said, "I was a very proud pitcher, very proud. That's the only reason I was a winner with a team like the Cleveland Indians. Not that they were bad guys, but we had no talent, and everybody knew it, and so did Gabe Paul. He was not trying to win a pennant. He was out to make money with the team, and that was it. He knew how to make it, no matter what. We knew we were going to be in last place when we left Spring Training.

"But I always tried hard, no matter what. I never wanted to be embarrassed on the mound, and I don't think I ever was. I always tried to give it everything I had out there."

Tom McGough
(Pitcher, 1977)

"It was Spring Training, 1976, in a Cactus League game against the San Francisco Giants in Phoenix that I had one of my most memorable baseball experiences," Tom McGough said. "My sole assignment for the afternoon, or so I thought, was simply to keep the pitching chart.

"But when Ray Fosse, who was rehabilitating an offseason knee surgery, came to the plate with two outs and nobody on base, the stage was set for my pinch running debut. [Manager] Frank Robinson looked at me and said, 'Mac, if Ray gets on, you're going to run for him.' At first I thought Frank was kidding. I was fast, and I always ran hard when we did wind sprints, but there is a big difference between that and being a base runner in a Major League game.

"Well, Ray hit a sharp double, and sure enough, I got the nod from Robinson to 'get in there.' It wasn't until I was actually standing on second base and heard my name over the loudspeaker that I realized that I hadn't even been on the base paths since high school. Of course, I didn't even know the signs. But I've never been one to back away from a challenge, so I was determined to do my very best for the team.

"As Duane Kuiper, the next batter, stepped to the plate, I couldn't help but hope that he'd hit a home run so that I could just jog home.

Instead, Kuip drilled a sharp single to right. I was moving on the pitch and got a good jump, but as I rounded third base [Coach] Joe Nossek signaled for me to stop. Then, suddenly, both of us noticed the throw from right field was going to sail over the catcher's head, so I continued home, now believing there would be no play on me at the plate. What I didn't see was the pitcher, Bob Knepper, backing up the plate.

"He caught the wild throw and fired a perfect strike to catcher Mike Sadek, who faked me to perfection as I was just a few feet from home. My eyes were riveted on the plate until I noticed the catcher turning toward me with the ball in his glove. It was anything but pretty, but somehow I contorted to a degree that would have made Houdini proud, and—well, *sort of*—dived successfully over Sadek, eluding the tag and scoring the run.

"Needless to say my teammates were highly amused, but my rebuttal to this day remains in the simple fact that I was, albeit quite comically, 'safe at home.'

"Also, needless to say, I was never asked to pinch run for anybody again—which didn't bother me a bit."

Cal McLish
(Pitcher, 1956–1959)

Cal McLish pitched for Brooklyn, Pittsburgh, Cincinnati, the Chicago White Sox, the Chicago Cubs, and Philadelphia, in addition to the Indians, during a 15-year Major League career. He was never a 20-game winner—although he came close in 1959 with the Tribe.

That was the season the Indians almost won the American League pennant but were beaten in the final week by Chicago.

It also was the reason McLish still bears resentment toward Frank Lane, then general manager of the Indians.

He recalled, "I'd won 19 games and was scheduled to start two days later, on Sunday in the final game of the season, which would give me a chance to win my 20th [against Kansas City, then one of the teams with one of the worst records in the league].

"But when I got to the clubhouse that Friday night, I was called into [Manager] Joe Gordon's office. Lane was there with Gordon and [Pitching Coach] Mel Harder, and Lane said, 'Cal, would you mind giving up your start on Sunday so Herb Score could pitch?'

"Well, I wanted the chance to win my 20th, but I liked Herbie a lot. He was still trying to come back from that [1957] eye injury . . . and I told Lane that I was willing to do it for Scores sake.

"What I didn't know, but found out later, was that Lane had already traded me to Cincinnati, even though it wasn't to be announced until later. That was the first year they had interleague trading and, naturally, if I had stayed and won 20, it would have been embarrassing for Lane.

"I found out about it after the season was over, when Hal Lebovitz called me and told me how it happened.

"So, in effect, while I thought I was giving up a chance to win 20 for Herbie, what I really did was give it up for Lane—which was really rotten of him. Absolutely rotten. I saw Lane once after that, but I didn't mention it. What good would that have done? It was too late to worry about it.

"I also thought it was rotten that Joe [Gordon] and Mel [Harder] didn't stick up for me. I kind of felt bad about that, too, but that's baseball. That's the way it is in baseball."

When asked about his given name(s)—Calvin Coolidge Julius Caesar Tuskahoma—McLish said, "It was my father who named me, but I don't know where the 'Calvin Coolidge' part of it came from. As far as I know my dad wasn't even a Republican. I guess he just liked the name, the same as he probably liked 'Julius Caesar.'" As for "Tuskahoma," McLish said it was the name of a town in the Indian territory of Oklahoma where his parents were born.

"Dad was 1/4 Chickasaw, and Mom was 1/16 Cherokee, which makes me 1/8 Chickasaw and 1/32 Cherokee," said McLish, who also is part Scottish, English, Irish, and Dutch.

Don McMahon
(Pitcher, 1964–1966)

It was a very hot and humid afternoon in Cleveland during a game in July 1964, and Manager Birdie Tebbetts, angered by the players' complaints, threatened to impose a $50 fine against the next player who grumbled about the weather.

An inning later, as he came off the field, relief pitcher Don McMahon grabbed a towel to wipe the sweat off his face and said, "Jeez, it is so hot out there . . ." and then, remembering Tebbetts' warning, quickly added, ". . . but I love it, Birdie, I love it. Honest, I do."

(He wasn't fined.)

Jose Mesa
(Pitcher, 1992–1998)

After ending his career with the Indians under less than friendly circumstances, Jose Mesa went on to pitch for San Francisco, Seattle, Philadelphia, and Pittsburgh. It was during the 2004 season, when Mesa regained his star status as a closer with the Pirates, that he was approached by a Cleveland sportswriter for an interview.

Before the scribe could even say hello, Mesa looked up and said, "Don't even ask," which ended the proposed interview before it even began.

Al Milnar
(Pitcher, 1936, 1938–1943)

"The Indians called me in 1933 after I'd pitched well in an amateur league in Cleveland and invited me for a tryout," Al Milnar recounted the beginning of his professional baseball career. "They gave me a bonus for going to the tryout—a streetcar fare from my home [on Cleveland's East Side] to League Park. That was it."

Milnar, who still lives in Euclid, pitched for the Tribe as a reliever briefly in 1936 and all of 1938 and was a starter in 1939 and 1940, compiling a 32–22 won-lost record before suffering an injury early in the 1941 season.

"I hurt my shoulder throwing sliders, which at that time was a new kind of pitch," Milnar said. "Johnny Allen, [a former teammate], taught me how to throw it, but looking back at it I wish he hadn't. In those days the doctors didn't know what to do about a sore arm. They just rubbed it with alcohol, and if you complained too much, well it was 'Goodbye Charlie.'"

Milnar's record fell to 12–19 in 1941, and he never had a winning season thereafter, winding up with a 57–58 eight-year Major League career record that included parts of 1943 and 1946 with the old St. Louis Browns and Philadelphia Phillies.

"Today, they can practically put a new arm on you and send you to the minor leagues for rehabilitation," Milnar said.

"But in my day you kept your mouth shut and didn't complain, or even say anything about a sore arm, because there always were a couple of guys on the bench ready to take your job. When my arm went bad, I just kept pitching, and my arm never got any better. It hurts me to this day.

"And we also weren't smart enough to hire agents in my day. But then, we didn't think we needed them. We felt lucky just to get a paycheck twice a month, and to play the game we loved."

"I don't remember too much about it anymore, it was so long ago, but I'm the guy who gave up the hits that extended DiMaggio's streak to 56 [on July 16, 1941]. The game was played at League Park, and the Yankees beat us, 10–3, before we [the Indians] stopped him the next night at the Stadium.

"Giving up the hit—actually, two of them [to DiMaggio]—bothered me, but what the hell, he hit in 55 games before that. The thing that bothered me more was that we lost the game.

"I always threw DiMaggio a lot of sliders, so it probably was a slider that he hit each time. In those days the slider was kind of an unknown pitch. In fact, Phil Rizzuto once told me that I was the first guy who ever threw him a slider."

Saturnino Orestes "Minnie" Minoso
(Outfielder, 1949, 1951, 1958–1959)

When Minnie Minoso played for the New York Cubans of the Negro National League in 1948, Joe Vosmik scouted the outfielder-third baseman for the Indians. In his report to then-Owner Bill Veeck, Vosmik called Minoso "the fastest thing on legs," and the Tribe quickly purchased Minoso's contract for $25,000.

After Minoso joined the Dayton (Ohio) Indians of the Class A Central League for the final two weeks of the 1948 season, Vosmik's subsequent report was even more glowing as Minoso batted .525 in 11 games.

"[Minoso] can hit Major League pitching right now—and if there is anything higher than Major Leagues, he'll hit that, too," Vosmik said.

In 1959 when Fidel Castro came to power in Cuba, the communist government seized Minoso's family's vast holdings in that country, leaving Minnie penniless. It was written that "an incalculable fortune was lost in a heartbeat," but Minoso refused to lament the loss.

"I come from the ranch," he explained. "I had one pair of shoes, but I had dignity because my mother and father gave me the idea that money wasn't everything."

Minoso "retired"—although he refused to use that word—in 1964 and managed and played in the Mexican League from 1965 to 1975.

He was activated by the White Sox for three games in 1976 when he was 49 (or 52, depending upon whose records you believe) and returned again for two games in 1980 at the age of 55 (or 58), giving him five decades in the Major Leagues.

At the time he said, "I sometimes think I am dreaming, and I don't want to wake up. I want to stay in baseball the rest of my life."

He wanted to be activated again in 1990, for a record sixth decade, but then-commissioner Fay Vincent would not give his approval.

"I liked Frank Lane. I liked him a lot. I used to call him 'Papa No. 2,' and he used to call me and say, 'I want to speak to my son, Minnie Minoso.' So somebody would come over to me and say, 'Some crazy guy on the phone wants to talk to you. He say to tell you that your daddy No. 2 wants to talk to you,' which is why I call him my Papa No. 2. He treated me good. Like a papa.

"One time he even introduced me to his daughter. He say to her, 'This is your brother, and I am his Papa No. 2.' "Lane was a good man. I know a lot of people in Cleveland did not like him, but I loved him. People no like him because he tell the truth, and anything he thinks is good, he'd do it. Even trade Rocky [Colavito]. He thought it was a good deal, so he did it."

Fernando Montes
(Strength coach, 1993–)

"On one of our flights I overheard Pat Borders [a Tribe catcher 1997–1999] say that he'd never been embarrassed during his Major League career. Several of the players also took note of it and decided they wanted to do something about it.

"A few days later when Pat was going to play in a Saturday afternoon game, I talked to the guys in the scoreboard room where they play introduction music for each player as he comes up to bat. I asked if they had anything from the old 'Hee-Haw' TV program, or some music like that, and they said they'd find something. I told them to play it when Borders stepped into the batter's box for his first at-bat.

"When he did, they played the theme song from 'Green Acres.' He looked into the dugout, and Kevin Seitzer and I are literally falling down laughing. And to make it even better—or worse for Pat—the catcher, Mike MacFarlane, turned to Pat and said, 'I hope that's your favorite song.'

"Pat struck out and came back to the dugout, threw his helmet down, and told us, 'You tell the guys up there that if they play that music again I'm going to kill somebody.'"

Terry Mulholland
(Pitcher, 2002–2003)

"It was during 1997 and 'Mo,' my nickname for Mulholland, was then pitching for San Francisco against the Phillies, one of Mulholland's former teams, in Philadelphia," recalled Joe Bick, a player agent for Mulholland. "He hit a home run—the ball was absolutely crushed and was measured at about 451 feet—which ended up being the second longest home run ever hit in Veterans Stadium that year.

"When the season was over, I was watching a game in the Arizona Fall League in Phoenix, where Mulholland lives. While we're sitting around shooting the bull one night I said, 'You know, Mo it amazes me that a guy who is as big and strong as you are and can hit a ball as far as you did in that game against the Phillies last season can't hit it a little more often.' He was a typical pitcher . . . you know, not much of a hitter.

"He said to me in all seriousness, 'Well, Joe, I think if you look back in the history of baseball you'd see that a number of premier power hitters never hit for much of an average.'

"And with that we both broke up."

In Terry Mulholland's perfect world, he would start every fifth day and make two relief appearances in between.

"You have to understand," he said. "I love pitching, and I love playing baseball. I've been this way since I was six years old. There is nothing more gratifying than when a manager gives you a baseball and tells you to go get people out."

As for his advanced age (his birthdate is listed in *The Baseball Register* as March 9, 1963), Mulholland—who pitched for 10 Major League teams, including Seattle and Minnesota in 2004, in a professional baseball career that began in 1984—said of himself, "I'm the youngest 41-year-old I know . . . and when I was 30, I was the youngest 30-year-old I knew."

Playing for a contract every year is not easy.

"It all depends on how much self-confidence you have and staying prepared to play baseball. You have to stay healthy, too," he says. "And don't complain about a lack of security [in baseball]. If you want security, learn how to work a monkey wrench."

In 2003, when he was both a starter and reliever for the Indians, Mulholland was called in to pitch in the middle of an inning when rookie Jason Davis was ejected from a game against Minnesota in mid-July. Although he was entitled to throw as many warmup pitches as he wanted, Mulholland took only eight and then promptly struck out Lew Ford on four pitches.

"That's the way you did it back home," Mulholland said. "You'd be playing right field in a summer league game, and they'd tell you to go in and pitch. Eight warmup pitches were all you got and all you needed.

"That's why big leaguers are such pansies. They're too coddled."

After pitching against—and beating the Indians—as a member of the Minnesota Twins on August 16, 2004, Mulholland said, "The thing I learned watching them is that you can't give them anything they can hit real hard. [So] I tried to tease them. Heck, I'll try anything. If I was allowed to take sandpaper to the ball, I'd do that."

Eddie Murray
(First baseman—designated hitter, 1994–1996; coach, 2002–)

During his induction speech at the Hall of Fame on July 27, 2003, as the 38th player elected on the first ballot, Eddie Murray said, "When Ted Williams was inducted 37 years ago, he said he must have earned it because he didn't win it because of his friendship with the writers.

"I guess in that way I'm proud to be in his company. I was never one much on words. I had a job to do. I'd seen people get caught up with doing well. I didn't want things like that to control me.

"For me, to focus a lot on the individual, that's not the way I learned to play the game. Baseball is a team game."

And to the youngsters in the audience during the Hall of Fame ceremonies, Murray said, "For every kid here today, I wish you could feel what I'm feeling, because I had a dream as a kid, and I actually lived that dream. It's unbelievable. I loved playing baseball. I still love this game."

Ray Murray
(Catcher, 1948, 1950–1951)

"I loved Bill Veeck, though I probably should have hated him. He had me up and down, between Cleveland and Oklahoma City like a damned yo-yo, in 1948.

"When I was called back to the Indians in September, my wife Jackie and I got into town around three in the morning, went to bed, and about eight o'clock the phone rang, waking us up.

"It was Veeck. He said, 'I want you and the wife in my office in 30 minutes,' because there was something he wanted to talk to me about.

"We were staying at the Hotel Cleveland [now the Renaissance Hotel on Public Square] and I told him, 'Hell, Bill, we've been traveling and we're tired. I'll come down later.' He said, 'No, I want to see you right away. Take a cab. I'll pay for it.'

"Well, he was the boss and what could I do? I didn't want to hurt my chances, so Jackie and I got dressed and took a cab to the Stadium. I didn't expect to be there long, so I told the cabbie to wait. "When we got to Veeck's office, he said, 'I appreciate the way you people have cooperated with me and I want to do something for you.'

"He held up a key and said, 'This is for a new Pontiac car. If you can find it, it's yours,' though he wouldn't tell me where to even look. He was laughing, but I knew he wasn't joking.

"Then I remembered, from when I was up with the club earlier in the season, that [Veeck] did business with a car dealer on the west side. I think it was called 'West Side Pontiac.' So Jackie and I jumped back in the cab and told him to take us there.

"We went in the showroom and there's a new Pontiac sitting over in the corner. I asked the salesman if I could try my key in the ignition, and when I did, VAROOM! The car started. How about that! We drove it out the door.

"It had to be worth about $4,800 at least. When the season ended, after the World Series, we drove that Pontiac home and kept it for a long time, all because I 'cooperated' with Bill, which means I didn't cuss and raise hell every time they sent me down.

"So, sure, I loved Bill Veeck. Why wouldn't I?"

Hal Naragon
(Catcher, 1951, 1954–1959)

"It was 1955, my second full season with the Indians, and Hank Greenberg and I just couldn't get together on my contract," said Hal Naragon, talking about how different salary negotiations are today, compared to his era. "In those days management was in the driver's seat and players didn't have much leverage. Finally Hank said that if

I was still on the club on June 15, he'd give me a $1,500 raise, so I signed.

"Then, sometime in May, we played the Yankees on a Friday night in front of a big crowd in the Stadium. Early Wynn pitched, and we won—and anytime we beat the Yankees it was a good game to win. I happened to get a hit or two and also, late in the game, I caught a foul ball down toward the third base line with men in scoring position. I called everybody off. . . . I wouldn't let anybody catch it except me, and it helped us win.

"The next day I went into the clubhouse and was called up to Greenbergs office. I thought, uh-oh, maybe they're going to send me back to Indianapolis, which then was the Indians' top farm club.

"But Greenberg told me he liked that play I made—the way I took charge of the foul ball—and said, 'You know the deal we had, the $1,500 part of it?' I said, 'Yes, sir,' and he said, 'It's yours,' even though it was long before June 15 [and] before he had to give it to me or not."

One of Naragon's favorite teammates was Mike Garcia, who threw all the standard pitches—fastball, curve, slider, change-up—and, occasionally, a spitball.

"We were playing Boston at the Stadium, I think it was in 1955, and Ted Williams was batting against Garcia, who'd load up a pitch every once in awhile—and boy, he had a good one. He didn't load up many, but he did when he felt he needed it. And when he loaded one up, Mike would shake his head and his glove so I'd know to expect it.

"So this time Williams is at the plate, we've got two strikes on him, and I got down and gave Mike a signal. I don't remember what I called for, fastball or curve or whatever, but Mike shook his head and his glove to let me know he was loading one up.

"He threw it and—honest to God!—it was right down the middle, about knee high, and when it got to the plate, the ball dropped about a foot.

"But even before the pitch got to the plate, Williams yelled, 'There's something on that ball!' Honest, he did.

"Of course, a spitter, most of the time, doesn't have much rotation and isn't really thrown very hard, but for Williams to see something on the ball like he did was amazing.

"I caught the pitch—it was a ball because Williams didn't swing and it dropped out of the strike zone—and right away I threw it back to Mike. The umpire, Hank Soar, walked around in front of the plate and yelled to Mike, 'Throw me the ball,' and Mike rolled it on the ground to him,' which cleaned it up.

"Then Williams turned to me and said, 'What was that pitch, Hal?' and I said, 'It was a sinker,' and that was the end of it."

Another "amazing" story—one that's even so scary that Naragon admits he researched its accuracy—involved Early Wynn and former Indians outfielder Gene Woodling.

"During the 1951 season when Woodling was then with the Yankees, we played them on June 24 in New York. Early Wynn was pitching for us and the score was tied 3–3 going into the bottom of the eighth inning. Woodling came up and hit a two-run homer, and the Yankees beat us 5–3.

"Exactly a month later, on July 24, we were in New York again, Wynn was pitching again, and we were leading 2–0 in the sixth inning. Woodling came up and hit another two-run homer off Early, tying the score, and the Yankees eventually won 3–2.

"Then, which is even more amazing—and kind of *scary*, too, to tell the truth—a month after that, on August 24, we played the Yankees again, and this time the game was scoreless in the eighth until Woodling, of course, hit another two-run homer off Wynn, and the Yankees won that game 2–0.

"All this happened on June 24, July 24, and August 24 of 1951— and to top it off, consider that Early Wynns uniform number was 24.

"You could say that it was fortunate for the Indians—and especially Early—that September 24, 1951, was an open date for us."

Indians pitchers of that era—the early to mid-1950s—were renowned as a fun-loving bunch, led by Bob Lemon and Early Wynn, which reminded Naragon of another story regarding his former batterymates.

"We were in Boston to play the Red Sox, when Lou Boudreau was their manager, and Al Lopez asked one of their writers who was pitching the next day. The writer said, 'We never know because Boudreau doesn't like to tell his pitchers when they are going to pitch because they'd get nervous and wouldn't have a good nights sleep.'

"Lopez said, 'Geez, I have to tell my pitchers so they *will* get a good night's sleep.'"

"Elroy Face had a terrific forkball [for Pittsburgh, Detroit, and Montreal from 1953 to 1969] that had made him a very successful relief pitcher, so good that he maybe should even be in the Hall of Fame.

"I knew him when I was a coach for the Tigers in 1968, which was about the time the split-fingered fastball—what they now call a *splitter*—was becoming very popular, and I asked him, 'What's the difference between the forkball that you threw and a splitter?'

"He said, 'Three million dollars.'"

Ray Narleski
(Pitcher, 1954–1958)

It all began for Ray Narleski, one of baseball's first relief specialists, in 1953 when he was pitching in the minor leagues for Indianapolis of the Class AAA American Association.

"It was strange the way it happened," he said. "I had lost a 12-inning game and was determined to find out what I'd done wrong. So I went out to pitch batting practice the next day, and a couple days later Birdie Tebbetts, who was the manager, said he wanted to talk to me. At first I thought he was calling me in for an attitude kind of thing, you know?

"But he said, 'Ray, I'm going to make you a reliever.' I said, 'The hell you are,' because, back then, relievers were old guys, guys who weren't good enough to be starters. Birdie said, 'No, this [becoming a reliever] can take you up to the big leagues.' He said he remembered seeing me throw the ball past Luke Easter and other good hitters in Spring Training, and said, 'You can throw it high and tight and low and away, and blow them away, which is a great thing.'

"It turned out he was right, and that it was good for me. No, make that very good."

★ ★ ★ ★ ★

"How hard did I throw? Well, I'll tell you. When I see these guys on TV and they say they are throwing 95 [mph], I know there were times, when I could go into my full windup, that I must have gone into the 100s. I know I did, compared to the 95s they say these guys are throwing. I could feel the ball explode right out of my hand. I really could. Boom! I could feel I had it. And I could go a long way, too. Not just one or two innings.

"I always wanted to be a starter, because starters get paid better than relievers. But looking back on it, I don't have any great regrets because I had a good career in Cleveland." (If saves were counted during Narleski's time as they are now, he would have had 13 in 1954 and 19 in 1955.)

Graig Nettles
(Third baseman, 1970–1972)

When the Indians played in Cleveland's old Municipal Stadium with its 80,000-plus seating capacity, crowds were sparse in what was known as the "bad old days"—the 1960s through the 1980s. That included 1970–1972, when Graig Nettles was one of the best third basemen in baseball.

Nettles also was known for his witty remarks, such as the time he was asked by a fan, "What time does tomorrows game start?"

Nettles replied, "Well . . . what time can you make it?"

After he was traded by the Indians to the Yankees in 1973 and played for New York for 11 years during the Bronx Zoo days, Nettles remarked, "Some kids dream of joining the circus, others of becoming a Major League Baseball player. As a member of the New York Yankees, I've gotten to do both."

Hal Newhouser
(Pitcher, 1954–1955)

Here's how close Hal Newhouser, a Hall of Famer and one of baseball's all-time best pitchers, almost played for the Indians as a teammate of Bob Feller.

"A bird dog scout for the Indians saw me pitch an amateur game in 1938 and invited me to Cleveland for a tryout. They put me and my mother up in a hotel where Bob Feller was staying. They wanted me to meet him, but Bob was out and didn't get back by the time we had to leave.

"The next day I worked out at League Park. Steve O'Neill was the Indians manager then and told me, 'Kid, you've got a real good arm, take care of it,' but all they told me was that they'd stay in touch, so my mother and I went home [to Detroit],

"I didn't hear from the Indians again, at least not until it was too late, and I've often thought about what might have been.

"Wish Egan, the famous scout for the Tigers, came to my home with Del Baker, then a coach for the Tigers. Egan laid five $100 bills on the table and told my parents, 'This is a bonus that Harold can do anything he wants with it, and here's a contract for him to play in the minor leagues for $150 a month.

"Remember, this was during the Depression and I was trying to earn money selling newspapers, making a half cent on each one; setting pins in a bowling alley; and collecting milk and pop bottles to get the deposit. My parents didn't have much money. Dad worked as a patternmaker in the automobile industry, and I was going to be a tool and die maker.

"So we signed the contract. I gave $400 to my parents and kept the other $100 for transportation and tuition to the trade school I was attending. I thought it was unbelievable that I would get so much money to play baseball.

"About 10 minutes after we signed the Tigers' contract, a big car pulled up in front of our house. It was a new Lincoln Continental. Two men got out and came to our door. One was Mr. Bracken, the Cleveland bird dog scout who'd seen me pitch on the sandlots, and the other was Cy Slapnicka, who was then the general manager of the Indians.

"Bracken said to my dad, 'Mr. Newhouser, here are the keys to that car out front. It's yours. And here's a check for $15,000 for Harold because we want to sign him. He will be Bob Feller's roommate, and we are going to have the two greatest young pitchers in baseball.'

"I looked at my parents and didn't know what to say. Neither did they. Finally I said, 'Mr. Bracken, I signed a contract with Detroit.' He said, 'When?' I told him, 'About 10 minutes ago.'

"With that, Slapnicka jumped out of his chair and yelled at Bracken, 'Damn you! If you hadn't insisted that we stop and pick up that car, we would have been here first.'

"With that, they left. I'm not sure if Slapnicka was angrier than the frustration my parents and I felt, but what could we do? I had signed with the Detroit Tigers and was a member of their organization."

Feller and Newhouser started against each other 19 times. Feller won 13, Newhouser won three, and three other decisions were credited to relief pitchers.

"We really brought the fans out when we pitched against each other, and I'd love to see something like that happen in baseball again," Newhouser said. "We were both tough competitors, but there never was any animosity between us.

"Ironically, in 1946, when Feller broke Rube Waddell's season strikeout record, he put me in the book with him. I was Bob's record-breaking victim—but I still think I was called out on a bad pitch. Not only was it out of the strike zone, it also was high. All hell broke loose in the stands when the umpire called me out.

"I was peeved at my teammates, because none of them wanted to be the one to strike out and give Feller the record. They were more concerned about *not* striking out than winning the game. I overheard some of them talking on the bench, saying things like, 'I'm going to swing at the first pitch because I'm not going to let [Feller] get two strikes on me.'

"After I struck out I went back to the dugout and said, 'Are you guys satisfied that it wasn't you? Now can we go out and win the damn game?'

"The reason I was so upset was that I had an agreement with the general manager that I would get back the 25-percent salary cut I had taken the year before. But I never got it. I won only 17 and lost 17 that season."

Phil Niekro
(Pitcher, 1986–1987)

"I'm sick of hearing I'm 47 years old," Phil Niekro said when he was acquired by the Indians in a waiver deal on April 3, 1986. "Everybody has to have a birthday. Somebody has to be the oldest player in baseball, and somebody has to be the youngest.

"I just happen to be the oldest . . . so give it a rest. Stop writing how old I am."

And when Niekro pitched the Indians to a 9–6 victory over Detroit on June 1, 1987, Phil and his younger brother Joe became the winningest brothers in Major League Baseball. They had a combined total of 530 victories, 314 for Phil and 216 for Joe, which was one more victory than the Perry brothers achieved—314 for Gaylord and 215 for Jim.

Jesse Orosco
(Pitcher, 1989–1991)

"At last count I've pitched in 41 ballparks," said Jesse Orosco, who finally retired in 2004 at the age of 47 after a 25-year career in professional baseball. "My favorite park always was Camden Yards in Baltimore. And my least favorite always was Municipal Stadium [in Cleveland]. Because it was so old, there always were so few fans, and it always seemed to be drizzly and cold."

Satchel Paige
(Pitcher, 1948–1949)

When Bill Veeck signed Satchel Paige to pitch for the Indians on July 7, 1948 the venerable J. G. Taylor Spink, publisher and editor of the *Sporting News,* ridiculed it as a cheap publicity stunt.

"To bring in a pitching 'rookie' of Paige's age [then thought to be 42] casts a reflection on the entire scheme of operations in the Major Leagues," Spink wrote in an editorial. He claimed it would "demean the standards of baseball in the big circuits," and that, "if Paige were white, he would not have drawn a second thought from Veeck."

Paige, who went 6–1 with a 2.48 earned run average to help the Indians win the pennant and World Series in 1948, tended—by his own statements—to agree with Spink.

"People don't come to see the ball game," he said early in his brief career with the Indians. "They come out to see me strike out everybody. Occasionally I didn't."

However, after Paige pitched a three-hitter to beat the Chicago White Sox, 1–0, on August 20, Veeck fired off a telegram to

Spink—and made it public—that said: "Paige pitching. No runs, three hits. He definitely is in line for *Sporting News* rookie of the year award.

"Regards, Bill Veeck."

Legendary were Paige's stories of the old Negro leagues, in which he pitched for more than two decades before getting his chance with the Indians. Of his former teammate, "Cool Papa" Bell, Paige said, "One time he hit a line drive right past my ear. I turned around and saw the ball hit his behind, sliding into second, that's how fast he was."

When the subject of his advanced years was raised, Paige insisted, "Age is a question of mind over matter. If you don't mind, it doesn't matter."

Once, at the end of Paige's career and the beginning of Nolan Ryan's, the old-timer asked Ryan if he knew what the best pitch was. Ryan recounted their conversation. "I said, 'Fastball?' and Paige said, 'No, the bow tie.'

"'The bow tie? What's the bow tie?' I asked Paige," said Ryan. "Satch told me, 'Fastball, right here,' and drew his hand across his neck. In other words, high and tight. That was my lesson from Satchel Paige a long time ago."

And Paige's rules for staying young: "Avoid fried meats which angry up the blood; if your stomach disputes you, lie down and pacify it with cool thoughts; keep the juices flowing by jangling around gently as you move; go very light on the vices, such as carrying on in society [because] the social ramble ain't restful; avoid running at all times; and don't look back, something might be gaining on you."

Gabe Paul
(President/general manager, 1963–1972, 1978–1986)

After joining the Indians as part owner, president, and treasurer in 1963, Gabe Paul remained at the helm of the club in one capacity or another until 1972. He left to join George Steinbrenner as president of the New York Yankees, serving in that position for seven years.

When F. J. "Steve" O'Neill purchased controlling interest in the Indians in 1979, Paul returned to Cleveland as the chief executive officer of the team. He did so, Paul said, because, "Cleveland is a sleeping giant. Give the fans a winning team and they'll flock to the Stadium as they did in the past."

One of Paul's best deals was the acquisition of pitcher Gaylord Perry (along with shortstop Frank Duffy) in a November 29, 1971 deal with the San Francisco Giants for pitcher Sam McDowell. Of the criticism Perry regularly faced because of accusations that he threw a spitball (or 'grease ball'), Paul said, "Gaylord Perry is an honorable man. He only uses the spitter when he needs it."

Mike Paul
(Pitcher, 1968–1971)

"It was 1970 or 1971, and we're playing Washington at the old Stadium, and Darold Knowles is pitching against us. He threw one at Graig Nettles' head that knocked him down and Graig was pissed. He swung at the next pitch, missed it, and threw his bat at the mound. Knowles had to jump to get out of the way of it. So all of us in the dugout started to charge out, thinking there's going to be a brawl. But Frank Howard, who was playing first base for the Senators, yelled out, 'Hold it! Stop right now.'

"Well, you know how big Frank Howard is [six-foot-seven, 260]. They called him the 'Washington Monument,' and when he yelled, 'Hold it!' you never saw so many guys freeze on the top step of the dugout. Then he said, 'That's one for you and one for us. Now let's play ball.' Which we did."

"Another time, it was during the 'Year of the Tiger' [1968], and it was my first trip into Detroit. We were in the eighth or ninth inning of the game, and I'm in there in relief and here comes a tough right-handed hitter, though I can't remember who it was. Alvin Dark came out and said he wanted me to go play first base. I said, 'What!' And he said, 'Yeah, I want you to play first base for one hitter while I bring in Stan Williams. Then I'll bring you back in to face Jim Northrup, or one of their other left-handed batters.

"So, I'm standing over at first base, and Emmett Ashford, the umpire, said, 'Make sure you keep your foot on the base.' I told him, 'Emmett, I just hope they hit a fly ball. I don't want any part of this.' People were yelling at me—remember, I was a rookie—and I was flat-out scared I was going to screw up.

"The batter got a base hit or something, and that was it. I went back to the mound and, because Dark took out Tony Horton for me to play first base, we didn't have another first baseman. Lee Maye, an outfielder, had to go to first base—and you can imagine what happened next.

"Northrup hit my first pitch, a slider, on the ground to Maye, and he botched it. It's like they always say, when you're playing out of position, the ball will always find you.

"It didn't find me at first base that night, but it sure as hell found Maye, and we lost the game because it did. That was the only time I played first base, thank God. I don't know if Maye ever did again."

"The first two Spring Trainings I was with the Indians, 1968 and 1969, Alvin Dark just made sure that everybody got in shape gradually. He didn't want anybody pulling any muscles, or getting hurt from doing too much. So we'd run maybe 10 foul lines—foul pole to foul pole—at maybe three-quarter speed, no all-out effort. Alvin wanted everybody to get into shape gradually. So we did that.

"The next year, when some of us got in early for Spring Training, everybody was kind of doing the same lollygagging, foul pole to foul pole thing, just taking it real easy, the way we did the year before.

"But then Dark came in and said, 'OK boys, we're going to change things this year. I want everybody to run three miles under 21 minutes, and I want you to keep running it every day until you can do it in 21 minutes.' Everybody started complaining that we weren't ready for it because we weren't expecting it, but we still had to do it.

"So, this one day I was running with Sam McDowell. Everybody took off. One of the coaches clicked the stop watch and, boom! Sam started running like a bat out of hell. But once he got to the far side of the field where it was out of sight from Alvin and the coaches, he pulled a pack of cigarettes out of his back pocket, lit one and stood there smoking as everybody went running by. Next trip around, Sam, after flat-out skipping a lap, joined us and was laughing like hell. I'm sure Alvin found out, but he never did anything.

"Sam got away with it . . . if you could pitch the way he could, you could get away with a lot of things."

Tony Peña
(Catcher, 1994–1996)

It was the highlight of Tony Peña's 18-year Major League playing career—his two-out solo home run off Zane Smith in the 13th inning of the first game of the 1995 American League Division Series. It enabled the Indians to beat Boston 5–4, propelling them to three straight victories into the League Championship Series and, ultimately, the World Series.

Peña's home run has been voted by Tribe fans as the most memorable moment in the 10-year history of Jacobs Field.

What most fans didn't realize—and which never was made public until Peña, as the manager of the Kansas City Royals admitted it during the 2004 season—was that he ignored a "take" sign by then-Third-Base Coach Jeff Newman on the pitch that he hit into the left-field bleachers for the game-winning homer.

The count on Peña, leading off the 13th inning, was three and zero.

"I didn't see [Newman's take sign]," he said. "I just saw the pitch and swung. Then I saw the ball go over the wall. Then I saw everybody waiting for me at home plate. It was the most beautiful moment ever.

"It was a moment I'm never going to forget, and nobody is going to take away from me. Actually, it wasn't just the best moment in this ballpark or the best moment I had with the Indians. It was the best moment of my career."

And this final clarification by Mike Hargrove, then the Indians manager. When Peña said he didn't see Newman's sign, Hargrove smiled and said, "Well, at first I gave the take sign, but maybe I took it off. . . . I just don't remember."

Gaylord Perry
(Pitcher, 1972–1975)

"You have to do what you have to do [to win]," Gaylord Perry always said when asked about charges that he threw illegal spitballs— or, more specifically, in his case, illegal "greaseballs"—although he never really denied it or admitted it.

"I just loved to make [opposing batters] *think* I was loading one up," he said.

When pointedly asked if he did indeed throw spitters or greaseballs, Gaylord chuckled and replied, "I always felt, and still do, that it's something for me to know and for the hitters to think about.

"I especially loved to pitch against the Yankees, because they were so easy to get going. With guys like Bobby Murcer and Reggie Jackson, all you had to do was put the thought [of a spitball] in their mind."

Murcer always insisted that Perry was a "cheater" despite Perry's claims that he was throwing a forkball and not a spitter. The former Yankees center fielder once said, "The only absolutely unhittable pitch I've seen in my whole career was Gaylord's hard spitter and, dammit, it wasn't a forkball."

And to keep the controversy alive in Murcer's mind, one Christmas Gaylord sent the outfielder a gallon of lard as a present.

Another who was really spooked by Perry was former Boston outfielder Fred Lynn. After going zero for four against Perry in a game in 1973, Lynn cursed Gaylord and said, "I saw only two pitches from Gaylord all night that were legal. He calls that thing a forkball, but there ain't a forkball alive that does what that thing does."

Once, in 1982 when he pitched for Seattle, Perry was ejected from a game by umpire Dave Phillips but insisted he was innocent, at least that time . . . and that he was a victim of circumstances.

"We were getting beat by California and [Mariners Manager] Rene Lachemann wasn't very happy," Perry said. "I didn't have much that day, and late in the game the Angels loaded the bases and Lynn, who was playing for California then, was the next batter. Lachemann came to the mound and told me, 'Dammit, Gaylord, put something on the ball.' He meant I should throw the ball hard, you know, that I should bear down, and I guess Phillips heard him.

"When my next pitch sunk about two feet, Phillips came running out from behind the plate screaming, 'You're out of here!' All I could say was, 'Thanks a lot, Lach.'"

After he was ejected by Phillips, Perry said he took a polygraph test and passed it with flying colors.

"F. Lee Bailey, the famous lawyer, gave me the test on a television program that was called *Lie Detector*. He asked me, 'Gaylord, did you put anything on the ball in the fifth inning of that game you were thrown out of?' and I said, 'No, I did not,' and I passed."

After he retired from baseball in 1984, Gaylord made a "fun video," as he called it. "It's about a [fictional] minor league ball team called the San Clemente Bulldogs that's losing every game by five or six runs. The coach gets mad because he wants to work his way up to the Major Leagues, but his team is doing so bad. So he tells them, 'I'm sending you to a baseball camp,' which is really the 'Gaylord Perry Baseball Camp.'

"They come and I teach them all these tricks, and they go back to San Clemente. Tricks, you know, like how to throw a spitter, scuff baseballs, cork bats, how to disguise them, how to hold on to a guy's belt when he's trying to get a lead off base.

"You know, all the things they do in the big leagues."

Did he teach the players how to throw "greaseballs"?

"Oh, no," he deadpanned. "I showed 'em how to *look* like they were loading up, how to make batters think things that bother them the way I bothered Bobby Murcer and Reggie Jackson. Remember? But you also should remember, none of those guys—Murcer, Jackson . . . all the others who accused me of cheating—didn't accuse me of throwing an illegal pitch when they hit a home run off me.

"I know a lot of guys on my team didn't like me too much because I pushed them. A great example involved Buddy Bell when he first came up. He was a third baseman, but we had Graig Nettles, so [Manager] Ken Aspromonte put him in the outfield, and one day a guy hit a ball to center field. Buddy went back to the fence, jumped up, and got his glove on the ball, but instead of catching it, it got away and fell over the fence for a home run.

"When the inning was over I was waiting for him in the dugout. I'm teed off and said to him. 'You don't have to help those guys. They get enough runs without you making it easier for them,' and Buddy said, 'Well, then, don't let them hit the ball so hard.'

"That got me instant respect for Buddy because he was right. I shouldn't have let the guy hit the ball so hard, and I knew right then and there I didn't have to push him anymore."

Jim Perry
(Pitcher, 1959–1963, 1974–1975)

"One of the games I remember so well was in 1960, Ted Williams' last year. I was pitching against the Red Sox and had a 1–0 lead going into the ninth inning and, to win the game, 1–0, the three guys I had to get out were Jackie Jensen, Frank Malzone, and Williams. I got the first two without any trouble, but Williams was a little different. I was still throwing pretty good, 94 [mph], but he kept pulling my pitches—even those on the outside—foul to right field.

"I finally got him on my fourth pitch, but it wasn't easy. He hit my fastball to right field. I turned and saw Tito Francona take one step in, but suddenly realized he shouldn't have—and jumped up and caught the ball. We were lucky on that one, and we won."

"People always ask me what it was like to pitch against my brother Gaylord. The first time we did was in 1970, in the All-Star Game. I was with Minnesota then, and Gaylord was pitching for San Francisco. I pitched two innings, the seventh and eighth, and gave up one run, and Gaylord pitched the sixth and seventh and also gave up one run. They [the NL] got a run in the ninth off Catfish Hunter and won, 5–4.

"The same thing happened three years later [in 1973], the only time we started a championship game against each other, when I was pitching for Detroit and Gaylord for the Indians. I was ahead by two runs after six innings, but Cleveland tied it in the seventh and neither of us finished the game—and neither of us was the winner or loser.

"Something else people always ask was if there was a big rivalry between Gaylord and me. There really wasn't. We both went out there every day and did what we were supposed to do for our team, no matter who was pitching against us. That's the way we were. The way we were brought up by our father. I know I always tried to pitch competitively, the same way if I had a one-run lead or a 10-run lead.

"I got to the big leagues before Gaylord. My last season in the minors was in 1958 when I pitched for Reading [Pennsylvania of the Class A Eastern League]. That was the year Gaylord signed with the Giants. He got a lot more money to sign than I did, but that was OK, because the money wasn't all that big when I started in pro ball [1956]."

"Gaylord used to drive the other teams—and the umpires—wild, the way he taunted them. Our clubhouse [at the old Stadium] and the umpires' room were real close, separated only by a short stairway, and one of the things Gaylord did was sneak up to where they dressed and put white flour in the resin bag. Then, when he was on the mound and used the resin bag, he made sure a lot of the powder got all over his hand, and when he pitched the ball it would come flying out all over the place which, most of the time, surprised the batter.

"We used to call it 'Gaylord's puffball.' "

Hank Peters
(Farm director/general manager/president, 1966–1971, 1987–1991)

"After the 1970 season, which had been another difficult year for us, I was farm director and [Owner] Vernon Stouffer met with the directors. They called me in and said the budget had to be cut, and it was going to be a very big cut, including between a 35 and 40 percent cut in our player development. And to make it even worse, we hadn't been spending that much money to begin with. It meant some major amputations had to take place.

"The directors didn't tell me what I had to do, they just told me this is how much money you are going to have, and it wasn't much.

"Vernon asked, 'Is this going to hurt us very much?' I asked him, 'Well, before I answer, let me ask, are you going to keep this ball club?' He bristled a little bit, then said, 'Why do you ask that question?' I told him, 'The things you do and don't do today, in player development, are never reflected immediately. So, if you intend to sell the club in the next two or three years, you don't need to be concerned. On the other hand, if you intend to keep the ball club, well, then you are committing suicide by cutting our player development budget as drastically as you are planning to do.'

"Which is what happened. He sold the club two or three years later, and when I think back on it, it was a nightmare.

"Vernon wasn't very happy when I told him what I did. But I was at the point where I didn't give a damn. We cut two or three minor league teams, leaving us with the minimum number, four, that Major League Baseball said we had to have. We eliminated all but eight or nine scouts, from about 16 or 18, which we'd been building up gradually, trying to improve, and which had helped us make some improvements.

"At the time, before I was ordered to cut the budget, I felt we had finally begun to show some progress. But when the directors ordered the cut back, we ended up releasing 30 or 40 [minor league] players, several of whom caught on with other clubs and made it to the big leagues.

"And that, in my opinion, is what happened to the Indians in what you guys in the media call the 'bad old days.'"

"Something else that contributed to the decline of the franchise in those days occurred in 1969, on July 4, to be exact. Stouffer put Alvin Dark in charge of all player personnel matters as both the general manager and manager, and took the GM duties away from Gabe Paul.

"At the time it happened, I was in the Carolinas, visiting one of our minor league teams, and I got a call from Stouffer. I told him I'd be returning to Cleveland in a few days, and he told me to meet him, that he had some thing he wanted to discuss with me.

"I did, and he dropped it on me. He said, 'I am making some changes. Gabe will continue as president, but won't have anything to do with the players. Alvin is going to run everything as general manager and field manager.' He also told me that Dark didn't know a lot of things about being the general manager, and he wanted me to help him.

"As you can well imagine, I couldn't wait to get away from Stouffer to call Gabe. And when I did, Gabe, of course, was at wit's end. He called Alvin just about every name you could imagine, privately, of course. Publicly he kept telling you guys [in the media] that he was a 'happy warrior' for the next year or two, or however long the new arrangement lasted. To tell you the truth, I think I was the only one who kept Gabe sane during that time.

"As for me, I was between them all. I had Vernon Stouffer and his son Jim on one shoulder, Alvin on the other, and if I had three shoulders, Gabe would have been on that one. I often wondered, what did I do to deserve this? It was a comedy of errors, which was reason enough for me to get out."

(Peters left the Indians in 1972 and served as president of the minor leagues through 1975).

Dave Philley
(Outfielder, 1954–1955)

"There's only one way to play this game . . . you've got to bleed and believe," said Dave Philley, who was one of 10 surviving players of the 1954 American League champion Indians who were honored in 2004 in observance of the golden anniversary of that team.

Other surviving members of the 1954 team that won a then-record 111 games: Bob Feller, Bill Glynn, Don Mossi, Hal Naragon, Ray Narleski, Rudy Regalado, Al Rosen, George Strickland, Wally Westlake, and Manager Al Lopez.

Jim Piersall
(Outfielder, 1959–1961)

"They've taken all the color out of baseball. Guys like me and Billy Martin and Leo Durocher—colorful guys like that—could never play today. They wouldn't have us.

"When I played, we didn't need teachers. We learned things ourselves. Today, you have to teach. That's what it's all about. Kids don't play enough, and they don't have the equipment [talent] to be good outfielders. A lot of today's kids are also dreamers, not workers."

"I used to get really pumped up when we played in Yankee Stadium. One time, Joe DiMaggio came up to me in a restaurant and said, 'Nobody gets them any better than you.' Willie Mays paid me the same kind of a compliment once. He said, 'Piersall is looney, but all he ever does is catch the ball.'"

Lou Piniella
(Outfielder, 1968)

The Indians re-acquired Lou Piniella from Baltimore in a minor league trade during the winter of 1965–1966. They originally signed him out of high school in 1962, and in 1963 traded him to the old Washington Senators who, in turn, dealt him to the Orioles in 1964.

After the Indians obtained Piniella, Frank Lane, then general manager of the Orioles, predicted, "The fans in Cleveland will love Piniella, mark my words."

Why? "Because Piniella looks just like that dago fruit peddler, Rocky Colavito," whom Lane had traded to Detroit five years earlier, incurring the wrath of Tribe fans everywhere.

As it turned out, Piniella played three seasons (1966–1968) in the Indians' farm system and made it to Cleveland for a brief trial in September 1968 when he appeared in six games without a hit in five at-bats. He was then claimed by Seattle in the 1968 expansion draft, but before playing a game for the Mariners, Piniella was traded to the Kansas City Royals and won the American League "Rookie of the Year" award in 1969.

Piniella recalled, "When I was playing for the Indians [Class AAA] farm club in Portland in 1967, I'd hit six or seven home runs early in the season, but I was batting only about .180. Johnny Lipon, our manager, called me into his office and asked if I wanted to stay in Portland or go down to Double-A ball. I told him I wanted to stay [in Portland], of course.

"The next day Lipon handed me a thick-handled, Nellie Fox model bat, and worked with me with that bat every day for the next several months. Until then I'd been strictly a pull hitter, but Lipon had me hitting only to right field or center the rest of the season.

"I ended up hitting .289, and because of Lipon's help I got to the big leagues in a couple of years. When I did, I told Lipon that he was the guy who helped me more than anybody.

"The ironic thing is that, Gabe Paul was the general manager in Cleveland when I was let go in the expansion draft, and knew how badly I wanted to make it to the big leagues with the Indians. And then, in 1974, when Gabe was president of the Yankees, he traded for me—so he must have remembered me."

Boog Powell
(First baseman, 1975–1976)

When Boog Powell returned to Cleveland for an old-timers game in 1991 and was issued the all-red—jersey and pants—uniform the Indians wore 16 years earlier, he said, "I swore back in 1975, once that season ended, I'd never wear this red-on-red [expletive] again.

"Some people said I looked like a blood clot, and others said I looked like a giant Bloody Mary. They both were right. It was awful. Those all-red uniforms were the only thing I didn't like about playing for Frank [Robinson] in Cleveland."

Vic Power
(First baseman, 1958–1961)

Vic Power recalled the night he tied a Major League record by stealing home twice in the same game against Detroit on August 14, 1958.

"We were losing and the first [stolen base] tied the game, and the second won it [9–8] in the 10th inning," he said. "A sportswriter came to me and said, 'How could you do that? You are too fat, and you are not fast. How could you do that?'

"I told him it was a night game, and nobody saw me coming. If it had been a day game, I could not have done it. They would have seen me and caught me."

It's a record that almost certainly will never be broken. As Power said, "Somebody will have to steal home three times in one game, and nobody can do that."

Power recalled the time that he and "Mudcat" Grant were in Cooperstown for an exhibition game with the Indians.

"We met Ty Cobb," Power said. "I had read about him, how hard he played and how hard he was on other players. He asked me how much I was hitting, and I told him '.319,' which I was very proud of. He told me, 'What's a matter, you in a slump?'

"Later I checked his record and he used to hit .380, .390, so I guess that's what he meant when he said I must have been in a slump."

Dick Radatz
(Pitcher, 1966–1967)

From 1962 to 1965, when he pitched for Boston and was the best reliever in baseball, Dick Radatz was nicknamed "The Monster" with good reason. He was six foot five, weighed 235 pounds, and had a fastball that was clocked in the high 90s, often reaching 100 mph.

But then, inexplicably, Radatz suffered, in his words, "a mental thing" and couldn't throw a strike if there was a batter at the plate.

"It was no problem warming up, but as soon as a batter stepped in against me, I couldn't throw the ball anywhere near the plate," he said.

The Indians traded for Radatz in 1966 in the hope of "rehabbing" him, as expressed by then-Tribe Manager Birdie Tebbetts, but to no avail. He went 0–3 with a 4.61 earned run average in 39 appearances.

"I tried everything. I even went to a psychiatrist who hypnotized me, but that didn't help, either," Radatz lamented.

After the Indians released him early in the 1967 season, Radatz tried again to recapture the rapture he'd known previously with the Red Sox in trials with the Chicago Cubs, Detroit, and Montreal. But it was all in vain, and his career ended in 1969.

Of his brief tenure in Cleveland, Radatz recalled, "Gabe Paul cut my salary 25 percent, the maximum allowed, from $42,500 to less than $32,000. When I complained to Gabe, he said to me, 'Dick, you're from Detroit, aren't you?' I told him I was, and he said, 'Well, if you don't like what I'm offering, get a job on the assembly line at the Ford Motor Co.'

"I said, 'But Gabe, I'm a college graduate. I have a college degree,' and he said, 'Then get a white-collar job at Ford.'

"That's the way baseball was in those days, before Marvin Miller and free agency. Looking back at what happened then is funny now, but it wasn't funny to me at the time."

Manny Ramirez
(Outfielder, 1993–2000)

"There are so many Manny Ramirez stories. . . . He is really funny, like the night we were in Oakland and he hit three consecutive home runs, each time with somebody else's bat, including mine for the third home run," Omar Vizquel recalled his former teammate.

"Three home runs with three different bats! That's an unbelievable story, but it's true."

During the 2003 American League Championship Series between Boston and New York, Red Sox Manager Grady Little offered this opinion of the former Tribe outfielder, who left Cleveland as a free agent during the winter of 2000–2001.

"It would take longer than this interview room would allow me to tell you about Manny. He has some weird ways, but I know if each baseball fan in the country had the time and opportunity to know the kid, they would probably not be thinking too many negative thoughts about him."

And this Ramirez story by his former Boston teammate Lou Merloni, a member of the Indians in 2004.

"This was [in 2003], just before our [Red Sox] starting lineup was set to run out on the field at the start of a game. Our starting pitcher was toweling off, getting ready to take the mound, and from the end of the dugout I hear, 'Let's go, guys.'

"So Manny runs out on the field, but everybody else stayed in the dugout. He went all the way to left field before he noticed that he was all alone on the field, and everybody else was still in the dugout. The fans loved it. They started cheering, and Manny tipped his cap and smiled. He got as big a kick out of it as everybody else."

Pedro Ramos
(Pitcher, 1962–1964)

It seemed that Pedro Ramos—a.k.a. "Pistol Pete"—was always under suspicion for throwing spitballs during his three seasons with the Indians, as well as previously with the Washington Senators/Minnesota Twins (1955–1961), and later with the New York Yankees, Philadelphia, Pittsburgh, Cincinnati, and Washington through 1970, when he ended a 15-year Major League career.

"Pete had a pitch that he called a *Cuban palm ball,*" said Doc Edwards, who not only was Ramos's catcher but also his roommate on the road.

Naturally, Edwards would not confirm that the Cuban palm ball was a spitter, although batters constantly made that accusation and often the umpires would go to the mound to check the balls Ramos threw.

"But they never found anything," Edwards said, "although one came close one night in 1962. It was veteran umpire Ed Runge, who got suspicious when several batters complained to him, and he noticed a large tobacco stain on Pete's uniform pants.

"Runge made Ramos go into the clubhouse and change, which Pete did. When he came out with clean pants and made a couple more pitches, Runge went out again and this time made Pete go in and change his jersey.

"But the same thing happened when Pete returned to the mound. Runge was still suspicious and then he ordered Pete to change his cap.

"When Ramos came back to the mound he was wearing a hard cap, a batting helmet, and all Runge could do was laugh."

Rudy Regalado
(Third baseman, 1954–1956)

"In the middle of the 1954 season, when we were fighting to win the pennant, we were scheduled—for some reason, I don't know why—to play an exhibition game in Jersey City against the Dodgers. It was a real hot and muggy day, and Al Rosen, our captain, complained especially loud about the weather, that it was so bad. There must have been a million mosquitoes buzzing around us that night, and our minds were on playing the Orioles in Baltimore the next night, not on a meaningless exhibition game in Jersey City.

"He suggested that we just go to the plate and hit the first pitch and get out of there as early as we could, which we did, and the game was played in only one hour and 35 minutes. We lost the game, 1–0, and I remember I went 0-for-4—hit the ball four times with four swings of the bat—but nobody cared."

"I guess I owe a lot to Bobby Avila for me being able to make the team in 1954. Avila was the Indians' second baseman then, and a good one, but was a holdout in Spring Training, though everybody said he had a visa problem getting out of Vera Cruz, Mexico. People nowadays just walk over the border, but then, well, I guess Bobby just wanted a big raise. At any rate, he was late getting to Spring Training.

"I was on the roster of one of the Indians' farm clubs and was planning to drive from my home in San Diego to Daytona Beach, where the minor league teams held Spring Training. I asked Hank Greenberg if it would be OK if I left home early and stopped off in Tucson en route to Florida so that I could get a couple of weeks of help from the Indians coaches [Red Kress and Tony Cuccinello]. Hank approved and when I arrived in Tucson I suited up and worked out with the big team. I didn't have a position, but I took batting practice every day and hit the ball pretty good.

"Avila still wasn't in camp when the exhibition games began and Owen Friend, another infielder who was on the roster, had a bad leg, and Cuccinello asked me if I'd ever played second base. I said no, that I'd played third base, shortstop, and the outfield, but never second base, though I'd sure be willing to do it if they needed someone. Tony worked with me for about an hour before the game—how to make the pivot on double plays and how to avoid the spikes of a runner sliding into second, that kind of thing—and I went out and played OK, even got two hits.

"The same thing the next day, and that was the start of a real hot streak for me. I hit 11 home runs and drove in 22 runs, and wound up with a .447 average that spring.

"Avila finally showed up, maybe because people began to say that he was losing his job to that Regalado kid, even though I was a third baseman, not a second baseman. After Bobby arrived in camp, the Indians found a place for me on the roster, and I never did go to Daytona Beach. Eventually Al Lopez put Rosen on first base, and I started the season at third.

"I don't know what happened that caused me to hit so well. If I knew, I would've stayed hot. I was just in a groove, like Tiger Woods gets in a groove and everything goes right. I stayed hot until about the middle of June and then they started throwing me that pitch . . . what do they call it? Oh, yeah. A curve ball . . . and I cooled off in a hurry."

Kevin Rhomberg
(Outfielder, 1982–1984)

"I don't know when or how it all began, but I was always a very superstitious guy, especially when I played ball.

"For some reason I felt it would be bad luck if somebody touched me, and I didn't touch him back. Don't ask my why, I just had to. It was really a superstition, though I've been called neurotic. Bert Blyleven thought I was crazy. Something else that was really important to me was that wherever I went I'd never turn right, I'd always turn left. Even if I had to make three left turns to go right. Why'd I do it? Well, think about it. There are no right turns in baseball, are there?

"A sportswriter in Texas once asked Rod Carew—who also was very superstitious—who was the most superstitious guy in baseball, and he said, 'That crazy kid in Cleveland,' which was me. It got around so much that, one time when I was stretching before a game, one of my buddies tackled me and everybody came over and touched me, but I couldn't touch them back because they were holding me down. Another time I was on second base and the shortstop came over, touched me, and got away before I could touch him back. That really bothered me at the time.

"It got to be pretty crazy. Fans were sending me things in the mail. Once I got a shirt that had a hand printed on it and it said, 'This constitutes a touch, and I got you last!' Another time [clubhouse attendant] Cy Buynak called me to the phone and said there was a guy on the line who said that talking with me constituted a touch. Crazy things like that. A magazine even wanted to do a story on it.

"I finally forced myself to quit it when I realized my kids had become aware of what I was doing. We were in a shopping mall and they started making left turns in order to make a right turn. That's when, when my family started getting involved in it, I figured it was time to end it."

Eddie Robinson
(First baseman, 1942, 1946–1948, 1957)

On July 6, 1947, Larry Doby joined the Indians as the first black player in the American League, and the second, to Jackie Robinson, in Major League Baseball. Between games of a double header against the White Sox in Chicago that day, Indians Manager Lou Boudreau told Doby he would play first base in the second game, which upset regular first baseman Eddie Robinson.

"Boudreau walked over to me and said, 'Hey Eddie, I want to borrow your glove. Doby is going to play first base," Robinson recalled. "He told me this after telling me a couple of days earlier, after I'd hit a couple of home runs, 'Don't worry, you're my first baseman.' Doby had never played first base. He was always a second baseman [in the Negro League]. Joe Gordon would have been happy not to play, but here Boudreau was taking me out of the lineup after telling me not to worry.

"I said to Lou, 'You can have my glove and my uniform, too. I'm quitting,' and remained in the clubhouse the first three innings, intending to shower and dress in street clothes and leave the clubhouse, when [Coach] Bill McKechnie came in.

"[McKechnie] said, 'Eddie, I know what this is all about. I know what's going through your mind. But what you and I know, it's not going to come out that way in the paper. It's going to look like you're doing this because of Doby being black. We know that's not the case, but it's not going to look that way in the paper. It's in your best interest, and for your future, to put your uniform on and come back out [to the field].'

"So I did, and that was it. The end of it, and McKechnie was right."

Frank Robinson
(Outfielder, designated hitter; manager, 1975–1977)

Upon being introduced as Major League Baseball's first black manager, and the 28th manager of the Indians on October 3, 1974, Frank Robinson said, "If I had one wish I was sure would be granted, it would be that Jackie [Robinson] could be here, seated alongside me today."

On the first day of Spring Training in 1975, Robinson was being interviewed by the three beat writers covering the Indians that year: Bob Sudyk of the *Cleveland Press*, Hank Kozloski of the *Lorain Journal*, and Russell Schneider of the Cleveland *Plain Dealer*.

Kozloski asked Robinson a question and, in answering, the manager called Kozloski "Russ." Kozloski said, "No, I'm Hank," and pointed to Schneider, saying, "He's Russ."

Robinson smiled and said, "Oh, OK, all you guys look alike."

Having played most of his Hall-of-Fame career with the Baltimore Orioles, Robinson was accustomed to winning. But the Indians hadn't won a pennant since 1954, and a World Series since 1948, to which Robinson quipped, "Pennant fever in Cleveland is a 24-hour virus."

In his inaugural season as manager of the Indians, Robinson had numerous battles with umpires, and on July 8, prior to a game in Oakland, he "rated" the arbiters in a newspaper story, which earned him a hefty fine by American League President Lee MacPhail.

In his evaluation, Robinson said that only ten of the 24-man umpiring staff was "creditable," 13 were "less than creditable," and that he had not seen enough of the one remaining member to express an opinion.

Twenty-six years later, in 2001, Robinson was appointed "vice president for on-field operations" by Commissioner Bud Selig, and one aspect of his job was to assess penalties against players who were overly aggressive in their complaints against umpires.

John Rocker
(Pitcher, 2001)

When John Rocker was acquired from Atlanta on June 22, 2001, in a trade for Steve Karsay and Steve Reed, then-Indians General Manager John Hart predicted great success for the controversial pitcher.

"With John Rocker we're bringing in a devastating left-handed late reliever," Hart said. "[Rocker] is 26. He's a dominant closer . . . a workhorse who has never been on the disabled list . . . and has [compiled] great numbers in the regular season and the postseason."

However, it turned out to be one of the worst trades in Hart's career. In less than a full season with the Tribe, Rocker appeared in 38 games with a 3–7 won-lost record, four saves, and a 5.45 earned run average, and was traded to Texas on December 18, 2001.

Upon joining the Indians, Rocker was asked by reporters about the angry reaction to a 2000 *Sports Illustrated* story in which he was quoted as being highly critical of New York and New Yorkers.

"Why is reaction such a big deal to you people?" Rocker snapped to reporters. "Who cares about reaction? The mound is still 60 feet [and] six inches from home plate. There'll be a guy standing there with a 32-ounce bat. Who gives a damn about reaction?

"I sure as hell don't."

Although most of his troubles concerned his erratic pitching, one day late in the season it was something else, as catcher Eddie Taubensee remembered.

"I went to the mound to talk to Rocker and to tell him that the umpire told me, 'Tell Rocker his fly is open,'" Taubensee said. "So I said, 'Hey, Rock, your fly's open,' and he said, 'Yeah, so what?'

"Well, the fans must have noticed it, too, because they really got on him that day—but I don't think it was only because they also saw that his fly was open."

Ricardo Rodriguez
(Pitcher, 2002–2003)

After Dmitri Young hit a 420-foot homer off Ricardo Rodriguez in a game against the Tigers on May 28, 2003, in Detroit, the rookie pitcher said, "I made a good pitch, and he it a long way. A real long way. All I can do is go like this," and he folded his hands and bowed his head in prayer.

Rich Rollins
(Third baseman, 1970)

"There was a game in Boston one night in 1970 that I'll never forget, even though I didn't play in it—which is the reason I'll never forget it.

"Ted Uhlaender was our center fielder, and the fans in the bleachers at Fenway Park started throwing things at him, probably because we were winning and they were mad at us, and Ted was the closest to them.

"Anyway, they started peppering Ted with bottles, batteries, all kinds of things, and finally he ran off the field and into the clubhouse. The game had to be held up because we didn't have anybody in center field, and Uhlaender flat-out refused to leave the clubhouse. He said, 'I'm not going to subject myself to that kind of abuse, because nobody is doing anything about it.' The cops, if there were any out there, just let the fans do what they wanted.

"The problem was that Alvin Dark, our manager, had nobody else to put in center field. No other outfielders at all, and the umpires were threatening to forfeit the game unless we got somebody—Uhlaender or somebody, *anybody* out to center field right away.

"Well, Alvin figured that, because I'd been Ted's teammate in Minnesota for seven or eight years, I could talk him into going back on the field. So I went into the locker room and said to Ted, 'C'mon, Alvin has nobody to put out there. Go back out there or they'll forfeit the game.'

"Finally he said, 'OK, I'll go back to the dugout, but I won't go out to center field unless I see a policeman up there [in the bleachers] every 10 or 20 feet in that front row. And if I don't see cops out there, I'm not staying on the field.'

"So, with that, the Red Sox made sure enough security people were stationed in the bleachers, Ted went back to center field and the game resumed.

"The reason it was so important to me was that Alvin had told me that if Uhlaender wouldn't go back in the game, I'd have to be the center fielder—and I never played the outfield in my life."

John Romano
(Catcher, 1960–1964)

"I was coming off a pretty good season in 1964 and thought I was entitled to a pretty good raise, but I had a lot of contract problems with Gabe Paul that winter [1964–1965]," John Romano said. "I'd hit .241 with 19 homers in 106 games, which was pretty good for a catcher, and I wanted more money than the $45,000 Gabe was offering.

"Finally, he called me at my home in New Jersey and told me to meet him in Cleveland, that he was going to take care of me. I figured he meant he was to settle my contract. But when I got to Cleveland, he really shocked me.

"Gabe said to me, 'Johnny, I want you to be the first to know we just traded you to the White Sox.' I was really surprised. I mean, I came all the way from New Jersey to be told I was traded away . . . that I wasn't getting the raise I wanted?

"When I finally recovered my voice, I said to him, 'Gabe, I want you to be the first to know that I am retiring,' and I went back home.

"A few days later Ed Short, the White Sox general manager, called and talked me into joining the White Sox—but not until he gave me the raise I was trying to get from Gabe. It was $9,000, the best raise I ever got in baseball.

'And you think times haven't changed?"

"I also think sometimes that if it hadn't been for me, Frank Lane would not have traded Rocky Colavito to Detroit for Harvey Kuenn [in 1960].

"Here's how I got involved. I was with the Indians then, and we were playing a Spring Training exhibition game in Memphis. I was sitting in the lobby of the hotel the morning of the game, and Lane came up to me and said, 'Johnny, I need to ask you something. If a game is on the line in the ninth inning and the other team has the tying run on third and the winning run on second, who would you rather pitch to, Rocky Colavito or Harvey Kuenn?

"I should have realized that something was in the works. In retrospect, Lane probably had already made up his mind to trade Rocky. He just wanted some reassurance that it was a good deal [for the Indians]. But at the time I never gave that a second thought. I just figured Lane was talking for the sake of talking, which he did a lot.

"I told him flat out that I'd rather pitch to Colavito in a spot like that. I mean, logically, if you're on the other team and had your choice, you had to pitch to Colavito because Kuenn was a much better hitter for average than Rocky. A day or two later Lane made the trade—Colavito for Kuenn.

"This sure is a funny game sometimes."

"After I was traded by the Indians [with Tommy John and Tommie Agee] to Chicago [for Rocky Colavito] in 1965, I hit a home run over the center field fence off Luis Tiant my first trip to the plate [in a game in late-July]. The next time I got up we had men on second and third and, with first base open, the proper strategy was to walk me. But Birdie Tebbetts wasn't about to put me on, not after trading me away.

"[Catcher] Joe Azcue kept looking over toward the dugout and asking, 'Should we walk him?' but Birdie just pointed to the sky and yelled, 'Don't walk him . . . he's gonna pop up.'

"Well, I didn't pop up, I hit another homer, this one for three runs. But even that's not the best part of the story, though it's the part I like to remember best.

"In the seventh or eighth inning, [White Sox Manager] Eddie Stanky brought in relief pitcher Hoyt Wilhelm, a guy I never caught before. So, as soon as they announced him, I walked over to the dugout and started taking my stuff off, my chest protector and shin guards, and Stanky said, 'What are you doing? Where are you going?' I said, 'I don't catch knuckle bailers,' and he said, 'Tonight you are.'

"What happened next—and this is the part I'll never forget, though I'd like to—Wilhelm struck out the first three guys he faced, but all of them reached, loading the bases, because I couldn't catch the third strike on each of them. After each one I looked into the dugout, and Stanky just motioned me back to the plate.

"We finally got out of the inning and I went into the dugout and started throwing my mask and shin guards around. Stanky, sitting on the top step of the dugout, said to me 'Now what are you doing?' and I said, 'Tell me, how do you catch this guy?"

"Well, somehow I did. The game went into extra innings, and I never missed another pitch from Wilhelm. I couldn't believe it. Neither could Wilhelm—or Stanky. "Did we win the game? That part I don't remember." (The White Sox won, 9–4.)

Al Rosen
(Third baseman/first baseman, 1947–1956)

Recalling the pressure-packed end of the 1948 season, when the Indians finished in a tie with Boston for first place in the American League, Al Rosen said, "After we lost the last game [to Detroit], forcing a playoff game in Boston the next day, believe it or not, just about everybody was half in the bag on the train going to Boston that night.

"But it didn't bother those guys [his teammates]. Nothing did. They were like the Three Musketeers, you know, one for all and all for one, except there were more than three; there were a lot of them.

"On the train to Boston, each table in the dining car had champagne and three or four bottles of booze on it. The whole thing was amazing. It was like everybody knew we were going to win. No sweat. I'd never seen anything like it.

"After I went to bed, Gene Bearden woke me up about one o'clock and asked me, 'Did you ever play first base? I said, 'No,' and he said, 'Well, you're playing first base tomorrow.' I got cold chills, I couldn't sleep the rest of the night. As it turned out, Bearden was wrong. I didn't play first base, Allie Clark did, and it probably was a good thing that I didn't."

Rosen almost won the Triple Crown in 1953 when he led the American League with 43 homers and 145 RBI, but his .335559 batting average (rounded off to .336) was .001612 behind Mickey Vernon's .337171 (rounded off to .337).

"In the last week of the season I went to [Manager] Al Lopez and said, 'I need at-bats, would you mind letting me lead off?' We were out of the race by then and Al said, 'If you want to do it, it's OK with me.' So I hit leadoff the last four or five games, and it worked out well because I was hot and getting a lot of hits. But so was Vernon.

"We went into the last game [against Detroit] and the first time up [Tigers third baseman] Ray Boone was playing back and, knowing I had to do something radical and different to catch Vernon, I laid down a bunt. The first one in my life. Never in the history of the game did I beat out a bunt—before or after. But I did this time, and was credited with a hit. The next time up, I doubled over the right fielder's head and got another hit later, so I was 3-for-4 going into my last trip to the plate. At the same time we were listening to what Mickey Vernon was doing in Washington and knew that he had two hits in four times at-bat, meaning that I needed another hit to beat him.

"Al Aber, a left-hander who was a little on the wild side, was pitching for the Tigers when I batted for the fifth time. He was trying to get the ball over the plate but just couldn't, and I kept fouling balls off, even though they weren't strikes, because I didn't want to walk. One of his pitches actually nicked me on the arm, and I yelled, 'foul ball, foul ball,' and the umpire went along with it, because everyone knew what the situation was.

"Finally I hit a high chopper to third base—though it also would have been ball four if I had taken the pitch—and I tried my darnedest to beat it out. My last step was a leap for the bag like a runner trying to reach the finish line, but I came up just short, and umpire Hank Soar called me out.

"Of course our bench erupted, claiming I was safe—and there are people I still hear from who say I was safe—though I knew I was out. Lopez came out to argue with Soar, but I told him, 'Al, I was out. [Soar] called it right,' and that was the end of it, and Vernon won the batting championship.

"I look back and think how great it would have been to win the Triple Crown, because there haven't been too many guys who have done it, but it didn't happen, and I've never dwelled on it. It's just one of those great stories that I like to tell."

★ ★ ★ ★ ★

Rosen worked for George Steinbrenner in 1978 and part of 1979, but for only a year and a half. "I had problems with George, and George had problems with me," he said. "My problem was that George was too dictatorial. He gave me responsibility, but not authority, and probably was the biggest second guesser I ever met in my life. A very difficult man to work for.

"And yet, I could probably call George Steinbrenner right now and say, 'George, I need $100,000,' and he'd probably not say a word and send a guy with the money.

"But working for him and being his friend are two different things. That's what I said when I left [resigned] the Yankees in July 1979. I said, 'George, I'd rather be your friend than work for you.'"

During Rosen's tenure as president of the Yankees, they finished the 1978 season in a tie with the Red Sox for the pennant, and it was

Rosen who made the call of a coin flip that determined where the one-game playoff would take place.

"I was in the American League office, and Haywood Sullivan [then general manager of the Red Sox] was on the phone. I told him, 'You call it, Sully,' but he said, 'No, you're right there, Al, you call it because you can see it.' George, of course, wanted the game in Yankee Stadium.

"Well, we lost the coin flip, and I had to call George and tell him. He asked me, 'What did you call?' I told him, 'Tails,' and he said, 'Dammit! What do you mean you called tails? Don't you know that the probable odds are that heads comes up more often?' "

As it turned out, the Yankees won the game, 5–4, on a home run by Bucky Dent, who hit only four home runs all that season.

Although he was with the Indians for only the final month of the 1948 season, Al Rosen remembers that team—which won the American League pennant and beat the Boston Braves in the World Series—as "a feisty, tough bunch of guys who took nothing from nobody."

And Rosen, a former collegiate boxing champion at the University of Miami fit in perfectly then and in his eight subsequent seasons as a leader of the Tribe.

On one occasion, late in his career, Rosen made clear his unwillingness to "back down" to anybody. It took place in Yankee Stadium against the team that the Indians, in Rosens era, always seemed to be fighting for the pennant.

A key member of the Indians claimed he couldn't play that night, complaining of a sore muscle in his leg as he lay on the trainer's table. Rosen stalked into the room and said, with sarcasm dripping from his voice, "Big men play big games."

The player on the table cursed at Rosen, and more profanity followed from both men.

Finally, Rosen said, "OK, I think it's best that you not say anything more to me, and I won't say anything more to you."

With that Rosen turned and walked to the door of the trainer's room when the other player called him a "yellow, no good son of a bitch." Rosen turned around, went back into the trainer's room, and a fight ensued. It took three men to pull them apart.

"Nobody calls me yellow," Rosen said of the fight.

How about "son of a bitch"?

"Well," he said, "that's bad enough, but don't ever call me yellow." Few ever did—and never a second time.

And as a postscript to the fight, both players played against the Yankees that night, Rosen with a black eye and a sore fist, and the other player with a swollen jaw—and a sore leg.

"I switched from third base to first base in 1954 so that Al [Lopez] could play Rudy Regalado at third because he'd had a monster Spring Training. If Al had asked me to walk across Lake Erie, I would have tried. After I switched to first base, I broke my [right index] finger, but I didn't know until the end of the season that it was broken."

"I endorsed Chesterfield cigarettes [after winning the MVP award in 1953]. I don't know why I did it. I didn't even smoke. They paid me $500, but after a while I felt so guilty about it I sent the money back. But there are still pictures of me out there with a cigarette in my hand. It's very embarrassing."

"George Steinbrenner and I tried to buy the Indians from Vernon Stouffer in [November] 1971, and it's still hard to believe the way it turned out.

"It was really a shocker because we thought the deal was all sewed up. We had a truly high-powered group of investors, including Gabe Paul and F. J. "Steve" O'Neill, and some very prominent Cleveland businessmen.

"Vernon Stouffer [then the Indians owner] led us to believe that he had accepted our offer. The bare bones of the deal called for us to pay Stouffer $8.3 million, which then was a large sum for a baseball franchise, and to assume a $300,000 debt the Indians owed the television station [that broadcast their games].

"Then we got a call from Stouffer that the deal was off, that he was going to sell to Nick Mileti. It was a real shocker."

(Mileti reportedly paid Stouffer $10 million for the franchise, although Paul, then the Indians president and general manager, later called Mileti's bid "only green stamps and promises.")

Hank Ruszkowski
(Catcher, 1944–1945, 1947)

The Indians had high hopes for rookie Hank Ruszkowski, a Clevelander who was their opening-day catcher in 1945, and played in 14 games that season before he was drafted and spent the next two years in the Army. He returned to play 23 games for the Tribe in 1947, but missed most of 1948 with a shoulder injury that required surgery.

Upon reporting to Spring Training in 1949 Ruszkowski had a theory that he believed would make him a powerful long ball hitter, though then-Manager Lou Boudreau vehemently disagreed.

As reported by Ed McAuley in the *Cleveland News,* Ruszkowski checked in with an assortment of new bats that weighed 48 ounces. At the time, the heaviest bat in the Major Leagues was one that weighed 44 ounces swung by muscular Johnny Mize.

Ruszkowski was quoted by McAuley as saying, "Babe Ruth used a 54-ounce bat, and Riggs Stephenson [a .336 hitter who played in the Major Leagues from 1921–1934] swung 56 ounces. I know I'm strong enough to use a 50-ounce bat, and I think it will give me more power to all fields."

Ruszkowski's theory: "Most hitters use an unnatural and unneces-sary motion when they bring their bat from their shoulder at the start of their swings. The only part of the swing that counts is the level sweep through the ball. So why not start the swing in that plane, instead of doing so with the bat on the hitter's shoulder?"

Boudreau didn't agree and tried to convince Ruszkowski to use the orthodox style, but the catcher refused. Finally the manager issued an ultimatum, and when Ruszkowski maintained his stubborn attitude, insisting upon proving his theory, he was demoted to the minor leagues and never got another chance with the Indians, who released him on May 3, 1949.

C.C. Sabathia
(Pitcher, 2001–2008)

After winning his final game for a 17–5 won-lost record as a rookie in 2001, C.C. Sabathia said, "Those [32] starts I had before today couldn't compare to this one. I never felt like I did today. The closest I can put it is this—when I was a little kid and my mom would take me to Toys 'R Us and, you know, you get that anxious feeling because you can pick out anything you want.

"That was what the feeling was like today. I was like a kid in a candy store"—or better still, a kid in a Toys 'R Us store.

Chico Salmon
(Infielder/outfielder, 1964–1968)

Although his versatility was his strength—he played every position for the Indians except pitcher and catcher—Chico Salmon hated to be called "Super Sub," according to Dino Lucarelli, then of the team's publicity department and later its public relations director.

But the fact is, it was Salmon's versatility that enabled him to play nine years in the Major Leagues, the last four (1969–1972) with Baltimore.

When he came to the Indians, Lucarelli said, "A story appeared that said Chico believed in ghosts, which is why, he said, he slept with the lights on in his bedroom. But everybody thought it was just a ploy so that Chico wouldn't be required to have a roommate, as did everybody else on the team in those days.

"One night he went on the *Sportsline* radio show with Pete Franklin, whom Chico always called 'Ben,' not Pete. Franklin tried to get Chico to admit that the ghost story was a hoax. 'Let's disprove it once and for all,' Franklin said. 'You don't really see ghosts, do you, Chico?'

"Chico replied, 'Tha's right, Ben. I no sees 'em . . . but I believes in 'em.'"

Another Lucarelli story about Salmon:

"One winter Chico wanted to get an off-season job and stay in Cleveland. I contacted some people and found out that Stroh's brewery was looking for a celebrity representative. I arranged a luncheon with five or six Stroh's executives to come in from Detroit to meet Chico. We sat down and everything was going great. We laughed a lot and the Stroh's people seemed to like Chico. Then the waitress came over to take our order and when she asked Chico what he wanted to drink, he said, 'I gonna have a Budweiser.' "He did not get the job."

In 1966, Birdie Tebbetts, then the manager of the Indians, "nominated" Ruthford Eduardo "Chico" Salmon for the American League All-Star team.

Salmon was incredulous, even speechless—almost—when Birdie's praise was repeated. "Man, what a t'rill that would be [to make the team]," he said. "Why, I'd be the biggest man in Panama. Everyone would want to talk to me. Imagine. I'd be the first boy from Panama to make the All-Star team. My mother would be amazed. I mean, happy. So would I. So happy I don't know what I'd do, man."

Richie Scheinblum
(Outfielder, 1965, 1967–1969)

One of the Indians' all-time favorite personalities was Richie Scheinblum, an outfielder who seemed to blush every time a reporter interviewed him or a fan asked for his autograph.

Richie compiled impressive statistics in the minor leagues but couldn't maintain his success in brief trials with the Tribe in 1965, 1967, and 1968, and after securing a place on the Major League roster in 1969, primarily as a part-time outfielder-pinch hitter. In that one full season with the Indians, Scheinblum, a switch-hitter, batted .186 in 102 games, after which his contract was sold to the then-Washington Senators.

Despite his inability to hit with the same degree of consistency he enjoyed in the minors, Scheimblum never lost his youthful naïveté and enthusiasm. In his first Spring Training with the Tribe in 1965 he was quoted in the *Plain Dealer*. "I'm rooming with Rocky Colavito . . . imagine that! He's a swell fellow and I really like him. All we talk about is baseball, and it's great.

"You know, we grew up on the same neighborhood in the Bronx. Of course, Rocky is older [by nine years] than I am, but my house was right across the street from Costona Park where Rocky was first scouted by the Indians. In 1958, when I was 14 and playing around the neighborhood, Rocky was a rookie and hit 21 homers. I kept track of every one of them. And now I'm rooming with him. I still can't believe it.

"And you know what else? We both have flat feet, probably from running on the same pavement on the streets in New York. How about that?"

During a Spring Training intrasquad game in Tucson, Arizona, in 1966, Scheinblum hit a 415-foot drive over the left field wall at Hi

Corbett Field. But instead of standing at the plate and admiring his handiwork, Richie put his head down and took off full speed. Early Wynn, who was coaching at first base, shouted to Richie, "Go hard . . . go hard," which Scheinblum did, without looking to see where the ball went (as it soared over the fence).

Scheinblum rounded first base and headed for second, still running hard—and still with his head down—and his teammates in the Indians dugout took up the cry, "Run, Richie, run, run, run," which Richie did, still without looking to see where the ball went.

When Scheinblum approached third base, Coach George Strickland waved for him to go home, which Richie did, still running hard and with his head down. The next Indians batter at the plate signaled for Scheinblum to slide, which he also did, thinking he had an inside-the-park homer. As he crossed the plate in a cloud of dust, the puzzled umpire told Scheinblum the ball had gone over the wall, that he didn't need to slide—after which Richie sat down in the dugout with his teammates and as usual blushed.

Jim Schlemmer
(Sportswriter, Akron Beacon Journal*)*

When he covered the Indians, which he did for 45 years until his retirement in 1969, Jim Schlemmer was noted for his critical, often sarcastic comments about the team's players, coaches, managers, and front office personnel.

He spared nobody, and nobody was invulnerable to Schlemmer's acerbic barbs, not even fellow sportswriters.

But the rotund and balding Schlemmer also was a character and, when the occasion presented itself, a hard drinker as well. Which was the case one night in Tucson, Arizona, during the Indians Spring Training in 1964. This time, however, what happened to Schlemmer was almost disastrous to a man of his position.

In his ground level room at the Highway House motel, Schlemmer imbibed too much—actually, *much* too much—one night after finishing his column and, after getting undressed for the purpose of taking a shower, he stepped through the door to his right that he thought led to the bathroom.

However, it was the door to Schlemmer's left that led to the bathroom. The door to his right, which he opened and walked through—and which slammed shut behind him—led instead to the parking lot. Suddenly Schlemmer, sans even his underwear, found himself in the parking lot, locked out of his room.

Fortunately, there was some shrubbery that he was able to hide behind, which he did for nearly two hours while fighting off mosquitoes and other assorted bugs that frequented the desert. Finally, with the clock approaching 2 a.m., a friend—well, a colleague who worked for a competing newspaper and on occasion was the butt of Schlemmer's acerbity—came along.

Schlemmer caught the man's attention and pleaded with him to obtain a spare key. The man finally did, but not until after he tormented the naked sportswriter from Akron who, thereafter, always made sure of the door he walked through, and/or was fully dressed before doing so.

Herb Score
(Pitcher, 1955–1959)

Buddy Bell once said of Herb Score, "He's such a nice guy, I bet he makes the bed in his hotel room when he wakes up in the morning."

Despite his great ability—and outstanding record before suffering a serious eye injury in 1957—Score never took himself too seriously.

Looking back on his career, Score once said, "A lot of pitchers don't use a wind up, but I deserve credit for being the first to do so. That's because I walked so many batters and had so many runners on base so often, it seemed I was always pitching from a stretch and I almost forgot how to wind up."

On May 1, 1955, Score, then a rookie, pitched the nightcap of a doubleheader against Boston, after veteran Bob Feller hurled the opener. It turned out to be quite a day for the two pitchers. Feller hurled a one-hitter to win the first game, and Score struck out 16 batters in a four-hit victory in the second game.

In a first page story the next morning, the *Plain Dealer* called Feller "a fading meteor" and Score "a rising star." It reported, "26,595 fans in the Stadium had the privilege of seeing the best pitcher of this generation [Feller] and his logical successor [Score] give sparkling performances."

In Spring Training 1957, after Herb Score had won 36 games and lost 19 his first two seasons with the Indians, Hall of Famer Tris Speaker, then a member of the Indians front office, said, "If nothing happens to Score, the kid has got to be the greatest."

Less than a month later, on May 7, Score was hit in the right eye by a line drive off the bat of the New York Yankees Gil McDougald, and didn't pitch again that season. Though he recovered from that injury, Score was never the same and retired in 1962 with a career won-lost record of 55–46.

After he became a broadcaster of Indians games, first on television and then on radio, Herb quickly became as big a favorite of the fans in his new capacity, as he was when he wore a uniform and toe plate, and struck out opposing batters.

Listening to Herb was like sitting next to a friend and watching a baseball game with his down-home style. He wasn't always perfectly articulate and, to be sure, he often was guilty of a *faux pas*. But nobody objected, as when he committed one of his—nay, one of the fans'—favorite comments during what was considered "the bad old days" of the 1980s.

When an Indians' batter hit a drive down the left field line, Score excitedly shouted into the microphone, "It could be fair, it could be foul . . . it is!"

But, again, the fans loved it, as they loved Score.

Phil Seghi
(General manager, 1973–1985)

Prior to Frank Robinson's first game as player-manager of the Indians—and Major League Baseball's first black manager—on April 8, 1975, against the New York Yankees, he was visited in the clubhouse by Indians General Manager Phil Seghi.

Seghi said to Robinson, "Frank, why don't you hit a homer the first time you go to the plate?" to which Robinson responded, 'Are you crazy, or what?'

An hour or so later, as the Indians' second batter to face Yankees right-hander Doc Medich, Robinson homered, leading the Indians to a 5–3 victory.

Richie Sexson
(First baseman and outfielder, 1997–2000)

Although he's one of the premier sluggers in the Major Leagues, Richie Sexson was drafted almost as an afterthought by the Indians in 1993. They picked him in the 24th round after more than 700 players had been taken.

So how does a 24th-round draft choice not only get to the Major Leagues, but also become one of the most prolific home run hitters? It was Sexson's will to succeed.

"I never worried about what round the Indians drafted me or how many players were picked ahead of me. It was no big deal. I knew I was drafted pretty late, but I knew what I wanted to accomplish—that I wanted to do this, play in the big leagues. I guess it was a matter of will. All I ever wanted to do was play professional baseball, and when you love the game and put a lot of preparation into it, good things can happen."

Mark Shapiro
(Assistant general manager, 1998–2000, general manager, 2001–)

"The day we traded Sean Casey is one of the more memorable days in my time with the Indians. I was farm director when John Hart and Dan O'Dowd made the [1998] deal with Cincinnati [for pitcher Dave Burba]. They asked my opinion, and I told them I couldn't be objective and shouldn't be involved in the decision. I could never trade Sean Casey, even though we desperately needed Burba.

"And, while I shared Sean's happiness, because he was going to get an opportunity that we both knew wouldn't happen here, I was simply too attached to him. I felt absolute sorrow because he was one of the very special people I'd ever been around, but wasn't going to be a Major Leaguer in a Cleveland uniform.

"So, we both were in tears as we shared some great discussion, and it was the basis for a friendship that still exists today.

"The bottom line is that it was a good deal, one of those deals that was good for both clubs. Burba provided what we desperately needed at that time by winning 15 games three straight years [1998, 1999, 2000], while Casey has become one of the best players in the National League."

"My favorite memory [since joining the Indians in 1992] involved Tony Peña in Game 1 of the 1995 Division Series against the Red Sox. It was Yom Kippur, so I wasn't there [at Jacobs Field]. I shouldn't even have been watching the game on TV. When Peña hit that home run in the 13th inning [that won the game, 5–4], it set the tone for a magical postseason."

In addition to Peña's game-winner, Shapiro also treasures the memory of Sandy Alomar's game-winning homer off New York Yankees closer Mariano Rivera in the 1997 Division Series. It sent the Indians on their way to their second World Series appearance in three years. "We were five outs from elimination when [Alomar] got that home run off the best relief pitcher in baseball," he said. "It symbolized hope for the team. It's etched in the minds of all our fans."

Sonny Siebert
(Pitcher, 1964–1969)

"The Indians always had the best fastball-pitching staff in baseball, back in the 1960s, and I'll tell you the reason why," Sonny Siebert said. "It was all because of Birdie Tebbetts. You didn't pitch for Birdie unless you could throw hard. When he was the manager [of] the Indians, they didn't even sign a pitcher unless he could throw the heck out of the ball."

Which Siebert could, as did his starting pitching partners of that era: Sam McDowell, Luis Tiant, and Steve Hargan.

"Sam McDowell and I were roommates and lockered next to each other most of the time. I used to listen to him being interviewed after games, and I never knew if he was kidding you guys, the way he'd answer your questions, when you'd come around to interview him after a game.

"One of the things he'd do was, when Bob Sudyk [of the *Cleveland Press*] would ask him, for example, what kind of a pitch he threw to strike out the last batter, Sam would say, 'Fastball.'

"Then, after Sudyk would leave and you [Russ Schneider of the Cleveland *Plain Dealer*] would ask him the same question, Sam would say it was a curve ball.

"Then it would be Hank Kozloski's [of the *Lorain Journal*] turn to ask what pitch he threw to get the last out and Sam would say, 'Change-up.'

"It amazed me. I had trouble keeping a straight face when I'd hear him do that. Once I asked him why, and Sam said, 'Oh, you know those guys. They all want something different, so I give it to them.'"

"The thing I remember so well about my no-hitter [2–0 over Washington, June 10, 1966] is similar to the time I came close to pitching a second no-hitter [for Boston five years later].

"Joe Azcue was my catcher with the Indians and, at the start of the ninth inning, he was a little nervous. He didn't want to do anything to spoil the no-hitter. When the first batter came to the plate, Joe got down in his crouch and put his fist down three times in a row without putting down any fingers.

"I called him out to the mound and asked him what was going on, and he said he didn't want to call for the wrong pitch. I told him I'd been throwing mostly fastballs, let's stay with it, which we did.

"I retired the first two batters without any trouble, and got two quick strikes on the third batter, Rabbit Saverine. He started to swing at my next pitch, but held back. Before the umpire ruled that he hadn't swung and that it wasn't strike three, everybody in our dugout jumped out on the field, and everybody in the stands started cheering.

"It took about ten minutes to get all our guys back in the dugout and even some fans off the field, and I thought for sure I'd lose the no-hitter. But then Saverine hit a routine fly to left, and that was it. I got the no-hitter.

"Then, in 1971, when I was with the Red Sox, almost the same thing happened. I took a no-hitter against the Yankees into the ninth and my catcher, Tom Satriano, came out and asked me, just as Joe did, how I wanted to work the hitters. I thought back to 1966 and told him the same thing. That I'd better stay with fastballs, even though, by then, I wasn't throwing as hard as I had a few years earlier.

"So what happened? The first pitch I threw to the first batter, Horace Clarke, was a fastball. He hit it up the middle and there went my no-hitter, so it didn't work twice in a row.

"Like somebody once said, sometimes you can think too much."

"At one time I thought, when I got out of baseball and became a businessman, I'd probably have to go by my given first name, Wilfred, instead of Sonny. I mean, when somebody named 'Sonny' reaches middle age, as I have, how can he still be called Sonny?

"But I don't know. I still get mail addressed to 'Sonny Siebert,' and I even get checks—most of them are small checks now—that some are made out to 'Sonny' and sometimes 'Wilfred,' so I guess it doesn't really make any difference. And my family and my friends still call me Sonny.

"Actually, I'm the third Wilfred in my family, which might be the reason I've always been called Sonny. My grandfather was the first Wilfred, though everybody called him Charley, but don't ask me why. Then, my father was the second Wilfred and people call him Joe, and I don't know the reason for that, either.

"So, there are three Wilfred Sieberts in my family, but none of us is called Wilfred, at least not all the time."

Duke Sims
(Catcher, 1964–1970)

"I always got a kick out of Luis Tiant, and I loved to catch him. He was a very funny man, even when he got mad. One time, I guess it was about 1966, Looie was pitching, I'm catching, and the umpire behind the plate was Frank Umont, who had a bit of a drinking problem at that time. It was a hot and very muggy day in Cleveland, Umont was sweating like hell and didn't smell too good. Everything he drank the night before was coming out.

"Looie, who always had great control, was throwing strikes, but Umont kept calling them balls. Looie got all bent out of shape and when I got back to the dugout I went to [Manager] Birdie Tebbetts and asked him, 'Birdie, am I doing something that would keep Umont from calling the pitches right?' Birdie said, 'No, I've been watching and you're not doing anything wrong. Umont is just horse [bleep], that's all.' Then Birdie said, 'The next time Looie throws a pitch that's a strike and Umont calls it a ball, you look into the dugout, and then I want you to go to the pitcher's mound.'

"So, we went back on the field and a couple of pitches later, Looie threw one right down Broadway, and Umont called it a ball. I looked into the dugout at Birdie, as he told me to do, then I called time and walked out to the mound. Looie was beside himself, he was so mad. I told him, 'Looie, look, Birdie is on his way out here, so I'm just killing time until he gets here. Don't worry about Umont. He's just having a tough time.'

"When Birdie got there he told Looie to look in at the plate at Umont and tell him when Umont was coming out [to break up the conference]. So, we didn't talk, we just stood there, Birdie and me with our backs to the plate, and waited for Umont to come out. When Umont did, he said, 'OK, Birdie, what's going on? You going to make a change?'

"With that, Birdie turned around and looked me right in the eyes and said, 'And you, Sims, you get one more good pitch from Tiant called a ball, I'm going to fine you five hundred bucks.' Then he turned around and walked off. Tiant started to chuckle, and I went back to the plate with Umont right behind me. When we got there, Umont said, 'Boy, Birdie sure is tough on you, ain't he?' and I said, 'No, Frank. Birdie was talking to you.' He said, 'Really?' and I said, 'Really.'

"And after that, for whatever reason, Umont got better—and Tiant won the game."

"My lifetime batting average was only .239 due to one of the most inept official scorers of all time," complained Duke Sims, whose memory obviously was much better than his batting eye. "It should be .240, not .239, because I was screwed out of a hit in 1968 on a ball that was ruled an error [charged to New York Yankees second baseman Horace Clarke].

"Because of that my career average [for 11 years in the Major Leagues] was .2394 and was rounded off—*down*—to .239. But if I had gotten credit for that hit, as I should have, my average would have been .2398, and would have been rounded off—*up*—to .240.

"Here's how it happened. We were playing the Yankees at the [old] Stadium and [southpaw] Steve Barber was on the mound for them. Now, being a left-handed batter, I seldom faced left-handed pitchers, especially not those who ate up left-handed batters the way Barber did. He was one of the nastiest left handers in the league. He had nasty, nasty stuff, but Alvin Dark left me in to face him for some reason—maybe because Joe Azcue was hurt or sleeping or something.

"Well, Barber threw me a sidearm low, inside fastball that I crushed. I really did, believe me. I hit it right at Clarke, and it handcuffed him [and] went through his legs, and after long deliberation, the official scorer called it an error. An error! I couldn't believe it. Neither could Clarke. I argued with the scorer after the game, and all he said to me was, 'That was an easy play for a Major League infielder.' I asked him, 'Does that mean Horace Clarke is not a Major Leaguer?'

"And because it was called an error, I wound up with one less hit [580] in my career [in 2,422 official at-bats for an 11-season batting average of .2394715]. If I had been credited with a hit, my average would have been .2398 [.2398843] and would have been rounded off to .240."

(Author's note: The "inept scorer" to whom Sims referred was Russell Schneider—yes, the author of this book—and states here that the play was called correctly. It was not a hit; it was an error because Major League second basemen are supposed to make that kind of play.)

When asked if the Indians won or lost the game in which Sims was "screwed" by the "inept scorer," his memory failed him.

Something else Sims recalled from his seven-year career with the Indians was a plan he crafted in 1968 to try to force then-General Manager Gabe Paul to give him and fellow catcher Joe Azcue big raises in 1968. Sims wanted Azcue to join him in holding out as a tandem, as Don Drysdale and Sandy Koufax did to the Los Angeles Dodgers in 1965.

"I told Joe that our position, catcher, was worth $100,000, because Johnny Bench had just signed with Cincinnati for 100 grand," Sims said. "I said to Joe, 'Lets hold out together, because the Indians needed either one of us and couldn't do without both of us. Each of us will get $50,000, but if Gabe negotiates with us individually, he'll break us apart and say that neither of us is worth $50,000.'

"The way I had it figured, Bench was the Cadillac catcher of both leagues, and not only that, Bill Freehan was making about $80,000 in Detroit. My rationale was simple—the [catching] position is worth $100,000, in our case, $50,000 for each of us.

"At the time I was making about $16,000 and Joe was making probably $25,000. So I figured it, Gabe had about 60 grand on the table for the position, and our combined numbers, Joe's and mine, were better than Bench's. It made sense for the two of us combined to get at least as much as Bench. The Indians were not going to let either Joe or me go to the plate 600 times, but together we would.

"Something else. Remember that a catcher works twice as hard as any other guy on the field—runs the defense, runs the pitching staff, and in order to be properly rewarded [with money] he has to be an offensive player, too. You could be a great catcher but never make any big money—not in my day anyway. In our case, Joe [a right-handed batter] faced all the nasty-ass left handers and I [a left-handed batter] got all the toughest right-handed pitchers in baseball.

"But Joe said, 'Oh, roomie, I got two kids and [the Indians] might release me. I cannot take that chance,' and wouldn't go along with me. But I held out anyway, though it didn't do me much good. I wound up getting something like $18,000 or $19,000. Joe never did tell me what he got."

Grady Sizemore
(Outfielder, 2004–)

How good a prospect did the Indians consider Grady Sizemore to be when he played—and starred—at Class AA Akron in 2003 and Class AAA Buffalo in 2004?

Teammate Corey Smith might have said it best: "When Grady rolls out of bed, he hits line drives. He is amazing."

And as Tribe director of player development John Farrell said when Sizemore first joined the team, "He has the potential with his tremendous ability and work ethic to be a team leader and become a star-caliber player at the big league level."

Joel Skinner
(Catcher, 1989–1991; coach, 2001–; interim manager, 2002)

"We were playing in Cleveland—I was with the Yankees then, I think it was 1988—and Richie Yett was pitching for the Indians. We had a man on third and Lou Piniella gave me the sign for a squeeze bunt. When I tried to lay it down, Richie pitched out, but didn't get it out quite far enough. I was able to reach out with one hand and bunt the ball down the first base line and got the run in.

"After they threw me out at first base, I circled around to the right and ran back to the [third base] dugout. As I went past the Indians dugout, I saw Doc Edwards, then the Indians manager, raise his right hand and punch the clip-board he was holding something awful. Pieces of it went flying all over the dugout, which made it even greater for me, knowing that it frustrated him so.

"I laughed about it later, though I never brought it up to Doc, which was a good thing because the next year I was playing for him [in Cleveland]."

After replacing fired Manager Charlie Manuel in July 2002, Joel Skinner led the Indians to a 35–41 record. When the season ended, he was considered a frontrunner for the full-time job based on comments by General Manager Mark Shapiro.

When asked to assess Skinner's assets, Shapiro listed them as "patience, positiveness, and his appreciation of the Cleveland Indians organization."

"I think he managed a game extremely well," Shapiro said.

A week later Shapiro signed Eric Wedge to a two-year contract to manage the Indians.

C. C. Slapnicka
(Scout/general manager, 1935–1941; scout, 1946–1970)

In a meeting with the Indians directors in the spring of 1936, C. C. Slapnicka, the team's head scout, said, "I suppose this sounds like the same old stuff to you, but I want you to believe me. This boy I found out in Iowa will be the greatest pitcher the world has ever known. His fastball is fast and fuzzy, never goes in a straight line, it wiggles and shoots around."

Slapnicka was talking about Bob Feller.

Shane Spencer
(Outfielder, 2003)

"When I was with the Yankees [1998–2002] and we came to Jacobs Field for the 1998 playoffs, my dad came up to see a game," Shane

Spencer recalled. "When I got back to the hotel after the game and my dad wasn't around, I asked my friends if they knew where he went, and they told me he went out with some Cleveland fans. Later he told me that the fans told him, 'We like your son, but we hate the Yankees.'"

Charlie Spikes
(Outfielder, 1973–1977)

As a No. 1 draft choice of the New York Yankees in 1969, great things were expected of Charlie Spikes when he was acquired by the Indians in 1973 in a trade that sent Graig Nettles to New York.

Nicknamed the "Bogalusa Bomber" (his home was in Bogalusa, Louisiana), Spikes hammered 23 homers and drove in 73 runs although he batted only .237 in 140 games his first season in Cleveland. His numbers improved in 1974—.271 average, 22 homers, 80 RBIs—but in 1975, with the arrival of Frank Robinson as baseball's first black manager, Spikes's career took a nose-dive.

"A lot of people were critical of Frank, saying that he put too much pressure on me, but it was my own fault, not his," Spikes said. "Everybody has differences of opinion, and Frank and I did, too. Let me say it this way. I was trying so hard to do well because I wanted Frank to do well as the first black manager.

"But I got off to a bad start. I went zero for 21, and Frank benched me. When I got back in the lineup, if I didn't hit well, he'd take me out again. But I don't blame Frank. That was me, my fault, not Frank's. I put pressure on myself. Frank didn't do it."

Spikes suffered a back injury a few years ago, underwent two operations, and was forced to give up his job in a textile factory in Louisiana.

"Nobody calls me the 'Bogalusa Bomber' anymore," he said.

Now they call him "Charles Leslie Spikes"—when he signs for his disability insurance.

Scott Stewart
(Pitcher, 2004)

Southpaw pitcher Scott Stewart said he knew he'd be booed when he was introduced for the Indians' home opener because of the poor record he compiled in Spring Training. He took it in stride, even tipping his cap to the fans as he took his place alongside teammates on the third base line.

"It was a respectable boo," he said. "Besides, I've heard worse, [and] it's better to be booed than spit upon."

A month into the season, with his won-lost record an abysmal 0–2 and with a 7.24 earned run average in 23 appearances—and the fans still booing—Stewart was designated for assignment and sent to Class AAA Buffalo.

George Strickland
(Shortstop, 1952–1957, 1959–60; coach, 1963–1969; interim manager, 1964, 1966)

"[The 1960s] were difficult times in Cleveland," George Strickland remembered. "There was so much politics involved, and there always seemed to be money problems. [Owner] Vernon Stouffer had pretty much put Alvin Dark in complete control of the club [in 1969], and it sometimes got to be very difficult.

"But when you check out the records of the pitchers we had then—Sam McDowell, Luis Tiant, Sonny Siebert, Steve Hargan, and some others—you have to wonder why we, the Indians, didn't do better. I guess it was because they were all too young then and became great pitchers after they left the Indians, which was a shame."

"If somebody had asked me when I was managing the Indians, 'Who had the best fastball in baseball?' I would have said, 'Sam McDowell.'

"And if I was asked, 'Who had the best curve ball?' I would have said, 'McDowell.'

"'How about the best change-up?' It also would have been McDowell.

"'The best slider?' Again, McDowell."

So why didn't McDowell do better, regardless of his drinking problem?

"I honestly believe that Sam was afraid of success," Strickland said.

Strickland—a slick-fielding, light-hitting shortstop—played for the Indians after being acquired from Pittsburgh in 1952.

"I was glad to go to Cleveland, which had a very good team then under Al Lopez, and I didn't mind leaving the Pirates, who were very bad then.

"We were so bad [in Pittsburgh] I think we were the only team in the history of baseball to be mathematically eliminated [from the pennant race] by June."

In 1954, when the Indians were in the process of winning a then-American League-record 111 games, Strickland was lost for six weeks after suffering a broken jaw when he was hit by a thrown ball while sliding into third base against the Yankees in New York on July 23.

Although the injury was serious—Strickland's jaw was wired shut for more than a month—there was a humorous aspect to the incident.

"One of the reporters [Jim Schlemmer of the *Akron Beacon Journal*] wrote that he had never seen courage like I showed that night, crawling to get to the base after I got hit," Strickland said, chuckling as he recounted the story by phone from his home in New Orleans. "When I read what Schlemmer wrote, I told him through my clenched teeth, 'Thanks for the kind words, and I hate to blow your story. But the truth is, I wasn't trying to get back to the base . . . I was just trying to find my denture.'

"Schlemmer told me, 'Well, don't say anything about it because everybody liked the story the way I wrote it, and I did, too.'

"I loved Jim. He was a fraud. He wanted people to think he was a nasty guy, a tough guy, but he was a real pussycat. It's like I always said, 'It's hard to meet bad people in baseball.' At least it was when I was up there.

"I was playing second base the night that Herb [Score] got hit by the liner off the bat of Gil McDougald. That was as bad as I ever saw. It happened so quickly. I ran to the mound, and Herb turned his head and all of a sudden he was bleeding from everywhere. His eyes, his nose, his mouth, his ears, everywhere. It was awful. Probably the thing that saved him was that the ball hit the side of his nose first. If it had gone right into the eye, it would have been worse. Very bad."

And when Strickland retired, he said, "I knew it was time to go when the players started bringing hair driers to the clubhouse, and you'd get on a team bus and eight or 10 guys would be carrying those boomboxes, and all of them tuned to something different."

Pat Tabler
(Outfielder/designated hitter/first baseman, 1983–1988)

"One thing that stands out in my memory from the years I played in Cleveland was the excitement of the fans, especially in 1986 when we went on a 10-game winning streak.

"After we won No. 10 in Chicago, we heard on the plane ride home how excited the fans were back in Cleveland. The next night, when we played Kansas City, the game had to be delayed for 20 to 30 minutes to let all the fans get through the gates. There were about 50,000 fans in the Stadium that night and, I'm telling you, it was very exciting—and different. The first three years I was with the Indians we were losing close to a hundred games each season, and not doing well at the gate.

"But in 1986 all my friends were calling me for tickets, and I had a huge pass list that night we came back to Cleveland to play the Royals. We went into the bottom of the ninth with the score tied, and when we loaded the bases, the Royals brought in Dan Quisenberry. I went up and got a hit that won the game, and I'll never forget the excitement that was generated, the way the fans went crazy.

"Like Gabe Paul said that Cleveland was a sleeping giant and that, if they ever had a really good team, the fans would really support the Indians, really get into it, which is what's happened. I think it's great.

"The following winter [1986–1987] we were on the cover of *Sports Illustrated* with the prediction that we were going to win the pennant in 1987—and the knuckle-headed reason was that five or six years in a row, a different team had won the American League East. So *S. I.* figured it was our turn, because we had a young, up-and-coming team.

"But we really stunk it up, finished last [with a 61–101 record]. It had been great to get the national recognition, but a lot of us knew we were a young team, and the sad truth was, we just weren't ready. We were not a complete team. Not then. Not against the Yankees and the Red Sox and the Orioles and the Brewers. Detroit ended up winning the division."

"One of the reasons we did so well for awhile in 1986, when we led the Major Leagues in hitting, was that any way it was possible to steal the catchers' signs, we did. Doc Edwards [then a coach] was in the bullpen, stealing the signs and relaying them to the hitters. That was right after we'd switched bullpens from right field to left field, the [publicized] reason being that [Manager] Pat Corrales could then see better from our [first base] dugout who was throwing in the pen.

"It started the night we were playing Baltimore and Doc discovered that [Orioles shortstop] Cal Ripken would hold his bare hand a certain way behind his back, depending on what pitch was being called, to let the outfielders know what the pitch would be so they could get a better jump. A closed fist was a curve ball, and an open fist was a fastball. Doc would raise his right hand in the air for a fastball, and lower it for a breaking ball. I think we scored, like, 15 runs that night [actually ten] and, I'll tell you, it's great hitting when you know what's coming. Left-handed batters at the plate could see Doc, but the signal had to be relayed from somebody in the dugout for right-handed batters. If it was a fastball, somebody in the dugout would whistle, and if it was going to be a curve ball, somebody maybe would yell out the batter's name. Not everybody wanted to know, but I sure don't know why not. I did, that's for sure."

Ed Taubensee
(Catcher, 1991, 2001–)

"It wasn't the most embarrassed I've ever been in baseball, but, yeah, it was pretty embarrassing," acknowledged Eddie Taubensee, talking about the only time in Major League Baseball history that a pitcher pitched both right-handed and left-handed in an official game.

The ambidextrous pitcher was Greg Harris, a natural right-hander who was on the mound for Montreal against Cincinnati on September 28, 1995. In the sixth inning, Reggie Sanders, a right-handed batter, led off, and was followed by left-handers Hal Morris and Taubensee.

Harris retired Sanders on an infield grounder, then, switching his glove to his right hand he pitched left-handed and walked Morris. Then it was Taubensee's turn to face Harris. "I took his first two pitches, which were slow fastballs . . . maybe 70, 75 miles per hour," said Taubensee. "Then I hit his third pitch—I think it was supposed to be a fastball, too—off the end of my bat, right back to [Harris], and he threw me out at first base.

"When I got back to the dugout, the guys were laughing. They got a big kick out of it," said Taubensee. "But, what the heck, it was no big thing"—even though it never happened before or since in the Major Leagues.

Birdie Tebbetts
(Catcher, 1951–1952; manager, 1963–1966)

In 1952, when the Indians, then managed by Al Lopez, signed Herb Score out of high school in Lake Worth, Florida, Birdie Tebbetts was a back-up catcher (with Joe Tipton) behind Jim Hegan. The Indians brought Score to Cleveland for a workout before they sent him to the minor leagues. Mike McNally, then the farm director, told Score, "Don't throw hard until you get good and loose, and let us see what you've got," according to a tale told by then-Manager Al Lopez.

Score was throwing to catcher Birdie Tebbetts when Lopez approached the young pitcher and introduced himself. Lopez stood behind the mound and, a few minutes later, asked Score if he was ready to "cut loose." Score said, "Yes, that's what I've been waiting to do," and Lopez told him, "Go ahead, but don't hurt yourself."

With that, Score said to Birdie, "Mr. Tebbetts, I'm going to let it out now," and the veteran catcher said, "You mean you haven't thrown hard yet?" Score said he hadn't, whereupon Tebbetts yelled to Tipton, "Hey, Joe, c'mon over here and catch this kid. I'm the next hitter [in batting practice]."

Tipton dutifully took Tebbetts' place and told Score, "OK, kid, let it come," which Herb did. His first pitch, a fastball, went over Tipton's head without the catcher even getting a glove on it. Lopez said, "Tipton turned pale because he knew if the ball had hit him, it would've got him right between the eyes, maybe even killed him. With that, Tipton yelled at Birdie, 'Tebbetts, you son of a bitch, you almost got me killed,' which was true.

"Then Tipton got down in a catchers crouch and told Score to throw another pitch. Herb did, it was a curve ball, and this one broke down and hit Tipton on the instep of his left foot. Now Tipton is really mad at Tebbetts. He threw down his glove and limped away. Hegan had to come out and finish catching Score, while Tebbetts hid behind a couple of players at the batting cage."

However, it was another left-handed pitcher who impressed Tebbetts even more. "Sam McDowell was the greatest talent I ever saw, period. There was none better, not Herb Score, not Bob Feller, not

Bob Lemon, not Early Wynn, not anybody, anywhere. He threw as hard as anyone, he had a great curve ball, a great slider, and a great change-up—and he also had a spit ball. But, like a lot of guys, he didn't know how to use his talent. He wasted it. He just couldn't put it all together."

Jim Thome
(First and third baseman, 1991–2002)

When Jim Thome became a free agent at the end of the 2002 season, he received and eventually accepted a six-year $85 million offer from the Philadelphia Phillies.

However, before he signed with the Phillies, Thome met one more time with the Indians, who were offering him $63.25 million over five years to remain in Cleveland.

Of his negotiations with Tribe General Manager Mark Shapiro, Thome said, "I called [Shapiro] up, and I said, 'Mark, if you will guarantee me a sixth year at the same money [$63.25 million] you're offering, I'll take it. I'm not asking for any more money, just one more year at the same amount you're willing to pay me for five. If you will, I'll sign this thing right now and get it over with.'

"[Shapiro] said he couldn't . . . but never explained why, except to tell me, 'My hands are tied.' Don't ask me what he meant by that. But that was it for me. The end [of negotiations with the Indians]."

Andre Thornton
(First baseman/designated hitter,
1977–79, 1981–1987)

"Something I learned early on, and was driven home to me many times, is that baseball is a game that teaches humility. I know it did to me. You play the game the way it's supposed to be played, and you don't get too cocky out there, because one minute you're up on cloud nine, and the next minute you can be humiliated in front of 30 or 40 thousand people.

"Like the time we were playing in Boston and I was swinging a pretty hot bat. First base was open and [Red Sox Manager] Don Zimmer intentionally walked the batter ahead of me. I got a hit and drove in a run, and when the inning ended, I went out to first base and was thinking, 'Who is Don Zimmer to walk a batter in order to pitch to me?'

"The next thing that happened, there was a pop-up between first and second base. I thought Duane Kuiper would catch it, and he thought I would, and the ball fell between us. It scored a run and immediately brought back to me a sense of humility."

"Humility can come in another form, too. Like the night my wife, Gail, sang the National Anthem prior to a game at the old Stadium in the late 1970s. We were playing the Yankees and afterwards Yogi Berra came up to me and said, 'Andre, your daughter'—he called Gail my daughter—'did a great job.'

"When I told Gail, she liked it, of course, though it made me think it might be time to retire."

"The day I hit for the cycle in 1978, the thing I remember most is that I went into Boston struggling like a dog as I was off to my usual slow start at the plate. I don't recall the sequel of the hits I got, although I remember the triple came in my last at-bat. People ask me, how in the world did I ever get a triple—although I wasn't all that slow.

"What happened was that the ball I hit almost went out of Fenway Park, and would have if it hadn't been to center field where the wall comes to a point. The ball ricocheted off the wall and away from the outfielders so that I was able to make it to third base easily.

"Another thing people kid me about is the game in which I hit an inside-the-park home run, the only time I ever did that. We were in Chicago, and Richie Zisk, the left fielder, for some reason was playing me over toward left center. Steve Stone was pitching for the White

Sox, and that was the day in 1977 that Kuiper hit the only home run of his career.

"I hit a towering pop fly down the left field foul line and when it came down it almost hit the chalk, out near the warning track. Zisk was so far away from the line that he couldn't get there, and—I guess because it had rained earlier in the day and the ground was wet—he couldn't stop. By the time he did, I was on my way home. But if it had been anybody other than Richie Zisk out there, I never would have gotten to home plate because he was slower than I was.

Luis Tiant
(Pitcher, 1964–1969)

"When I got called up by the Indians [from Class AAA Portland on July 19,1964] I did not want to go. We were in San Diego and I was supposed to pitch that night. They canceled me, but didn't tell me why. The next day [Portland Manager] Johnny Lipon called me into his room and told me, 'You have to go to New York. The Indians want you, Luis Tiant.' I left San Diego at seven o'clock at night and arrived in New York at 7:30 the next morning. When I got to my room at the hotel I got a call from Gabe Paul. He said, 'Come to my room to sign a new [Major League] contract. It was for $5,000. The minimum salary that year was $6,000, but they only gave me $5,000 because it was July, not the start of the season.

When he was in his prime with the Indians in the late 1960s, Luis Tiant had a "corkscrew" windup/delivery that entertained fans as much as it confused batters.

"I didn't do it for show," Tiant said. "I did it to get batters out. They would say, 'We can't tell where the ball is coming from,' which is what I wanted them to worry about. I gave [the batters] my shoulder, back, foot, and—finally—the ball."

Tiant also talked a lot to hitters he was facing.

"I'd tell them, 'Hit this one, if you can.'"

Most of the time they couldn't.

When Tiant joined the Indians as a rookie in 1964, one of his teammates was third baseman-outfielder Al Smith, who said he had played against Tiant's father, Luis Sr., in the Negro League in 1946 and 1947.

"If this kid is half as good as his father, we've got us a helluva pitcher," Smith said.

Indeed, Tiant proved to be more than "half as good" as his father had been, and it turned out that the Indians did have a helluva pitcher.

Luis, Jr. went 10–4 as a rookie and in 1968 led the American League with a 1.60 earned run average with a 21–9 won-lost record.

"I pitched for Los Angeles [1958–1962] when the Dodgers had [Don] Drysdale and [Sandy] Koufax and for the New York Yankees [1963–1964] when they had [Ralph] Terry and [Mel] Stottlemyre before I came to Cleveland," said Stan Williams, who pitched for Cleveland in 1965 and from 1967 to 1969, "and in my opinion Luis Tiant probably was the greatest right-handed pitcher I ever played with.

"Not only was he a great pitcher and a great competitor, Looie also was one of the funniest men I've ever known. He kept everybody loose with his antics—like, he'd smoke a big cigar in the shower, run around the clubhouse naked, swing from the overhead pipes like a big gorilla, crazy things like that.

"One of the funny things that I remember so well is what he did to our first baseman, Tony Horton, a big, six-foot-four strapping guy— and a very serious guy. Steve Hamilton, he of the famous 'blooper'—or what he called his 'eephus' pitch—was on the mound for the Yankees and threw his blooper to Horton during a game in 1968. Tony took a vicious swing at the ball and popped it up to the third baseman, who'd been playing deep and had to charge in and dive to catch it.

"When it happened, Tiant ran out of the dugout and—in front of all the crowd—put his finger under Hortons chin like it was a fish hook and literally dragged Tony back to the dugout."

Bill Veeck
(Owner, 1946–1949)

On June 22, 1946, the Indians were purchased for $2 million by Bill Veeck, who built them into a World Series championship team in 1948. Veeck spent a great deal of time in the stands, mingling with fans, and said, "I have discovered in 20 years of moving around a ball park that the fans' knowledge of the game is usually in inverse proportion to the price of the seats they are occupying."

On July 3, 1947, Veeck purchased the contract of Larry Doby for $10,000 from the Newark Eagles of the Negro National League. Two days later, Doby became the first African-American to play in the American League and second (by 11 weeks to Jackie Robinson) in the Major Leagues.

Several years later, in recalling Doby's first time at-bat for the Indians as a pinch hitter against the Chicago White Sox on July 5, 1947, Veeck related the following in a national magazine:

"He swung at three pitches and missed each by at least a foot. [Doby] was so discouraged . . . he sat in the corner [of the dugout], all alone, with his head in his hands. Joe Gordon was up next . . . and missed each of three pitches by at least two feet and came back to the bench and sat down next to Doby, and put his head in his hands, too."

It was a nice story that Veeck told, but the fact is, Gordon was on third base when Doby batted, as reported in a book about Doby entitled, *Pride Against Prejudice.*

Other Veeck-isms: "Baseball is almost the only orderly thing in a very unorderly world. If you get three strikes, even the best lawyer in the world can't get you off."

"I try not to break the rules . . . merely to test their elasticity."

"We didn't win the pennant in 1948. We won it on November 25, 1947, the day I rehired Lou Boudreau [as manager of the Indians]."

Mickey Vernon
(First baseman, 1949–1950, 1958)

"The best thing about being traded to the Indians [December 14, 1948] was that I won't have to bat against Bob Feller, Bob Lemon, Gene Bearden. It should add at least 20 points to my average [because] instead of facing the Indians, I'll be batting against Washington pitching."

(A year later he was traded back to Washington.)

Omar Vizquel
(Shortstop, 1994–2004)

"When I was growing up [in Venezuela] Davey Concepcion was my idol, and I always wanted to be a ball player. But when I went to a tryout camp, they told me I was too small . . . that I should go to the racetrack and be a jockey."

"There are so many things that happen during your career, you could write a book about it," Omar Vizquel said. "One of them was the time I made three errors in one game [in 1994], which I never had done before and haven't done since. I never thought I would have a game like that. The fans started screaming names at me, saying what are you doing here and why didn't I stay in Seattle—instead of being traded here—things like that.

"I knew I had to do something to try to get the fans back on my side and to regain the confidence of my teammates. So I went the next two months without making an error, something like that, and everything was forgotten. I finished the season with only eight errors and won my first [of nine consecutive] Gold Gloves."

"So many funny things also happen in a player's career. Like the time we were losing 12–2 [to Seattle in 2001] and came back to win. Charlie Manuel came to me in the fifth inning when we were still down by six or seven runs and said, 'Be ready because you are going to be the hero of this game.'

"I came up in the ninth inning with the bases loaded and hit a triple to tie the game and we went on to win.

"Stuff like that. Sometimes it's hard to believe."

"Another time I was fielding a ground ball, and it rolled up my arm to my chin and went down inside my shirt. The runner just kept running, and all I could do was hug him because I couldn't get my hand on the ball. Everybody started yelling, and at first the umpire didn't know what to call although he finally called the guy safe because I couldn't tag him—the ball was still inside my shirt."

When Coach Buddy Bell was asked to rate Vizquel as a shortstop, he said, "If Ozzie Smith is in the Hall of Fame, Omar has to make it, too. I've seen them both a lot. Ozzie was more flamboyant, but if you put a gun against my head, I'd have to say Omar is better overall. He's the smartest player I've ever been around."

And this praise for Vizquel from another outstanding shortstop-third baseman, Alex Rodriguez of the New York Yankees, "[Omar] is a phenomenal defensive player. He's like an artist. It's fun to watch all the defensive styles, and his is the most unique. All the barehanded plays he makes.

"He's an innovator."

Rick Waits
(Pitcher, 1975–1983)

"One of the funny things I remember about my career is that, my first day in the Major Leagues, when I was with Texas before I was traded to the Indians, I had three managers within a 24-hour period.

"I was called up by the Rangers in September [1973] after I'd gone 14–7 and won the Triple-A championship game [for Spokane of the Pacific Coast League]. Whitey Herzog was the Texas manager then and said he was going to give me a start. But three hours later, at about five o'clock, Herzog was fired, and the Rangers made Del Wilbur, who'd been my Triple-A manager, the interim manager. I figured I'd surely get in some games, because Wilbur knew me from Spokane. But right after that first game, the door to the clubhouse flew open, and here came a bunch of TV cameras following Billy Martin, who'd just been named the new manager of the Rangers, my third manager in less than 24 hours.

"Under Billy I pitched only one inning in that final month, and got a save. But that's all. No starts, as Whitey had promised, or as I expected to get with Wilbur.

"As it turned out, that was the only inning I ever pitched for the Rangers. They sent me back to the minor leagues in 1974, and I was still there [until June 13, 1975] when the Indians traded Gaylord Perry to Texas for Jim Bibby, Jackie Brown, and me, and cash. I heard it was $250,000, because there always was a lot of money involved in deals the Indians made in those days.

"After that a lot of great things happened to me in Cleveland. At the time we—Bibby and Brown and I—thought it was a tough trade for Cleveland to make, giving up their best pitcher for three young guys and cash. But one thing the three of us remember—and we always kept track of it—is that the three of us always combined to win more games for Cleveland than Gaylord did for Texas."

"Playing for Frank Robinson was good. He gave me the ball. He gave me the chance to pitch, which Texas never did, even though I had won at every [minor league] level I played. That first half-year with Cleveland in 1975 was great. I was 6–2 with a two-something [2.96] ERA, and I'll be forever thankful to Frank for giving me the chance.

"But that's not the only reason I thought Robinson was a great manager. Remember, we did not have a real great ball club those seasons

[1975–1977], and when he was fired [June 19, 1977], I thought it was way too soon to pass judgment on him. At the time we were playing pretty decent ball, but had just gone into a little spin. I think they made the change just for the sake of change when they gave the job to Jeff Torborg.

"Jeff was a great friend, he'd been my bullpen coach and changed some things that made me a better pitcher. But still, I thought Frank knew the game as well as anyone. He was a tough guy, very aggressive, and nobody liked to win more than Frank Robinson—even when he played a game of cards—and I enjoyed pitching for him. I sure did."

Bill Wambsganss
(Second baseman, 1914–1923)

If ever a man was in precisely the right place at precisely the right time, it was Bill Wambsganss, better known in baseball history as Bill Wamby.

Wamby's right place at the right time was about three strides to the right of second base at Cleveland's old League Park in the fifth inning of the fifth game of the World Series against Brooklyn, October 10, 1920.

Because he was, Wambsganss was able to make the only unassisted triple play in World Series history, helping the Indians win the game, 8–1.

"You'd have thought I was born the day before and died the day after. The only credit I deserve is for being in the right place at the right time," Wambsganss said. He speared a line drive off the bat of Willie Mitchell, his momentum carried him to second base, where he doubled Pete Kilduff, and then turned and tagged Otto Miller, who was running from first.

"After the game I was interviewed by one newspaperman. A guy from Brooklyn talked to me. He asked me how it felt to make an unassisted triple play. I said it was the chance of a lifetime, which it was," Wambsganss said.

Jim Warfield
(Trainer, 1971–2002)

"In my 30 years as a trainer for the Indians, I've had a lot of 'favorite' players, so don't ask me to name my most favorite. There are too many. But one of them is Gaylord Perry, who also goes down in my book as one of the classiest, most dedicated, professional, conscientious, and hardest workers I've ever been around, in baseball or anywhere.

"The mention of his name brings back a memory that I'll never forget; it took place during the 1974 season. That was not a good year for the Indians, though it certainly was for Gaylord, who went on to win 21 games.

"But it was a game he didn't win that I remember so well. It was played on July 8 in Oakland, with the A's on their way to a third straight World Series championship. Gaylord went into the game with 15 consecutive victories, needing one more to tie the American League record [held by Smoky Joe Wood, 1912; Walter Johnson, 1912; Lefty Grove, 1931; and Schoolboy Rowe, 1934].

"Something else that made all those victories by Gaylord even more impressive was the fact that many of the 15 games—in fact, the last six or seven in a row—he won while pitching with a badly sprained right ankle that nobody knew about. He didn't want the press to find out because, if they wrote about it, he was afraid opposing batters would bunt on him, and he probably was right.

"Vida Blue pitched for the A's against Gaylord that night and, even though it was a Monday and the game wasn't scheduled to be televised back to Cleveland, the station sent a crew to Oakland to cover it; it was that big back home.

"Oakland scored first on a two-run homer by Gene Tenace [in the second inning] and was ahead, 2–0, until we scored in the fifth and went ahead, 3–2, in the seventh when Dave Duncan hit a two-run homer. But Oakland tied it, 3–3, in the ninth, and won in the tenth [on a walk, sacrifice bunt, and pinch hitter Claudell Washington's first Major League hit, a single to left]."

"Gaylord was great, but Blue was just as tough against us, and retired the last ten batters in a row [through the top of the tenth], after Duncan's homer. That's how Gaylord's winning streak was stopped."

But that didn't end Warfield's story.

"After the game, as I always did, I cut the tape off Gaylord's ankles, took off the hot applications and cream that he used on his arm, and helped him with some shoulder exercises, then he went in and took his shower. Through it all, Gaylord never said a word, and he still didn't when he came out of the shower, and we did some more shoulder work, as we always did. When I was finished, he just got up off the table and walked out, still without saying a word.

"The next day Gaylord came to the Coliseum about eleven o'clock in the morning with his son Jackson and said to me, 'Pardner,' which is what he always called me, 'there was a reason I didn't say anything to you after the game last night. It's because that was the toughest defeat of my career, and I just didn't want to talk about it. I hope you understand.' Of course I did."

Eric Wedge
(Manager, 2003–2009)

How anxious was Eric Wedge to start his career as a Major League manager?

"After getting the job [on October 29, 2002], I was very excited. [I] spent the winter in Cleveland preparing for everything and decided to drive down to Winter Haven, [Florida], with my [new] wife, Kate."

They were married November 16, 2002.

"Winter Haven is about a 17-hour drive from Cleveland, and we planned to go halfway and stop en route at least one night. But once I started driving, my mind got to working and I got to thinking about Spring Training and how excited I was to get it going. The next thing I knew we were 10 hours, 11 hours, 13 hours on the road and were getting to the point where it was almost too close to stop—so we didn't.

"We ended up driving all day and through the night . . . all the way straight to Winter Haven in a little more than 16 hours. That was February 9 and 10, and although Spring Training didn't start for another week, I didn't think anything of it. I felt good and just wanted to get started. There probably were about a million different thoughts that popped through my head.

"After we arrived, [General Manager] Mark Shapiro asked me where we stopped, and I told him we didn't. I thought he might scold me, but he didn't. He just laughed. A few other guys joked with me about it but it just seemed like the thing to do. I wanted to get down here. I wanted to get started."

What was the biggest thing Wedge learned in his rookie season as a Major League manager?

"[That] it's always harder *not* to say something than it is to say something," he replied.

And, when asked to comment on the early-season hitting problems of first baseman Travis Hafner, Wedge said—in what could be construed as "Stengelese"—that Hafner "needs a consistent approach to be consistent. That's where his inconsistencies lie."

Fred Weisman
(Eldest son of Lefty Weisman, the Indians' trainer from 1921–1949)

"I used to play the piano for my dad, who loved to sing, especially Irish songs," said Fred Weisman, now a prominent attorney in Cleveland. "Dad had a pretty good voice and so did Joe Shaute [who pitched for the Indians from 1922 to 1930]. They would harmonize together and were really good, especially Shaute, who was a great tenor. In fact, he sang the national anthem a few times before games during his career with the Indians. He and my dad used to do a little barbershop, that kind of stuff.

"Another one who had an excellent voice, and who also loved to sing, was Jim Hegan [a Tribe catcher from 1941–1942 and 1946–1957]. Hegan and a friend of his, a priest from Lynn, Massachusetts, came over to the house a lot, and they'd sing with dad while I played the piano.

"In 1946 when the Indians celebrated my dad's 25th anniversary as the team trainer, my dad sang at the Stadium before the game that night, and [Owner] Bill Veeck hired a trio that backed him up. Dad loved it. So did the fans.

"I can't imagine something like that happening today. But then, times were a lot different then. I guess everything was."

Jed Weisman
(Youngest son of Lefty Weisman)

"When I was born [in 1933], Alva Bradley, then the owner of the Indians, suggested to my dad that I be named for the teams starting outfielders, who were Joe Vosmik in left, Earl Averill in center, and Dick Porter in right. So my name, Jed, was a combination of 'J' from Joe Vosmik, 'E' for Earl Averill, and 'D' for Dick Porter.

"I'm often reminded how lucky I was to be named Jed, because, at that time, another outfielder named Bob Seeds was fighting Vosmik to be the starting left fielder. If he had won the job, my name might have been 'Sap,' for Seeds, Averill, and Porter, instead of Jed. I guess I should always be thankful that Vosmik was better than Seeds."

★ ★ ★ ★ ★

"I enjoyed being around the players, and my greatest memory probably goes back to 1948 when the Indians took me on a western swing, to Detroit, Chicago, and St. Louis. Before one game, I think it was in St. Louis, while the Indians were taking infield practice, Lou Boudreau called me out on the field and told me to take ground balls at shortstop while he went into the clubhouse. Imagine that! They let me do everything except take the catcher's throws at second base—they probably thought I'd miss the ball and maybe get hurt—but I did pretty well, if I do say so myself.

"As my brother Fred said, we weren't allowed to call the players by their first name, although one day Steve Gromek said to me, 'Either you call me Steve, and not Mr. Gromek, or I'll call you Mr. Weisman and not Jed.' So I did, but never around my dad."

"One of the things I remember so well about the time my dad was the Indians trainer is that a lot of the players were always coming over to our house to visit, especially Jim Hegan, Joe Gordon, and Ken Keltner," said Jed Weisman, who's also a Cleveland attorney.

"In those days most of the games were played in the daytime, and the guys would come over, munch on the chopped liver my mom made, and have a few beers with my dad. Hegan didn't drink much, but Gordon and Keltner could put it away pretty good.

"It was really funny. Everybody in our neighborhood grew up knowing that somebody from the Indians would be coming over from time to time, and all the kids wondered, 'Who's going to be there tonight?' It was always a thrill for them. They'd come over for autographs, and I'm sure they envied my brother and me, but it was no big thing to us. It was always fun.

"I also got to know Earl Averill pretty well. He was one of the nicest guys in the world but acted real tough in the clubhouse. He'd grab me, put me on the rubbing table in the trainer's room, pick up my dad's scissors, and threaten to cut my ears off. He scared the hell out of me the first time he did it, which probably was the reason he continued to do it. But I liked him a lot. I liked all the guys, but Averill probably was my favorite."

Jake Westbrook
(Pitcher, 2001–2010)

"A lot of people expected me to be disappointed when I was traded here by the Yankees, but I wasn't, not in the least," Jake Westbrook said.

"It wasn't anything new, not to me, anyway. I was traded a couple of times before the Indians got me, and I always knew that trades are part of baseball, the way the game is played, which I should know as well as anybody. I was drafted by Colorado in 1996, was traded to Montreal after the 1997 season, and dealt to the Yankees after the 1999 season before I came to the Indians."

(Westbrook was acquired with pitcher Zach Day to complete a July 25, 2000, deal for David Justice.)

"Actually, nobody likes to be traded, because it tends to make you feel unwanted, but I knew that coming to the Indians would be a good opportunity for me. Besides, I didn't feel I had a real good chance to do much with the Yankees and that it would better for me here, which it was—and is."

Dr. William Wilder
(Team physician/medical director, 1970–2000; medical consultant, 2001–)

"If anybody ever wondered about how stressful it can be to manage a Major League Baseball team, I can relate a couple of instances that will prove that it is very stressful, beginning with Ken Aspromonte [who managed the Indians from 1972–1974] and continuing with his successor, Frank Robinson [1975–1977].

"Aspromonte found out about it when he walked into the locker room for a ball game and there was Robinson, putting on a uniform. It was right after that that Aspromonte's wife, Laurie, came to our house and borrowed our typewriter to type Kenny's resignation speech that he gave to the players.

"There are a million Bert Blyleven stories, a lot of which can't be told, but one I can tell you goes back to the early 1980s, and we were giving the players their pre-Spring Training physicals," Dr. William Wilder said. "I still get on Bert about it when he comes in with the Twins [as a broadcaster]—and he never lets me forget it either. It was about the time I gave him a prostate exam, you know, the digital rectal exam.

"That night in Tucson, after I'd finished the physicals, my wife and I were going out for dinner. Pete Franklin, the broadcaster, was there in the lobby of the hotel doing his radio show and was interviewing Blyleven.

"When Bert saw me he said to Pete—on the air and heard by 38 states and half of Canada—'Oh, here comes Doc Wilder. He just gave us our physicals today.' Pete said, 'How'd it go?' and Bert said, 'Fine, the doctor checked my prostate, but something I don't understand— he had both of his hands on my shoulders.' Pete just about died and finally said, 'We're going to take a break.'"

"There also is a good Gaylord Perry story. One night he got hit in the left shin with a line drive and had to be taken out of the game. I went into the clubhouse and asked him where it hurt. He put his hand on his right leg and said, 'Here and here and here,' but every time I poked around it didn't seem to bother him no matter what I did.

"Well, he let me go through it all—his shin, his ankle, his knee, everything—and finally I said, 'Gaylord, it looks pretty good,' and he said, 'Doc, you're poking around the wrong leg.' That was Gaylord; he loved to bait me like that.

"And, on that subject, I have to say I certainly agree with what [late trainer] Jimmy Warfield always said, that Gaylord had the greatest pain tolerance of any player he ever worked on. Gaylord was famous—or maybe that should be infamous—for the hot stuff Jimmy used on Gaylord before a game. It was so hot Jimmy wore rubber gloves when he massaged Gaylord's shoulder. None of the other players could stand it.

"But Gaylord, you've got to give it to him, had his own routine, his own set of exercises, everything. He always did his own thing, never mind anyone else, and it worked. He's in the Hall of Fame, isn't he?"

(Perry was inducted into the Hall of Fame in 1991.)

Stan Williams
(Pitcher, 1965, 1967–1969)

"I pitched for Los Angeles [1958–1962] and the New York Yankees [1963–1964] before I went to the Indians, and when I was with the Dodgers in the winter of 1960–1961, I had a contract problem with [General Manager] Buzzie Bavasi. He argued that I walked too many guys and, because I did, he was refusing to give me the $2,500 raise I wanted that would have jumped my salary up to $10,500.

"Buzzie said, 'Tell me why I should I give you a $2,500 raise,' and I told him, 'Because I'm going to do these five things for you: First, I'm going to walk fewer than 75 batters, I'm going to pitch 230 innings, win 15 games, strike out 200 batters, and have an ERA under 3.00. Buzzie said, 'That's fine. But don't just tell me you're going to do it, do it and I'll pay you.'

"As it turned out, I made three of them; I won 15 games, pitched 235 innings, and struck out over 200 batters [205], though my ERA was a little more than 3.00, and my walk total was over 75 [108], so I didn't get the $2,500.

"But I tried hard, especially to keep from walking a lot of guys. Anytime I'd get behind in the count on a batter, like 3-and-0, or 3-and-1, I just went ahead and drilled the s.o.b. because nothing was said about HBPs [hit batters].

"But I couldn't do enough of it. Word got around about what I was doing, and guys got harder for me to drill.

"And, no, Buzzie never did give me the $2,500."

"Of all the games I pitched in the big leagues [482], one of my best, maybe the best, was in 1967 [August 10]. The Indians had brought me back after I'd had a sore arm and had been out of the big leagues for almost three full seasons.

"We were in Baltimore, and Sonny Siebert was supposed to start, but he told [Manager] Joe Adcock he needed one more day. So Adcock asked me if I could pitch and I told him, 'That's what I'm here for.' I started the game and went all the way, 13 innings, and won, 2–1.

"The reason it's one of my favorites is because I struck out two Hall of Famers nine times—Luis Aparicio five times and Frank Robinson four times.

"The first three times Robinson batted, I struck him out on a fastball, the second time with a curve, and the third time with a slider. The fourth time he came up I got him 0-and-2 and I'm thinking, 'What is he sitting on? What should I throw him?' I'd already struck him out on a fastball, curve, and slider.

"Then it occurred to me that I hadn't thrown him a spitball—and I had a good one. So I turned my back to the plate, loaded one up and threw him a helluva spitter, low and away. He swung and missed it by about two feet.

"Imagine that. There I am, a guy who'd had a bad arm and was out of the big leagues for three years, who came back and threw a 2–1 victory, went all 13 innings, struck out 15 and just pitched a helluva game.

"But the next day the headline in the paper was, 'Robinson accuses Williams of throwing a spitter'—even though that one was the only one I threw the whole game."

"In 1968, when Alvin Dark managed the Indians, on two occasions he brought me in with the bases loaded, two outs, and a three-and-two count on the hitter," Stan Williams remembered. "The second time he did it, after he gave me the ball and started to walk back to the dugout, I called him back to the mound and asked him, 'Skip, how do you want me to pitch to this guy?'

"He just looked at me and said, 'I don't care. Just get him out,' which I did and says a lot for our pitching strategy back then, compared to all the fancy stuff everybody in the game likes to talk about now."

Rick Wise
(Pitcher, 1978–1979)

"There have been a couple hundred no-hitters in the history of Major League Baseball. But mine, when I beat Cincinnati, 4–0 [June 23, 1971] was the only one of its kind, because I also hit two home runs in it. I'm in my own company, and that makes it very special to me."

"It was difficult for me when I was traded to Cleveland from the Red Sox during Spring Training of 1978 and I had to join the Indians in Tucson [Arizona]. I'd had some very good years in Boston. We had gone to the World Series in 1975, and I'd had some personal highs while I was there, although, at the time I was kind of on the outside looking in with Don Zimmer [the Red Sox manager]. He'd shuffled some of the pitchers between the starting rotation and the bullpen, and back again, so I wasn't really surprised when the Red Sox traded me.

"But surprised or not, I was disappointed because Boston was a strong and contending club, and Cleveland wasn't. It also was disappointing to have to pick up and go all the way across the country for Spring Training without knowing my teammates, really not knowing anybody with the [Cleveland] club.

"The way the fans were in those days also made it difficult. It probably took ten games or so to put as many fans in the seats in Cleveland to equal what the Red Sox would get for one day, for just about every game they played.

"It also was difficult playing in Cleveland, because the Stadium then was really a football stadium, not a baseball park like Fenway, or like so many parks today, including Jacobs Field. We'd need 80,000 to fill the stadium, but we'd be lucky to get six or seven thousand for a game in July and August.

"But I've got to say that the guys on the Indians, to their credit, played as hard as they could, no matter the problems. It's just that, for the most part their talent level was not as good as the rest of the league, though we had some outstanding individual players. We just couldn't put it all together as a team. We didn't have the consistency you need to be a winner in Major League Baseball."

Early Wynn
(Pitcher, 1949–1957, 1963; coach, 1964–1966)

"There I was, getting out guys like Joe DiMaggio, King Kong Keller, Bill Dickey, Joe Gordon, Red Rolfe, and Tommy Henrich, but I lose the game because that little pip squeak [Phil] Rizzuto hit a home run," said Early Wynn, after a 1–0 loss to the New York Yankees on September 26, 1941. "From that game on, I always thought bad things about anyone who hit a home run off me."

Early Wynn, nicknamed "Burly Early" and renowned for his gruff demeanor and tough style of pitching, once was asked if it were true that he was so competitive he'd throw a high, hard fastball at his own mother if she were batting against him.

Wynn replied, "It would depend on how well she was hitting."

A former teammate who could testify as to Wynn's temperament was George Strickland, the Tribe shortstop from 1952 to 1957 and 1959 to 1960.

"The first game I ever played behind Early Wynn, he was having some minor problems—minor because he never had big problems. I looked into the dugout, and [Manager] Al Lopez motioned for me to go over and talk to Early, to settle him down or whatever," Strickland recalled.

"I called time, walked toward the mound, and before I got halfway Early turned, glared at me, and said, 'Where the hell do you think you're going? Just turn around and get your ass back to your position and don't bother me.'

"So I did, and when I looked in the dugout again, there was Lopez and a couple of guys laughing. He set me up good. Boy, did he ever."

Speaking of the Tribes 1954 pitching staff that many—Al Lopez included—consider to have been the best in baseball history, Lopez said, "The only guy who gave me trouble when I went to take him out of a game was Wynn. He'd really get upset when he was having a bad game, although he didn't have many of them.

"Once when I went out to get him, which was my second trip to the mound that inning and meant I had to bring in a relief pitcher, Early was arguing with the umpire, Bill Summers. Early must have been giving him a bad time, because just as I got there, I heard Summers tell him, 'One more word out of you and you're gone.'

"Early looked at Summers, then at me, and asked the umpire, 'Why the hell do you think [Lopez] is coming out here—to bring me a ham sandwich?'"

Of the Indians pitching staff of 1954, when he and Bob Lemon led the American League with 23 victories each (and Mike Garcia won 19, Art Houtteman 15, Bob Feller 13, and relievers Don Mossi, Ray Narleski, and Hal Newhouser combined to win 16), Wynn said, "I don't know for sure if we were the best staff ever, but give it to me and I'll take my chances against any other team in history."

In 1957, during Kerby Farrell's ill-fated season as manager of the Indians, he went to the mound to either replace or simply talk to Wynn. The gruff pitcher, who was not happy about the way the game was progressing, greeted the manager by saying, "What the hell do you want? Get the hell out of here. I can take care of this myself," whereupon Farrell turned around and dutifully returned to the dugout.

On another occasion, when Al Lopez managed the Indians (1951–1956), he went out to get Wynn. It was Lopez's second trip to the mound that inning, which meant Wynn had to be replaced by a relief pitcher. Just as Lopez reached the mound umpire Bill Summers, who had been a target of Wynn's wrath, told the pitcher, "One more word out of you, and you're gone."